AF517779

The Earth Has No Corners

The Earth Has No Corners

Felicitation Volume on the 70th Birthday of Dr. Karan Singh

Editor
K.L. NANDAN

ISBN : 81-7541-088-4

First Published in India in 2001

The Earth Has No Corners

Published by :
SHIPRA PUBLICATIONS
115-A, Vikas Marg, Shakarpur,
Delhi-110092 (India)
Ph : 2458662, 2200954 Fax : 91-11-2458662
Email : siprapub@satyam.net.in

Laser Typeset by :
Sunshine Graphics
Delhi-110032

Printed at :
Chaudhary Offset Process
Delhi-110051

Photograph on cover by Siddharth Mishra
Cover Design by Kishan Singh

Contents

Editor's Note

A Universal Man

From the perspective of a poet and journalist, I have always held Dr. Karan Singh in high esteem as a poet-philosopher. I have also watched with great interest the public career of this prince-philosopher who has been an intimate witness to a turbulent era of our history during the latter half of the 20th Century. His unique personality as the universal man has always been a source of inspiration for me to know and understand him better. What fascinates me is an extremely sensitive aspect of the personality of this poet among princes. He considers himself "a plaything of Lord Shiva" and, in his prayer to the Lord, he lyrically prays,

"You can fill me with light and power,
So that I shine like a meteor,
Against the darkness of the midnight sky;
Or You can extinguish my spirit,
So that I sink forever,
Into the deep and fathomless ocean of time".

Looking at the two aspects of creation and protection of that mighty symbol of the eternal cosmic force, the savant-devotee chants in supplication to the great Lord,

"You can smile at me with the radiance
That kindles the universe,
Or You can open your eye of fury
And reduce me to a heap of ashes".

Our celebrated seers and sages of the great Vedic era were endowed with a vision of entire mankind being a family, and their perception transcended narrow precincts to embrace the entire universe. The poet and the philosopher in Dr. Karan Singh is blessed with such an endowment and his vision breaks through the narrow confines of family and community to embrace the universality of mankind. He is in the mould of that Vedic vision of the Universal Man, the Global Citizen.

The more I knew him, the more I wanted to know him. To understand him better, one has to delve into his friendless childhood. Born on 9 March 1931 in the fashionable resort of Cannes on the French Riviera, he was the only child of Maharaja Hari Singh and Maharani Tara Devi of Jammu & Kashmir. Imagine the loneliness of the adolescent. Immediately after being appointed Regent at the age of 18, he was left alone in his hotel room by his parents who departed with their staff. Recalling the moment he says, "For half an hour, I sat absolutely alone in my hotel room, poised between the weight of the past and the burdens of the future". These words provide us a glimpse of a mature approach to life in a person so young. Besides the loneliness, he had his share of physical pain and suffering. The physical suffering and the pain of loneliness moulded his inner self, giving it a meaning and knowledge well beyond his age. Sri Aurobindo's philosophy gave it a higher dimension.

My pleasant journey of knowing him spanned the decades, and now he has turned 70. But his youth defies age. Speaking on 'ageing', he once observed that "Ageing is sometimes termed a problem; but the way I look at it is that older people represent a national asset. With their experience and their maturity, if that could be used for creative purposes, they can do a great deal of development of society and the nation". George Bernard Shaw had said, "youth is a wonderful thing, what a pity it is wasted on the young". Youth found Dr. Karan Singh so fascinating that it decided never to leave him. Grow old he did, ageing he defied. The poet, Robert Browning had said, "grow old along with me, the best is yet to be".

This 'yet to be' is a never ending process, and in this process of evolution of the inner self, Dr. Karan Singh was deeply influenced by that visionary Prime Minister of India, Jawaharlal Nehru and India's philosopher-President, Dr. Sarvepalli Radhakrishnan. Jawaharlal Nehru, whose writings deeply impressed and influenced him, brought him into the political arena. Dr. Radhakrishnan opened his mind's window on the riches of philosophy. Two other great men who profoundly influenced him are Swami Vivekananda and Sri Aurobindo. Their thoughts shaped his psyche. He developed a sense of revolt against the feudal mindset and tendencies and spearheaded the transition to democracy. He reminiscised that "If my father landed a good catch, there was merriment, but if he had a bad day or lost a big fish, he would be in terrible mood. This almost invariably meant that some unfortunate shikari was sacked in the middle of the night and this added to my growing alienation from the order in which I was born. Here was authority without generosity, power without compassion".

Early in his public life, he resolved to renounce the use of the title of Maharaja. When Indira Gandhi moved to abolish the Princely Privy Purses, he voluntarily surrendered it by putting the entire sum into the Hari-Tara Charitable Trust set up to commemorate his parents and dedicated to the service of those people in the country who are socially and economically challenged. He converted his exquisite Amar Mahal Palace in Jammu into a library and museum, housing a priceless collection of Pahari miniature paintings and contemporary Indian art as well as a personal library of over 20,000 volumes, many of them rare and of historical significance.

His father, Maharaja Hari Singh, initiated him into the splendourous realm of Indian classical music. The renowned Ustad Vilayat Hussain Khan of the Hindustani classical music's Agra Gharana coached him for some time, and later Bahram Singh Rawat and Pandit Uma Dutt Sharma taught him several ragas. Remembering the days of his music apprenticeship, he said, "Once the seed of new tune was planted in me, it would germinate and grow until I would find my whole being pulsating to its rhythm".

But the rhythm of life swept him in a different direction. In 1949, at the intervention of Prime Minster Jawaharlal Nehru, at the age of 18, Maharaja Hari Singh appointed him the Regent of Jammu & Kashmir. Shri K Natwar Singh has aptly put it that "few individuals have made so spectacular an entry into history as Dr. Karan Singh". Thereafter, for 18 years, he was continuously the head of the State, first as Regent till 1952, as elected *Sadr-i-Riyasat* from 1952 to 1965 and as Governor for two years from

1965. Looking back on his life, Dr. Karan Singh says, "Curiously my life seems to fall neatly into eighteen year periods. The first 18 years were spent as a student in India and a patient abroad, while no sooner had I turned 18 that I found myself catapulted into the office of Head of the State which I held under three different appellations - Regent, *Sadr-i-Riyasat* and Governor - for exactly eighteen years. Within a few days of my thirty-sixth birthday, I was invited to join the Union Council of Ministers, and for the next eighteen years, until 1985, was active in national politics as a Member of Parliament, including over ten years as Cabinet Minister".

As Heir Apparent, his vision of the State of Jammu & Kashmir can be judged by two events. One was Lord Louis Mountbatten's visit to Srinagar to impress upon Maharaja Hari Singh the desirability of acceding either to India or Pakistan. Remarking on this incident, Dr. Karan Singh says, "the Maharaja, after entertaining the guest lavishly and arranging for a fishing trip, quietly avoided sitting down for a discussion on the plea that he had suddenly developed severe attack of colic". The second incident was the arrest of Jawaharlal Nehru by his father. He writes, "I was stunned. Here was the most charismatic leader of the national movement for freedom, the author of "An Autobiography" and "The Discovery of India", the declared future Prime Minister of Indian republic and, instead of welcoming him and seeking his co-operation, we had arrested him".

Despite the underlying emotional and ideological distance between the two, he had profound respect towards his father because of his deep-rooted philosophical insights into our ancient cultural traditions. When his father passed away, he was out of the country but rushed back to perform the last rites as the son. With overwhelming emotion, but at the same time with exemplary insight into the ultimate truth, Dr. Karan Singh writes, "Twelve years ago, my parents and I were taken out in a similar procession after my return from America. This time I was alone, my mother had donned the white clothes of the traditional Hindu widow and all that was left of my father's body was a handful of ashes in the urn that I gently cradled in my hands. How much in the end does a man weigh!"

His is a unique personality, and the uniqueness of his approach to life has always fascinated me. I fully agree with the other eminent devotee of Sri Aurobindo, Manoj Das who opines that, "Had Maharaja Hari Singh been keen to bring up his scion on his own image, the flow of events over this subcontinent would have been twisted into another bizarre bend". It remains a mystery as to what twist of destiny made the sole heir to the fabulous throne of Jammu & Kashmir emerge as a musician, a poet of distinction and an acknowledged scholar of philosophy, religion, spirituality and mysticism. He acknowledges with warmth and nostalgia the refulgent influence of his deeply pious mother, Maharani Tara Devi, in the fashioning of his psyche. He is a deeply religious person, but his Hinduism is a liberal religion which allows an individual the freedom and capability of response according to his own 'samskara'. 'Hinduism', he believes, 'is basically a pluralistic religion which has many different paths to the divine – Ekam Sad Viprah Bahuda Vadanti (the truth is one, the wise call it by many names), tremendous freedom and flexibility". He considers this universal aspect of Hinduism as most appropriate for the emerging global society.

That he was entirely different from the scions of other princely families was visible early in his life. It was reflected in the subject he chose for his doctoral study, the political thought of Sri Aurobindo, an uncompromising revolutionary and a valiant fighter against British rule in India. The Bharatiya Vidya Bhawan subsequently published his doctoral dissertation in their series of prestigious publications. In the preface to the book, "Prophet of Indian Nationalism", Jawaharlal Nehru wrote, "It is significant to note that he should have devoted himself to his studies and, more particularly, to this analysis of the political thoughts of Sri Aurobindo during a crucial period of our history, instead of occupying himself with the normal activities of Indian princes, that is shikar, polo and high society". Dr. Karan Singh was not a run-of-the-mill prince. He was different and has remained different. How deeply Sri Aurobindo's thoughts have influenced him is seen from his life-long quest for higher consciousness of man, the pursuit of the spiritual dimension of the human psyche. His study of Sri Aurobindo's philosophy led to a long association with Auroville near Pondicherry, a unique experiment in international living inspired by The Mother. He later became the first Chairman of the Governing Board of the Auroville Foundation, and also held the Sri Aurobindo Chair at the Benaras

Hindu University.

In 1967, Prime Minister Indira Gandhi inducted him into the Union Cabinet. At 36, he was the youngest person ever to become a Union Cabinet Minister in India. His first assignment was the portfolio of Civil Aviation and Tourism, where he made a marked impact by his vision and dynamism. He moved to Health & Family Planning in 1973 and brought the important but ignored subject of population stabilisation centre stage by making it a national commitment and framing the first national population policy in1974. He was also Minister of Education & Culture in 1979. First elected from the Udhampur Parliamentary constituency as Member of the Lok Sabha (Lower House) in 1967, he was re-elected from there in 1971, 1977 and 1980. Presently, he is elected to the Rajya Sabha (Council of States) from Delhi.

Of his days in the Union Cabinet under Indira Gandhi, he recalls, "Indira Gandhi had always been friendly and supportive, and was hurt that I did not support her when the second party split came. It was difficult to explain to her the twin impact of the Sanjay and Sheikh Abdullah factors, which obliged me to part company with her. While I did not join the Congress (I) as most other did, I am glad that I had personal reconciliation with her sometime before her tragic death. She was indeed a remarkable woman who left a powerful impact on the Indian political scene, and my ten years as Minister in her cabinet were for me a period of valuable education and experience in administration and politics". This shows that Dr. Karan Singh has the rare quality of managing conflicts and reconciling them at personal and humane levels, and the ability to confront the turbulence of public life with equanimity and poise.

Dr. Karan Singh's creative expressions, through a large number of books that he has authored, reflect his varied and wide-ranging concerns and commitments as poet, scholar, statesman, humanist, environmentalist, man of peace and an eternal seeker for truth and the essential nature of things. One of his earliest works is "Varied Rhythms", a collection of essays and poems published in 1960 when he was not yet 30. It brings forth the richness of his language and imagery that, to this day, bewitches his readers. Because of his scholarship and thinking, he is acknowledged the world over as a living bridge between science and spiritualism, between religion and material world, and between India and the world. Among his most fascinating works is his "Autobiography". He was not only a witness to many tumultuous happenings but also an active participant in many of them. His autobiography is an intimate but rich tapestry of his life and times intertwined with a turbulent period of India's history that included the dawn of freedom, momentous politics of Jammu & Kashmir's accession to India and its aftermath, the conflicts with Pakistan and China, and the era of Jawaharlal Nehru and Lal Bahadur Shastri.

Along with chronicling political and other developments within the country, the autobiography also sensitively probes Dr. Karan Singh's inner growth, his spiritual quest, and his search for the profounder truths. A distinctive candour, insight and the lack of rancour and prejudice are reflected in every page as he analyses the events to which he was witness. In some places, it reads like a novel. He describes the tribal invasion of Srinagar in October 1947 thus, "On that fateful day, I was left virtually alone in the palace while my father and the members of staff were attending the Durbar in the beautiful hall at the city palace on the Jhelum with its richly decorated papeir machie ceiling. Suddenly the lights went out - the invaders had captured and destroyed the only power house at that time, which was at Mahura, on the main road from Domel to Srinagar along which the invasion was proceeding. In the pitch darkness, I sat alone in my room on the wheel chair. After a few minutes, the eerie silence was broken by the sudden, blood chilling howls of the jackals. Weirdly, the cacophony rose and fell and then rose again into a mad crescendo. Death and destruction were fast approaching Srinagar, our smug world had collapsed around us, the wheels of destiny had turned full circle".

In spite of the onerous duties as Head of State, he pursued his education with single-minded devotion. After qualifying in his Senior Cambridge examination with distinction from the prestigious Doon School in Dehradun, he graduated from the Jammu & Kashmir University of which he himself was the Chancellor in his capacity as Head of State. In 1957, he took the MA in Political Science from the Delhi University, creating a University record by securing a distinguished first class first, and then went on to take his doctorate.

Among his many pursuits is his deep interest in eclectic education as an instrument of the integral efflorescence of the human personality. An acknowledged scholar of Sanskrit, he is deeply interested in reviving our ancient literature and culture and integrating them into the modern system of education. During his brief tenure as Union Minister of Education & Culture in 1968, he took credible steps in this direction. He was the only person from South Asia to be invited by the UNESCO to join its select International Commission on Education for the Twenty-first Century chaired by the distinguished French intellectual, Jacques Delors, formerly President of the European Union. His contributions to the Commission's deliberations and recommendations were widely acknowledged. With his deep insight into the Indian cultural tradition as well as his wide exposure to Western literature and civilisation, Dr. Karan Singh is now recognised the world over as an outstanding thinker. A spellbinding orator in the mould of Dr. Sarvepalli Radhakrishnan, he has lectured in five continents on philosophy, culture, politics and the environment. For many years, he was Chancellor of the Jammu & Kashmir University as well as the Benaras Hindu University.

Dr. Karan Singh was India's Ambassador in Washington from mid-August 1989 to mid-March 1990. In February 1989, Rajiv Gandhi spoke to him about the significance of improving Indo-US relations and enquired whether he would agree to go as Ambassador to Washington. On his agreeing, Rajiv Gandhi gave him the personal rank of Cabinet Minister and also conveyed to President George Bush Sr. that the new Ambassador had the Prime Minister's personal confidence. During the credentials presentation ceremony, President Bush said "The Government of India has done us great honour by naming as its Ambassador a man of so many distinguished achievements as a public servant, author, environmentalist and poet."

Of his brief sojourn as Ambassador, Dr. Karan Singh writes "Within the first few days of my stay in Washington I realised that relations between India and America were far from satisfactory. It was all very fine to talk about the two greatest democracies in the world, but the fact was that for a variety of reasons—historical, ideological, economic—we were really in considerable difficulty". Speaking of the steps that he initiated to remedy the Indo-US relations, he recalls "I decided to aproach them on the basis of seven Task Forces, each dealing with a significant area of the relationship. The areas that I delineated were the Congress, Defence, Academics, Culture, Media, Corporate Business and the Indian-American community. Each of these represented a significant segment of the overal relationship between the two countries, and I felt that what was needed was intensive activity in each area involving not only the Mission staff but also other qualified and effective persons drawn from a wider sphere."

Dr. Karan Singh is actively associated with myriad fields of activity. As Chairman of the Temple of Understanding, an international Interfaith association with headquarters in New York, he has been actively promoting the Interfaith dialogue and through it religious harmony from many fora around the world. As member of the UNESCO's International Commission on Education for the Twenty-first Century, he stressed that "Our educational systems today around the world seldom preach religious harmony. On the contrary, in many societies there is indoctrination in favour of one and against other religious traditions, so that millions of young people are growing up convinced that their highest destiny is to destroy other people belonging to different religions. This is no longer an acceptable situation". He believes that educational programmes, not only for formal education but also non-formal methodologies using the latest Information technology, should be directed towards introducing an element of Interfaith awareness and dialogue among the people of the world. The fact that he finds acceptance cutting across religious divisions is reflected by both the Benaras Hindu University and the Aligarh Muslim University conferring on him honorary Doctorates.

His persistent quest for world peace has a strong underpinning of Vedantic philosophy. Addressing the conference on "God, the Contemporary Discussion" in France, he emphasised that, "the quest for world peace is now no longer merely a mystical vision or an idealist utopia. It has become a sheer necessity for the very survival of the human race. The growth of weapons technology has become so awesome that with nuclear weapons we can destroy not only the human race but also all life on this planet. Even a non-nuclear conflict, like the Gulf War, has caused massive casualties and appalling damage to the biosphere and the environment of our planet. Therefore, it is imperative for us to find mechanisms for a peaceful resolution of disputes between nation states". He believes that one of the reasons for such disputes is the fact that "the human psyche today is fractured and fragmented and can be healed only by the inner processes which are to be found in all the great religious traditions of the world." He urges that, "let us never lose sight of this fundamental truth enshrined deep within the recesses of our consciousness, for it is only through a profound inner dialogue that we can access the divine within ourselves".

A lifelong conservationist, he was the first Chairman of the biggest wildlife conservation programme, "Project Tiger" and was also the Chairman of the Indian Board for Wildlife for several years. He is presently President of the People's Commission on Environment & Development (India) and is a Member of the Board of the Green Cross International.

While putting together this felicitation volume, I was privileged to view this many-splendoured personality from the perspective of some of the tallest men and women of our times in several countries. As the varied images passed before my eyes, the realisation grew on me that here is a person in whom each sees his version of light and understanding, even though their fields of pre-eminence are quite different. The eminent scientists, scholars and spiritualists, representing three major streams of human mind and intellect, find a converging point in him. While the eminent scientist, Dr. A. P. J. Abdul Kalam sees in Dr. Karan Singh "an integrated man of value systems", the other equally eminent scientist, Dr. M. S. Swaminathan sees in him a forceful "champion of human security". The thinker-philosopher from Japan, Daisaku Ikeda, speaks of his shared concern with Dr. Karan Singh for the "culture of peace". The renowned American scholar and diplomat, Professor John Kenneth Galbraith, from his sick bed, considers it a privilege to felicitate him on his momentous journey through life. President Vaclav Havel of the Czech Republic, carrying with him the nostalgic fragrance of the great Prague Spring, considers him a "kindred spirit in the world of humanists and the lovers of freedom of man".

It is thrilling to find the Jagadguru Sri Sankaracharya Swamigal of Kanchi Kamakoti Peetham showering his benediction on him and focusing on the linkages between "Kanchi, Kashmir & Sri Karan Singh". The leading disciple of the great Swami Sivananda, Swami Satchidananda, who set up the well-known Yoga Vedanta Centre in Yogaville (USA) with its unique revolving statue of

Nataraja, speaks of his notable contributions to the Interfaith dialogue. Professor Ervin Laszlo of the Club of Budapest shares with Dr. Karan Singh his deep concern regarding the responsibility of science and religion for human survival. Professor Suheil Bushrui is reminded of Khalil Gibran, that great poet who sang of the culture of peace within and without human beings. Professor T R Anantharaman sees in him the personification of our ancient concept of "rajarshi". Ms Aster Patel of Auroville investigates through "Being in the making" the world in transition, which has been of special interest to Dr. Karan Singh, while Professor Roger Walsh explores the mysteries of "the psychological effect of meditation".

Professor Chaturvedi Badrinath examines the aspects of, "Forgiveness or Use of Force", a theme of prime concern to Dr. Karan Singh. Dr. Lokesh Chandra discusses "the flow of civilisation", while Professor P. N. Dhar steers us through the concerns and issues about Kashmir. Professor Raimundo Panikkar analyses "politics, religion and interculturality" and the poet P Lal delves into the overwhelming sincerity of the human and the poetic in Karan Singh. The author Manoj Das watched "the wheels whirl across time and space" in his reflections on Dr. Karan Singh's autobiography. Professor Emeritus of the UN University for peace and former UN Asstt. Secretary-General Mr. Robert Muller emphasises absolute and urgent need for proper earth government. The eminent astro-scientist, Dr. Jayant V. Narlikar seeks to share with him his jigyasa, the wondrous quest for "cosmic puzzles and speculations". The elder statesman of Kashmir, Syed Mir Qasim speaks of him as "truly a prince among men" and the renowned environmental scientist, Dr. T. N. Khoshoo finds him a champion of "sustained development in developing countries". Shri K. Natwar Singh sees in him the "gentleman scholar", while constitution-expert and luminary with field of law, Dr. L.M. Singhvi calls for a dialogue among civilizations and faith traditions. Dr. Ponna Wignaraja considers him a champion of coherence of "culture, development and democracy". Professor D. P. Chattopadhyaya shares his thoughts on the "evolution of human consciousness", a subject of abiding interest to Dr. Karan Singh. Professor Vidya Nivas Mishra and Professor Rafael Argullel discourse on "understanding each other".

World celebrities from diverse disciplines of knowledge and human activity from different parts of the world have contributed to this felicitation volume. I am deeply beholden to all of them for their insightful contributions. I am also grateful to all my friends, and to Shri Yogendra Bali in particular, for their help and co-operation in putting this volume together. I sincerely thank the staff of Dr. Karan Singh, particularly Shri Rajendra Prasad, for their help with relevant informations from time to time. Shipra Publications must be commended for bringing out this publication in record time with such production quality.

In the end, I place on record my deep sense of gratitude and indebtedness to Dr. Karan Singh himself for allowing me to undertake this challenging task, and for the privilege of serving him through this publication. I wish him many more years of fruitful life. I am confident that, with the blessings of the great Lord Shiva, whose ardent devotee he is, Dr. Karan Singh will have many more roles and responsibilities to serve India and humanity in this new century.

New Delhi — K. L. Nandan
9 March 2001

Dr. Karan Singh: An Integrated Man of Value System

•

A.P.J. Abdul Kalam

Dr. Abdul Kalam is among the tallest of living Indian scientists, a Scientific Adviser to the Prime Minister of India and the guiding spirit and inspiration for many impressive Indian scientific breakthroughs in the fields of nuclear, missile and space researches.

"The discussions started from the famous Chidambaram Temple, the cosmic dance of Lord Nataraja, the ancient spiritualism and the thoughts that transmitted through the sculptors, and moved to the space galaxies moving in the galaxy of millions of stars in dynamic motion and within the stars number of planets orbiting around the star, the sun. After all these exchanges I had with Dr. Karan Singh, a poem emerged from me, which highlights that the mankind belongs to one of the smaller galaxies that is Milky-Way."

Society, culture and education are among the areas of interest close to Dr. Karan Singh. He is an ardent advocate of education of the society and not that of mere literacy. Dr. Karan Singh emphasises the true test of education which should be its current impact on daily life and society. He champions education as a tool to address the religious tolerance, bring about inter-faith dialogue, evolve spiritual unity and lay the foundation of a global order and world society. His knowledge of Indian culture, tradition and civilisation is unfathomable, and together with the understanding of religion and exposure to the social structure and fabric of the West it has transformed him into a class of singularly gifted global thinkers and philosophers. His essays and books on culture, society, religion and common social issues like poverty are a window to his thoughts and philosophy.

Dr. Karan Singh follows science as a keen observer of its impact on the society. He is a staunch advocate of the use of science in improving the quality of life of the mankind through innovative technologies. He looks upon the magnificent achievements of science as a means to make the dream of a global society come true, yet at the same time he abhors its destructive power. He compares science and religion and draws parallels between their brilliance in providing comfort, succour and peace, and also their destructive power that can annihilate the entire world if human reasoning and love do not feed positive action oriented thoughts. He propounds and stoutly promotes the development of a new paradigm to evolve a global ethic that would enable the world to tread and navigate safely through the hazards it faces from both science and religion. He fervently appeals for a peaceful and creative progress in turning the planet into a living heaven for mankind on earth.

His vast knowledge of the Indian heritage has brought *Yoga* and the Indian Systems of Medicine close to his heart. He had encouraged and promoted scientific research in both disciplines in the well-known national medical institutions when he held the portfolio of Health and Family Welfare as a Union Cabinet Minister.

When we come into close contact with the studies and works of Dr. Karan Singh, we are in an environment of spiritual vision. His remarkable book titled "Prophet of Indian Nationalism", on the thoughts of Sri Aurobindo Ghosh (1872-1950) is indeed thought provoking. As we go through the Foreword by Pandit Jawaharlal Nehru, we see the right political thoughts coming out of a princely environment.

I had a great experience, a decade ago. Even though I had read and also known Dr. Karan Singh as a Cabinet Minister for Civil Aviation, Education and Culture, Health and other ministries, during his political career and also as Head of State or *Sadar-i-Riyasat,* my close contact with Dr. Karan Singh happened two and a half years back during a flight from Delhi to Bangalore. I had a very intimate and detailed philosophical discussion with him. During the discussion, we realised that I came from Rameswaram, the holy centre of Lord Rama, and Dr. Karan Singh from Kashmir, the seat of holy temple Vaishno Devi, and so the discussions entered into the unison of Indian culture. The discussions led me to get deeply immersed in the super vision of Dr. Karan Singh. The discussions started from the famous Chidambaram temple, the cosmic dance of Lord Nataraja, the ancient spiritualism and the thoughts that were transmitted through the sculptors, and moved to the space galaxies moving in the galaxy of millions of stars in dynamic motion and within the stars number of planets orbiting around the star, the Sun. After all these exchanges I had with Dr. Karan Singh, a poem emerged from me, which highlights that the mankind belongs to one of small galaxies that is the Milky-Way. In the Milky-Way galaxy, we belong to the smallest star-the sun, and our habitat is the earth, one of the insignificant planets, but yet man is proud to be a ruler, who can transform the planet into a beautiful and peaceful living habitat or a hell.

After the flight with Dr. Karan Singh, I started reading some of his books. In his autobiography, Dr. Karan Singh, at the Preface brings out an incident which inspired in me the importance of spiritual mission, which I quote, '*...In the sixties I built a Nataraja temple in the great Sri Raghunath temple complex in Jammu, probably the first in North India. Apart from the images, I got a German friend to fabricate a thirty-inch high lead crystal shivalingam which is installed there, under which in due course Asha's and my ashes will lie...*" I was moved with his thoughts and actions of building a place for his abode. May the Almighty bless him and his family live long and contribute.

Dr. Karan Singh is an immensely enlightened, suave, polite and down to earth person. The multiple contours of his imagination and intellect on the vast horizon of his thinking on a variety of subjects and his firm belief in humanity have given him rightly a place as a philosopher par excellence. It is my privilege to know such a rare personality in person and enjoy his friendship. It gives me great pleasure in felicitating Dr. Karan Singh on this happy occasion of his 70th birthday. ❑❑❑

The Raja-Rishi In Our Midst

•

T.R. Anantharaman

Prof. Anantharaman, formerly Director, Institute of Technology and Rector, Banaras Hindu University, is also the founder Chancellor of Ashram Atmadeep, the World Headquarters of a unique Movement for the Third Millennium to usher in a New Social Order inspired by the Spiritual Vision of Vedic India.

"In fact, it was Yoga that brought Dr. Karan Singh and me close together over twenty-five years ago. Dr. K.N. Udupa, the then Director of the Institute of Medical Sciences at the Banaras Hindu University, Varanasi, and I (then Professor and Head, Department of Metallurgy, Institute of Technology, BHU) sought a meeting early in 1973 with Dr. Karan Singh, then Union Minister for Health and Family Planning at New Delhi, to seek his support for the establishment of a centre for Yoga at our university. Unlike most ministers of today, Dr. Karan Singh was easily accessible, responded quickly and graciously to our request and gave us time to meet him in his office at the earliest convenience."

At the very beginning of the great epic Ramayana, the hermit-author Valmiki asks Narada, distinguished guest of an evening at his Ashram, the following question:

"कोन्वस्मिन्सांप्रतं लोके गुणवान्कश्च वीर्यवान्।
धर्मज्ञश्च कृतज्ञश्च सत्यवाक्यो दृढव्रत:।।

चरित्रेण च को युक्तः सर्वभूतेषु को हितः।
विद्वान्कः कः समर्थश्च कश्चैकप्रियदर्शनः।। (I.1. 2 and 3)

"Today in our world, is there anyone virtuous and also valorous, who understands *Dharma* and is also of righteous conduct, who speaks the truth and is steadfast to his principles, who is endowed with a lofty character and is well-disposed to all living creatures, who is learned, capable and also of pleasing appearance ?"

After observing that each of the many qualities enumerated by Valmiki is rare to come by, Narada speaks of Sri Rama, the illustrious son of King Dasarath, as the one person who fulfills all the exacting requirements referred to by the poet. If today Narada were to visit *Ashram Atmadeep* and a similar question put to him by me with reference to Delhi and around, I feel sure that Narada would name Dr. Karan Singh as such a unique person and then go on to describe this scholar-statesman's sterling qualities and his many-splendoured achievements during the last half century.

As every educated Indian ought to know, Sri Rama belonged to the famous solar dynasty boasting of a long line of great kings, the so-called *Ikshvakus*, who were not only outstanding rulers, but also custodians of the sacred *Yoga* tradition. In the *Bhagwad-Gita* Sri Krishna informs Arjuna that he taught *Yoga* to Vivasvan, the founder of the solar dynasty, who, in turn, initiated his son Manu in the same. Arjuna is then told as follows:

"एवं परम्पराप्राप्तमिमं राजर्षयो विदुः।
स कालेनेह महता योगो नष्टः परंतप।।
स एवायं मया तेऽद्य योगः प्रोक्तः पुरातनः।।
भक्तोऽसि मे सखा चेति रहस्यं ह्येतदुत्तमम्।। (IV. 2 and 3)

"Thus transmitted in succession from father to son, Arjuna, this *Yoga* was known to the *Raja-Rishis* (Royal Sages) of the solar dynasty. It got lost, however, through efflux of long time. I am imparting to you today the same ancient *Yoga*, which has been a supreme secret, because you are my devotee and friend."

So the *Yoga* tradition was *puratana* (ancient) even at the time of the Kurukshetra war, fought perhaps over 3000 years ago! Having a pre-Vedic origin in the mature Indus Valley Period (3000-1800 B.C.), lost and regained in some parts from time to time, this magnificent Yogic heritage of India has however enjoyed all along the safe custody and zealous protection of *Raja-Rishis*. With his deep interest and committed involvement in *Yoga*, Dr. Karan Singh surely belongs to this long line of Royal Sages.

In fact, it was *Yoga* that brought Dr.Karan Singh and me close together over twenty five years ago. Dr. K. N. Udupa, the then Director of the Institute of Medical Sciences at the Banaras Hindu University, Varanasi, and I (then Professor & Head, Department of Metallurgy, Institute of Technology, BHU) sought a meeting early in 1973 with Dr. Karan Singh, then Union Minister for Health and Family Planning at New Delhi, to seek his advice and support for the establishment of a Centre for *Yoga* at our University. Unlike most ministers of today, Dr. Karan Singh was easily accessible, responded quickly and graciously to our request and gave us time to meet him in his office at the earliest mutually convenient date. Of course, Dr.Karan Singh had already held the exalted position of Chancellor of the Banaras Hindu University and was known for his keen interest in the growth and well-being of this unique National University established in 1916 through the monumental efforts of a great Indian, the late revered Mahamana Madan Mohan Malviya. His missionary zeal for *Yoga*, particularly for Sri Aurobindo's *Poorna Yoga* (Inter-Yoga), was also well known. Following our fruitful discussions with him, Dr. Udupa and I sought and obtained the blessings of Dr. K. L. Shrimali, then Vice-chancellor of our University. Things then moved fast and within a few months the *Yoga Sadhana Kendra* (Centre for Yoga) came into existence as an inter-disciplinary academic unit of the University, for study, research and propagation of *Yoga* in all its theoretical and practical aspects on a modern scientific basis. On Dr. Shrimali's request I took over as the first Hony. Director of this Centre and served in that capacity for four years *i.e.*, till 1977, when I was appointed the Rector of Banaras Hindu University.

For all those, including Dr. Karan Singh, who were concerned with the rather difficult fledgeling years of the BHU Centre for *Yoga*, it is a matter of some satisfaction that this Centre is very much alive and is still serving the students and staff of this University through its well-organized Certificate and Diploma Courses and through scientific researches, mainly at the *Yoga* Research Laboratory of the Institute of Medical Sciences. However, at the global level, we have a long way to go to win, for *Yoga* its rightful place in education and research, as assigned in a routine way today to many modern scientific and technological disciplines in schools, colleges and universities. It is my earnest hope that Dr. Karan Singh will give priority now to this challenging task and help ensure that the third millennium makes the enormous benefits of *Yoga* available to one and all in the human family.

Needless to say, the present time just on the eve of a new millennium is most opportune for a systematic study *de novo*, as also critical evaluation of the full potential, physical, mental, intellectual and also transcendental, of classical *Yoga* from both the spiritual-philosophical and scientific-practical angles. To begin with, it is necessary to appreciate and highlight the enormous importance and as yet unfathomed depths of the *Yoga Sutras*, the earliest and perhaps the most systematic treatise of the classical *Yoga* traditions, consisting of just 195 *sutras* or aphorisms in Sanskrit, collected and codified by sage Patanjali over 2000 years ago. The second step is to re-orient the study, research, teaching and propagation of *Yoga* so as to bring the theory and practice of *Yoga* in tune with the spirit of enquiry, objectivity and openness characterizing our Age of Science and to pave thereby a clearer and surer way than hitherto, for establishing a stabler, less careworn, happier and more harmonious human family on this earth.

Incidentally, modern science has in recent decades modified its hard and uncompromising attitude to all that was considered non-science and hence *non-sense*(!) earlier *viz.*, to all knowledge that went under the labels of Spirituality, Mysticism and Religion. The advent of quantum mechanics has had a lot to do with this welcome development. Some significant contribution to this happy change in attitude has been made by recent advances in neurophysiology in unravelling the role of the left (or rational) and right (non-rational) hemispheres of the human brain. It is appropriate here to record what Max Planck, the German physicist widely regarded as the father of quantum mechanics, wrote as early as 1936:

> "Science means unresting endeavour and continually progressing development towards an objective which the poet's intuition may comprehend, but the scientist's intellect can never fully grasp."

Gradually the *rational* part of the human psyche, typified by Science, has begun to merge again with the other part, ignored by western Science for three centuries, namely our *irrational* or *supra-rational* side *i.e.*, Spirituality.

During the last four decades, despite the denial of whole-hearted recognition and support from the Government and its funding agencies, many medical scientists of our country have taken to *Yoga* research and conducted many a pioneering albeit preliminary study on the physiological as well as neuro-physiological changes brought about in *Yoga* practitioners through *Bahiranga Yoga i.e.*, *dharana dhyana* and *samadhi* experiences. These systematic scientific studies have established beyond doubt the therapeutic value of many yogic practices, besides their enormous contribution to positive health and sense of well being of the practitioners. In this connection, apart from the encouragement to such researches during Dr. Karan Singh's tenure as Union Health Minister, special mention is in order for the dedicated work of research groups at the All India Institute of Medical Sciences, Delhi; the Institute of Medical Sciences, BHU, Varanasi; the Medical College, Chennai; the National Institute of Mental Health and Neuro-Sciences, Bangalore; and the Defence Institute of Physiology and Allied Sciences, Delhi. The names of Dr. B.K. Anand (Delhi), Dr. K.N. Udupa (Varanasi), Dr. B. Ramamurthy (Chennai), Dr. T. Desiraju (Bangalore) and Dr. W. Selvamurthy (Delhi) come naturally to one's mind in relation to these pioneering researches. Thanks to the recent efforts of some medical scientists, particularly Dr. B. Ramamurthy (Chennai) and Dr. P.N. Tandon (Delhi), the field of human consciousness has come to the forefront in the context of researches on the functioning of the human brain. As a sequel to these initiatives, the *National Brain Research Centre* has just recently come into existence in Delhi to develop bridges across different disciplines ranging from philosophy to computational sciences, physics and neurosciences. The Round Table discussions organised by this centre at Allahabad in October, 2000 are likely to lead to more intense activity in the field of consciousness than even before in our country in the coming years.

In fact, at the global level, ancient *Yoga* and modern science have already started rubbing shoulders following the recent almost explosive revival of scientific interest in human consciousness. This exciting development has been due partly to the successes achieved in probing the secrets related to more than a billion interconnected "*neurons*" estimated to be active in a normal human brain. Increasingly powerful scientific tools are presently in use in Neuroscience laboratories, ranging from microelectrodes to magnetic resonance imaging and positron emission tomography. The modern world is also gradually coming round to recognize the validity of 'Sri Aurobindo's diagnosis that the present serious crisis in human society can be resolved *only* through transformations in consciousness *i.e.,* subtle neural changes brought about by normal evolution combined with conscious efforts of the *Yogic* type, and *not* through further technological changes in the outer physical world.

Many brilliant scientists of the west, notably Nobel Prize winners Brian Josephson, Francis Creek and Gerald Edeeman, as also the mathematician Roger Penrose and the neuroscientist Christof Koch, have developed keen interest in the last two decades and also taken seriously to studies in the realm of consciousness, still the most elusive, even though inescapable, of all phenomena. Among many seminars and conferences in this exciting field, special mention needs to be made of the two Inter-Disciplinary International Conferences held in April 1994 and April 1996 respectively on the theme "Towards a Scientific Basis of Consciousness", at the Health Sciences Center, University of Arizona, Tucson, USA. The second conference attracted over 1000 "consciousness scientists" and led to an astonishing consensus *viz.*, "Consciousness cannot be explained within the paradigms of our current science."

The above-referred developments are indeed exciting, even epoch-making, but where do we go from here and what has India, the home of *Yoga* for over 4000 years, to offer in this field in the coming years? This is where the *Raja-Rishi* in our midst has a central role to play. He has to ensure that the authentic voice of *Yogic* and Vedic India is raised to bring some clarity in the midst of the prevailing confusion in regard to defining and understanding consciousness. The need of the hour is to bring together scientists and scholars with a feel and empathy for India's Vedic and pre-Vedic traditions to research *together* with an open mind, starting from two age-old *Maha-Vakyas* (Seminal Utterances) of the Vedic *Rishis* (seers):

"प्रज्ञानं ब्रह्म — Brahman is Pure Consciousness.

सर्वं खल्विदं ब्रह्म — All this is verily Brahman."

□□□

Forgiveness or Use of Force: Which is Superior?

•

Chaturvedi Badrinath

Chaturvedi Badrinath is an eminent intellectual and scholar of Indian philosophy. He has lectured on various facets of Indian philosophy in several Indian and foreign universities, institutions and societies of learning.

"Karan Singh's familiar vision has been that of the world as a family. And life in a family is lived, as we all know, not so much on the basis of thoughts and ideas, but on the basis of feelings above all. His concern has been with the conflicts and violence we create in the name of religion, faith, political ideology, and even truth. I thought the best way for me to greet Karan Singh on his 70th birthday would be to bring up a question that has always been at the centre of human experience."

I feel honoured in being invited to contribute to this volume of essays to celebrate the 70th birthday of Dr. Karan Singh. I met him for the first time in 1970 at Frankfurt. He was then a Minister in the Government of India. We happened to be staying at the same hotel. My colleague, Suresh Mathur, Indian Consul General, had come to take me to his home for lunch later in the day and to see Dr. Karan Singh and his wife off on their one-day visit to Baden Baden. I was introduced to them. On learning that I was to give the next day a talk on some aspects of Indian philosophy at Marburg University, Karan Singh, on a most friendly impulse, invited me to spend the day with them, not knowing that I was not free to do so. I was greatly touched by Karan Singh's invitation to me on impulse: but I was touched no less that Suresh Mathur had come as arranged previously, to take me to his home, and there was no question that I would have gone with him. But Suresh relinquished me to Karan Singh as graciously as Karan Singh had invited me to go with them.

It was a most charming day for me, and also blessed. No sooner did the car journey to Baden Baden begin, in a Mercedes 600, that Sri Aurobindo appeared, and remained with us almost throughout. Karan Singh's earliest work was on his political philosophy. Sri Aurobindo listened attentively when Karan Singh began to explain to me some intricate turns in his later philosophy; but he looked vastly amused when, in turn, I mounted a criticism of his *The Life Divine*. Philosophical contentions vanished, though, when, on a happy impulse again, Karan Singh began to sing, in his very melodious voice, some songs he had composed in *Dogri*, his mother tongue. That was beautiful. Mrs Karan Singh, Princess Yasho Rajya Lakshmi, showed an endearing sense of humour. At one point in our cruise in that Mercedes 600, a tourist bus drew parallel to it, and the men and women in that bus began to applaud and cheer happily. I said to Mrs. Karan Singh: "See, they are cheering you." And she replied: "No, no, they are not cheering *me*, they are cheering the Mercedes 600." At this, Sri Aurobindo laughed as well. And he looked captivating when he laughed. I remember wanting to say to him, but did not have the courage, "Sir, if only you laughed like that, and more frequently than you are known to do, you would be a philosopher of human *feelings*, and not a philosopher just of super-consciousness."

Karan Singh's familiar vision has been that of the world as a family. And life in a family is lived, as we all know, not so much on the basis of *thoughts and ideas*, but on the basis of *feelings* above all. His concerns have been with the quality of life which, in that family, we create for ourselves and for others. His concern has been with the conflicts and violence we create in the name of religion, faith, political ideology, and even truth. I thought the best way for me to greet Karan Singh on his 70th birthday would be to bring up a question that has always been at the center of human experience, in collective relationships quite as much as in our personal relationships. It is the question concerning the need of forgiveness and reconciliation, *kshma*, in the face of the human instinct to avenge hurt and insult. And nowhere has this question been discussed in greater details, not in the abstract, but in the numerous contexts of concrete daily living, than in the *Mahabharata*, While *kshma* or forgiveness and reconciliation, is primarily a feeling, as hurt is, it has its undeniable rationality as well. Why forgiveness? Why not revenge?

Yudhishthira, the eldest of the royal five Pandava brothers, and the legitimate heir to the throne, had lost a second time in the game of dice, the dice being fraudulently loaded. He had put, successively, his brothers, and then his wife, on stake, and had lost each time. They were banished from the realm for thirteen years, as an agreed penalty to whoever lost the game. They had nothing that they could call their own except each other. One evening, sitting in a humble cottage in a forest, they were having a conversation about the state they were in. Draupadi, their wife, was arguing most forcefully for regaining through war what they had dishonestly been deprived of by their first cousins, the Kauravas.

Draupadi says to Yudhishthira: "When we were set off on this life of misery and deprivation, clothed in garments mean and coarse, there were tears in the eyes of all-excepting those four, wicked and evil: Duryodhana, Karna, Shakuni, and Dushasana. They had a mocking smile on their lips, and not a tear in their eyes. Seeing what we are reduced to, and its injustice, how *can you be not angry?* A Kshatriya who does not use force when time demands it, invites from everybody contempt only. No, not for a moment must you entertain towards our enemies the feelings of forgiveness and reconciliation: for this is the time for force."

Ever since Draupadi was insulted and humiliated, by Dushasana chiefly, her inner space was wholly occupied by the memory of that event. He had tried to disrobe her in the royal assembly,into which she was brought, dragged by her hair. She had resisted when she was told that she was now a slave, having been put at stake by her eldest husband Yudhishthira, in that game of dice which, through a dishonest device, he was made to lose. She was burning with a great many feelings, with the desire for revenge most of all. And it is in that, in the feeling of revenge, most of all, that Yudhishthira finds the root of never-ending violence in the world.

He advocates, on principle, forgiveness and reconciliation. He unfolds its rationality in simple and quick steps. He says to his wife: "Draupadi, if your appeal to anger and force were accepted as just principle of conduct, then what kind of world would this be? There would never be peace among men: for anger is the root of all conflicts:"

> आक्रुष्टः पुरुषः सर्वं प्रत्याक्रोशेदनन्तरम्।
> प्रतिहन्याद्धतश्चैव तथा हिंस्याच्च हिंसितः।।
>
> हन्युर्हि पितरः पुत्रान् पुत्राश्चापि तथा पितृन्।
> हन्युश्च पतयो भार्याः पतीन् भार्यास्तैव च।।
>
> एवं संकुपिते लोके शमः कृष्णे न विद्यते।
> प्रजानां संधिमूलं हि शामं विद्धि शुभानने।।
>
> If everybody is angry, then anger is returned with anger. Hurt, he hurts; violated, he violates.
>
> Fathers would kill sons, and sons would kill fathers; husbands would kill wives, and wives would kill husbands.
>
> In a world where there is only anger, Krishne, there can be no peace. For you must know, dear one, that reconciliation is the root of peace among people. —Vana-parva, 29. 27-29.

Therefore,

> क्षमा ब्रह्म क्षमा सत्यं क्षमा भूतं च भावि च।
> क्षमा तपः क्षमा शौचं क्षमयेदं धृतं जगत्।।
> क्षमा तेजस्विनां तेजः क्षमा ब्रह्म तपस्विनाम्।
> क्षमा सत्यं सत्यवतां क्षमा यज्ञः क्षमा शमः।।
> Reconciliation is the essence of the universe.
> Reconciliation is truth; is the past and the future.
> Reconciliation is sacrifice, and purity.
> It is reconciliation that holds the world.
> Reconciliation is the force of the forceful.
> And it is the ultimate aim of the austere.
> Reconciliation is the truth of the truthful.
> Reconciliation is sacrifice, and it is peace.
> —Vana-parva, 29.37,40.

But Draupadi had never disputed any of this. Neither had she ever advocated anger and force as the decisive factors in relationships *always*. She was a woman of intelligence that was as luminous as her beauty. She had moments earlier argued that to separate forgiveness and reconciliation from *desa* and *kala*, and also from *patra*, that is, 'the place', 'the time' and the character of 'the person' concerned, and then place upon it an absolute value regardless, is to invite disrespect and not peace. She gives numerous examples of it from daily life. She recounts a parable which, she says, she had heard as a little girl on her father's knee. It was about a question Bali had put to his grandfather, Prahlada, and the latter's answer. The question was: 'Between force and reconciliation, which is superior?' And the answer was: सततं तेजों न नित्यं श्रेयसी क्षमा: neither force, nor reconciliation, is good *always*. He who forgives, always is considered weak, and is taken advantage of, by his servants, relatives, his children, and by his wife no less. He who uses force always, in his speech and conduct, offends everybody to such a degree that he soon destroys himself. There is a time for force; and there is a time for reconciliations; a time for being gentle, and a time for being hard.' Draupadi's argument simply is that,

> The man who is gentle, is disregarded by everybody; and the man who is harsh keeps hurting people. He who knows the occasion to be one or the other, is truly a great king.
>
> —Vana-parva, 28.36

The argument now becomes a question of judgement, about which there can be two conflicting perceptions. Yudhishthira settles that swiftly by saying that, in *his* judgement, that time was not for force. Draupadi, equally swiftly, questions his judgement, and says, gesticulating sarcastically, that his mind is confused, mistaking a general principle about forgiveness to be also a right feeling. "I bow to that God, and to that Fate, who has cast your mind into confusion": then, even more sarcastically, this: "I have heard the enlightened people say that, protected, *dharma* protects: but you, protecting *dharma* always, are now unprotected by it."

Then she questions, as countless human beings have done since, sometime or the other in their lives, God's justice and mercy. "On the contrary, He plays with human beings as children play with toys", she says. "Nor do I see him treat the living beings like father and mother would: He acts, as ordinary mortals do, with caprice. This view of mine is only strengthened when we see those who are good suffering privations of every kind, and those who are wicked enjoying pleasures of every variety. when I see the prosperity of Duryodhana, and your humiliation and pain, I condemn that God who behaves so capriciously."

The *Mahabharata* demonstrates, what can be clearly seen everywhere in human affairs, that when feelings are disregarded, and only some abstract ethical principle drummed instead, then judgements about a human situation get thoroughly muddled—with distracting emotions. Until then, in that long conversation, Yudhishthira had been addressing his wife with endearing words like *priye,* or 'darling', *shubhanane,*, or 'the dear one', or *shubhe,* 'the good one'. But now, irritated, he addresses her as *raja-putri,* or 'Princess', or simply as *daughter* of *Yajnasena'*. Courteous to her all the same, he responds by saying: "I heard carefully what you said, Princess, and what you said was said in a very elegant language. But you are now propounding atheism." "I have not adopted *dharma* with an eye on some material advantage out of it; for in that case I would be a merchant of *dharma*. I do what I do because I must. *Dharma* never remains without giving its fruits, and that is true of *dharma* as well. Because the fruits of *dharma* are not quickly manifest, you must not, for that reason, cast doubt either on *dharma* or on God. The man who acknowledges the evidence only of human intelligence, and regards this sensible world, to which he attaches himself sensuously, as the only reality, must forever remain confused as regards the reality unseen. Dear queen, you must not, like a fool, either doubt or accuse *dharma* and God."

Draupadi saw that the conversation between them had taken a different turn. Yudhishthira was talking like a professor of philosophy, unmindful of feeling and their force: she was talking like a woman deeply hurt and insulted. "Never will I disregard, or disrespect, *dharma*—much less God', she replied. "Take it that, hurt and wounded, I am crying as if I was mad. Why, I shall cry even more, and you listen to me with a calm mind."

Following this, she mounts, in sixty verses, a powerful argument, clear and consistent, from human efforts as the means of gaining everything of worth. She engages in an issue that is central to the question of ordering human relationships including the question of forgiveness and reconciliation: Is a person free to be what he, or she, is? Or is one determined by some *other*—Time, or Fate, or God, or History? If the latter, than I am no more free to forgive or not forgive than the other person was free or not free to behave towards me unjustly. The substance of what she said is: "At this moment we are in great adversity. Without arguing endlessly the question of human freedom, or whether you will or will not achieve success—if you devote yourself to efforts, and have no doubts as to its efficacy, we can regain what you have lost. She concludes by saying:

> "Taking into consideration time and place, and judging through intelligence one's capacities and strength, let a man, with untroubled mind, make effort and increase in blessings."
>
> "Let no man show disrespect to himself. For, defeating himself thereby, he can never gain anything good."
>
> —Vana-parva, 32.53,58.

She was also meaning to say that, in their particular context, it was no use bringing up the question of forgiveness and getting entangled in its evident complexity, when two opposite views concerning it are both as reasonable as they are forceful. The question was one of fighting deceit and injustice.

To forgive or to remain irreconciled, keeping the memory of the past alive is a question that can never be decided one way or the other as a matter of principle in the abstract. It can be decided only at the level of *feeling.* Hurt is a feeling: to forgive is a feeling too. In its absence, hurt is not just a memory. In not forgiving, hurt is lived again and again, and is perpetuated—this time by myself. Feelings of revenge are self-consuming and self-destructive. Even before I destroy the other, I would have destroyed myself. This is as true in a collective sense as it is true in a personal sense. Forgiveness is thus primarily directed towards one's self; for then it is a feeling—of freedom from the prison of the past.

□□□

Dr. Karan Singh: A Personality Rich in Cultural Heritage

•

Mrs. Sarala Birla

Mrs. Sarala Birla is a moving spirit behind the landmark cultural and literary institutions of the famous Birla family, considered not only amongst the greatest industrial dynasties but also the greatest cultural dynasties of India.

"He has the fragrance of the fresh breeze of wisdom and vision of Kashmir. Kashmir which gave birth to great celebrities like Keyyat, Kalhan, Rudrat, Vilhan, Mammat, Udbhat, Anandvardhan Acharya and Abhinavgupt Acharya. He also represents the experience and tradition of the rulers of Kashmir. Dr. Karan Singh is also a soft-spoken and thought provoking ora tor. When he gives a speech, words come like the flow of a mountain waterfall."

I was happy to know that a felicitation volume was being published to mark Dr. Karan Singh's completion of 70th year of his life. This is a life replete with action and achievement.

His services in the varied fields of politics, religion, philosophy and culture have always been pronounced. He gave a special distinction and prestige to any responsibility he held, whether as an honourable minister or in a prominent position in an institution.

He is truly the "Son of Himalayas" endowed with superconsciousness, clean and pure in thought, committed to serve mankind and easily accessible to all.

He has the fragrance of the fresh breeze of wisdom and vision of Kashmir. Kashmir which gave birth to great celebrities like Keyyat, Kalhan, Rudrat, Vilhan, Mammat, Udbhat, Anandvardhan Acharya and Abhinavgupt Acharya who represent the experience and tradition of the rulers. Dr. Karan Singh is also a soft-spoken and thought provoking orator. When he gives a speech, words come like the flow of a mountain waterfall. The listeners are hypnotised when he recites the Vedic *Richas*, the *mantras* from the Upanishads and ancient prayers or *shlokas*. It's like the sound of music from a stringed instrument. He is a living affirmation of the magnificience, magnanimity and tolerance of our ancient culture and also a synthesiser of tradition and modernity, seeking to establish a link and harmony between ancient culture and modern contexts. Therefore, in his spoken and written word, the ancient dons a modern visage.

We have enjoyed friendly relations with Karan Singhji for the last 40 years. Very often he has graced the programmes of our institutions as a speaker.

The Birla Academy of Art and Culture was inaugurated on January 9, 1967. Dr. Karan Singh was the Chief Guest on that occasion.

He has served for many years on the Jury of the G.D. Birla International Award. We continued to recieve encouragement and cooperation from him in that capacity.

We installed an impressive 62 feet high idol of Ashutosh Bhagwan 'Maha Mangal Dev' on the Delhi-Gurgaon national highway. It was on March 10, 1994 on the auspicious Maha Shiv Ratri, that *Pran Pratishtha*, or life-breath ceremony of the grand idol was performed. On that auspicious occasion Dr. Karan Singh, brimming with devotion delivered a very meaningful discourse on Shaivism. Expressing his deeply touching sentiments, he had said at that time: "If I am unable to go to Kashmir for a darshan of Lord Shiva, I shall be able to fulfill the desire of my heart by his darshan here, now."

I am convinced that felicitation of Dr. Karan Singh, so rich in personal virtues and achievements, will be a great source of encouragement and inspiration for all.

□□□

Kahlil Gibran: The Poet of the Culture of Peace

•

Suheil Bushrui

Suheil Bushrui, Professor in the University of Maryland in the United States, using the life and works of great poet Kahlil Gibran seeks to raise the challenges before the 21st Century, pointing out that the work of peace-making is still far from complete.

"Those of us who love India have come to know her through her great teachers such as Kabir, Gandhi, Tagore and Vivekananda, the ambassadors of spirituality who have bestowed upon us India's enriching gifts of the mind and the spirit. India has built for the world a kingdom of the imagination and the spirit; and today His Excellency Karan Singh is India's noble prince in that kingdom, a world teacher held in honour by all those who share his vision of world unity."

Kahlil Gibran occupies a unique position in the pantheon of the world's great writers. His best-known work, *The Prophet*, has been translated into forty different languages, enabling it to be read and appreciated in places as far apart as Tokyo, Manila, Delhi, Nairobi, Rome, Paris, London, and New York. In the celebration of its 60th anniversary, the prestigious Penguin Publishing Company named Gibran as one of the most important authors of the 20th century. His stature and importance increase as time passes, for although he died in 1931 and his finest work was published over 70 years ago, his message remains as potent and meaningful today as when he was writing. With its emphasis on the healing process, the universal, the natural, the eternal, the timeless, his work represents a powerful affirmation of faith in the human spirit.

Events around the world in the last decades of the 20th century have underlined all too clearly the continuing relevance of Kahlil Gibran today. The dismantling of the Berlin Wall, the end of the cold war, the move towards federalism in Europe, and the growing role of the United Nations Organisation all reflect his passionate belief in the oneness of mankind and the need to remove man-made barriers, a vivid contrast to the fashionable emphasis on cynicism, anxiety, and despair of much of the 20th-century literature. Yet despite these promising developments, much ground remains to be covered. In Gibran's own homeland, and in the middle east in general, conflict and religious intolerance still prevail. The natural environment, whose sanctity he constantly proclaims, remains under threat from pollution and exploitation. In a world still riven and divided, Gibran's message of peace, unity, and reconciliation still urgently demands a hearing.

Of all his contemporaries, it is perhaps William Butler Yeats who parallels Gibran most closely. Both were profoundly preoccupied with the question of unity and its achievement in a fragmented world. In Ireland as in Lebanon, partition of many kinds threatened this vision: religious, cultural, social, and geographical. As Gibran achieved equal fluency in his Arabic and English writings, and drew on Christian, Sufi, and Bahái traditions and imagery, Yeats attempted to blend the Anglo-Irish literary tradition, the riches of Gaelic myth and poetry, and the purely English background in a new, overarching combination of the best in all three. Philosophically, Yeats and Gibran shared a passion for unity at every level: not the bland, faceless "globalisation" of the late 20th century, a stirring of diverse cultures into a featureless, indiscriminate blend, but a reconciling and recognition of individual traditions enabling them to live in harmony together to the mutual benefit of all. At a personal level, Yeats's experiments with the Japanese Noh theatre and Gibran's discovery of the English language brought both of them a new creative vigour and rejuvenation. Both, in their awareness of the violence and destruction threatening a world running headlong into chaos, assumed the role of prophets, warning mankind of the terrible consequences of pursuing a path of disunity and anarchy. As Yeats put it in "The Second Coming":

> Things fall apart: the centre cannot hold;
> Mere anarchy is loosed upon the world,
> The blood-dimmed tide is loosed, and everywhere
> The ceremony of innocence is drowned;
> The best lack all conviction, while the worst
> Are full of passionate intensity.

In the pages that follow I propose to show how Gibran, who, unlike Yeats, did not live to see the rise of Hitler and Mussolini and the splintering through civil war of Spain, another country where the Christian and Muslim traditions had nourished a rich and ancient culture; foresaw in specific areas the dangers encroaching on the whole of humanity if these forces where not checked. In his impassioned appeals for unity, he speaks as cogently and forcefully at the beginning of the 21st century as when he first took up his pen.

Indeed, in his own person Gibran seems to embody the process, delicate and costly as it is, of forging unity between widely disparate cultures and traditions, languages and literatures. At first sight it may appear paradoxical and implausible that one man could weld together influences as diverse as Nietzsche, Christianity and Islam, the Romantic poets such as Blake and Wordsworth and their contemporaries, and the artistic environments of Paris and New York. Yet he triumphantly achieved this, and in so doing stands as a proof and symbol of a unity which informed his vision in the widest sense of a world in which rights of many kinds—those of women, human kind in general, its many religions, and the whole of creation—would be secured and respected, releasing the people of the world to lead a new life free from acrimony and conflict.

Gibran's Sufi masters in Arabic literature, ibn al-Arabi, ibn al-Farid, and al-Ghazzali, taught him about the Unity of Being and inspired a deeper vision of the nature of the universe. The key passage, or root metaphor, that may serve to symbolise the vision of Gibran is that passage from Iran: *The City of Lofty Pillars*, where he emphasises the interdependence of the whole of creation:

> All things in this creation exist within you,
> and all things in you exist in creation;
> there is no border between you and the closest
> things, and there is no distance between you
> and the farthest things, and all things, from
> the lowest to the loftiest, from the smallest
> to the greatest, are within you as equal things.
> In one atom are found all the elements of the
> earth; in one motion of the mind are found the
> motions of all the laws of existence; in one
> drop of water are found the secrets of all the
> endless oceans...

Such a vision requires a radical rethinking of the present situation of humanity that it is nothing short of revolutionary. Yet it is easy to forget that Christianity, in its early stages, was equally revolutionary in its rejection of the conventions of the schematised and hierarchical social structures of the Roman Empire. St. Paul's proclamation (Galatians 3, xxviii) that;

> There is neither Jew nor Greek, there is neither bond nor free, there is neither male nor female: for ye are all one in Christ Jesus.

boldly abolishes at a stroke the cherished distinctions on which that society rested. It is ironic to reflect that, with the adoption of Christianity as the official state religion, certain sayings of Paul were taken out of context and used to support oppression and restriction, especially when applied to women, who were enjoined to cover their heads and refrain from speaking in church. Gibran himself, coming from a Maronite Christian background, was brought up on the Bible, whose cadences and vocabulary powerfully influenced his own literary style. Yet he was also receptive to the influence of Nietzsche, renowned above all for his virulent attacks on Christianity and his statement in *The Gay Science* that "God is dead," as well as for some remarks in the same work about women which are distinctly unpalatable to the modern reader.

To achieve unity, it is necessary first of all to identify the forces that militate against it. For Gibran, organised religion as the world had experienced it, was one of these forces. Like Nietzsche, the son of a Lutheran pastor, he came of clerical forebears; his maternal grandfather, Istifan Rahme had been a Maronite priest. Yet he saw how obedience to the norms of organised religion, exploited as a means of social control and coercion (a view also common to Kierkegaard) could warp and wither the life of the individual, particularly in the case of women, and perpetuate hatred and suspicion between adherents of different traditions, existing in a state of mutual intolerance. He shared with Blake a distrust for the divisive external practices of institutionalised religion, attacked in *The Marriage of Heaven and Hell*, whose ministers, the baleful "priests in black gowns," fetter and thwart natural desires and, in *A Little Boy Lost*, prey upon the innocent. In "*The Crucified*" Gibran writes: "Jesus was not sent here to teach the people to build magnificent churches and temples...He came to make the human heart a temple, and the soul an altar, and the mind a priest," [*Secrets of the Heart* (1992), 215]. He also inveighs against the conventional insipid "meek and mild" portrayal of Jesus which, among others, turned Nietzsche himself against Christianity:

The Nazarene was not weak! He was strong and is strong! But the people refuse to heed the true meaning of strength...He lived as a leader: He was crucified as a crusader; He died with a heroism that frightened his killers and tormentors. Jesus was not a bird with broken wings; He was a raging tempest who broke all crooked wings, (ibid., 214).

The only work of Nietzsche's which Gibran is definitely known to have read is *Thus Spake Zarathustra*, but its influence on him was profound and far-reaching. During his time in Paris he wrote to his friend Adele Watson:

Yes, Nietzsche is a great giant—and the more you read him the more you will love him. He is perhaps the greatest spirit in modern times, and his work will outlive many of the things we consider great. Please, p-l-e-a-s-e, read *Thus Spake Zarathustra* as soon as possible, for it is—to me—one of the greatest works of all times.

At first this attraction might seen unlikely, not only on account of Nietzsche's attitude to religion but because of some of the more notorious passages of his work, frequently quoted out of context, concerning war and women, such as, "Man should be trained for war and woman for the recreation of the warrior: all else is folly (*Thus Spake Zarathustra* I: "Of Old and Young Women"). Surely this suggests an improbable source of inspiration for a poet of the culture of peace? Yet, as we shall see, the views which Nietzsche expressed about women were largely shaped by factors and circumstances very different from those in Gibran's case. It was his intellectual vigour, iconoclastic spirit and freedom from cant and hypocrisy which delighted Gibran, and also his supple and lyrical poetic language. While in Paris, Gibran had also read Voltaire and Rousseau, whom he described as "the conscience of France towards the end of the eighteenth century," and found himself especially in sympathy with Rousseau's revolt against materialism and injustice, his belief in nature as a teacher, and his sense of the unity of being, all of which were to be central to his own thought. Nietzsche fulfilled a similar function in nineteenth-century Germany. During a period of rapid industrial and material progress and the boom years which followed Bismarck's wars of expansion in the 1860s, culminating in the Franco-Prussian War of 1870-71, Nietzsche viewed with horror the bombast and complacency which were replacing the cultured atmosphere of the smaller German courts which were swallowed up in the new Empire whose proclamation in 1871 left even its ruler, Wilhelm I, sufficiently dubious to write to his wife that it was the unhappiest day of his life; instead of Prussia being absorbed into Germany, the opposite had occurred. Facing the increasing vainglory, materialism and philistinism which ensued, Nietzsche directed a series of urgent warnings and pungent invective against his fellow countrymen. Fighting against the current of his times, he became what Gibran described as "probably the loneliest man of the nineteenth century and surely the greatest" (recalling Ibsen's statement in *An Enemy of the People* that "the strongest man is he who stands most alone"). In a society which he saw as spiralling into madness, he fittingly used the voice of a madman to express some of his most devastating apothegms, notably the already quoted "God is dead. God remains dead. And we have killed him" (*The Gay Science*, 125), a device which was to influence Gibran when he came to write *The Forerunner*.

Fools and madmen figure frequently in literature as beings privileged to utter that which is forbidden to those in their "right" minds. *The Arabian Nights* is full of such characters and Gibran could not have missed in his early readings of those famous folk stories of Arabia the character of "al-Bahlul," whose foolish words are the epitome of all wisdom. We may recall the Fool in Shakespeare's *King Lear*, interspersing words of wisdom with his unchecked folly, or the *yurodivy*, "holy fools," who recur throughout Russian literature, most notably, perhaps, in Pushkin's

Boris Godunov (1825-31). In Pushkin's story, the Simpleton fearlessly confronts the usurper Tsar with the murder of the true heir, the child Dimitri, and assures him " I cannot pray for a Tsar-Herod...the Mother of God would not be pleased," and, in the noisy tumult which, at the end of Mussorgsky's opera, greets the arrival of a false Dimitri, who is left alone, a solitary, clear-eyed prophet of the woes in store for Russia. Sharing a child's candour and straightforwardness, such beings also share their impunity: as Kipling puts it in his epigraph to his story *Tods' Amendment*:

The World has set its heavy yoke
Upon the old white-bearded folk
Who strive to please the King.
God's mercy is upon the young,
God's wisdom in the baby tongue
That fears not anything.

In his affinity with Rousseau's belief in the innate innocence of natural man, Gibran likewise found the figure of a madman a fitting mouthpiece for his convictions, as in *The Forerunner; Yuhanna the Mad*, *The Madman* and, in *The Forerunner*, the poem "God's Fool," the vision of a man imbued with purity of vision who remains full of wonderment at all he surveys although his bizarre activities lead to his arrest. To achieve peace and unity, a similar sense of wonderment was a step towards universal respect for creation in its entirety, transcending artificial barriers and obstructions in a simplicity and honesty of vision which was a precondition for the establishment of harmony. A speaker who stood outside such norms and limitations, whether in Nietzsche's world or Gibran's, was the natural (in every sense) choice to express outspoken criticism of the prevailing order and to foretell the consequences if it remained unchanged. And such criticism had to be voiced if a lasting state of peace was to result, founded on sincerity without any attempts to gloss over sources of friction. As Blake writes in *A Poison Tree*:

I was angry with my friend;
I told my wrath—my wrath did end.
I was angry with my foe;
I told it not—my wrath did grow.

Despite stylistic similarities between Nietzsche and Gibran, such as the use of parables and figures such as the madman and gravedigger, their overall messages remain different, mainly because Gibran never felt impelled to challenge the cosmological order or to question the nature of divinity in its deepest sense. There was another important area of difference between them, however, and this, as previously mentioned, was in their attitudes to women and their rights.

Although both Nietzsche and Gibran had a more important relationship with their mothers than with their fathers, the nature of these relationships differed significantly, which in its turn was to influence their views on and relationships with other women throughout their lives. Nietzsche's clergyman father died when his only surviving son was not yet five; the boy was raised with his younger sister Elisabeth by their mother and aunts in an atmosphere of suffocating, narrow-minded piety which did nothing to inspire him with intellectual respect for Christianity. Shy and ill at ease in the company of women, he never married or-achieved a satisfactory long-term friendship or deeper bond with a potential mate. His philosophy was also influenced by Schopenhauer, whose troubled relationships with, and general contempt for the female sex were proverbial. Although Gibran's father survived until 1909, their relationship had always been fraught, disrupted by the older man's fecklessness and taste for drink, and permanently weakened when the rest of the family emigrated to the USA in 1895 after a scandal whose details remain obscure, leading the elder Gibran to be left behind. It was through the industry of the poet's mother, Kamila, that the family survived in its new environment; she earned money to support Kahlil, his elder half-brother Boutros (Peter) and his two younger sisters Marianna and Sultana, by peddling fabrics in the wealthier parts of Boston with such success that after a year Peter was able to open a dry goods store on the proceeds, together with the family's savings, in which the two girls worked as assistants while Kahlil continued his schooling. It was Kamila who held the family together through the precarious years of her son's childhood and adolescence, and her death from cancer in 1903, when he was twenty, was a grievous blow, following those of Sultana and Peter from tuberculosis the previous year. In later years he recalled her thus:

> I never saw her when to the least being she was less than a sister or to the greatest less than master. She gave me to understand, even when I was three years old, that the tie between us was as between any two other people, a tie of liking each other—and that we were two separate beings brought

together by life and by shame. She was the most wonderful being I have known—I can see her face now, so thin; and yet it grew only more beautiful.

After Kamila's death, Marianna, the one surviving sister, not only kept house and cooked for her brother, caring for him devotedly and never marrying, but also supported them both by working as a seamstress for $60 a month after the sale of the grocery store. This reversal of the traditional values of the close-knit Lebanese community caused Gibran to be despised and even ridiculed, but allowed him to pursue his literary and artistic ambitions single-mindedly. The wholehearted support of his mother and sister in both practical and emotional terms, and the industry and practicality with which they combined the daily business of running a home and earning a living, gave him a deep respect for women's capabilities, as did his important friendships with the young Boston poetess Josephine Preston Peabody, journalist, novelist, and suffragette Charlotte Teller, and most significantly of all, with Mary Haskell, the headmistress of a girls' school who was to become his patron, mentor, collaborator, and sometime fiancée, although she subsequently married another man, sensing that the bond between them was not destined to end in marriage.

In attempting to formulate a culture of peace, Gibran could not overlook that microcosm of conflict and harmony—the home—and the relationship between the sexes on which it rests, especially in view of his own parents' domestic troubles. He was only too aware of the power of organised religion to cramp and distort women's lives in subservience to a narrow view of authority; his own mother had previously been married to a cousin who had left her with a young son to seek his fortune in Brazil before dying prematurely. Her second marriage, as we have seen, was no more fortunate. Gibran realised that only through justice and equality for both sexes could a better future for all be achieved. In several of his writings he directly addressed the theme of women's rights in the context of problems faced by oriental women, trapped by misogyny and arranged marriages based on the material interests of an oppressive patriarchal system: "it is tragedy writ in the blood and tears of womanhood, which a man reads and laughs at because he understands nothing of it," as he wrote in *Spirits Rebellious* (1908), a collection of four stories dealing in outspoken and defiant terms with the oppressive social conditions in Lebanon and attempting to offer positive solutions. Two in particular, "Warde al-Hani" and

"The Bridal Couch," focus on the rights of women in the Middle East and their oppression through forced marriage and the sublimation of true love to social customs, reinforced by the dictates of a legalistic view of religion far removed from his own concept of a God who gives men and women alike "spirit wings to soar aloft into the realms of love and freedom" and a faith which "makes us all brothers equal before the sun." He would later explore this theme in his Arabic novel *The Broken Wings* (1912), the story of Selma Karamy, compelled to marry a bishop's nephew, in a society where a woman "is looked upon as a commodity, purchased and delivered from one to another," and where men view women "from behind the sexual veil and see nothing but externals."

Gibran's view of women and their right to equality was not merely an idealistic or theoretical one which broke down when faced with the practicalities of everyday life, like Coleridge and Southey's plan for a community based on the ideals of Pantisocracy, which foundered on the mundane demands of housekeeping and childbearing. His discussions with Mary Haskell's circle, his correspondence with May Ziadah, and above all his first-hand experience of the courage and resilience of the women of his own family convinced him of women's equality in all respects with men and their right to similar privileges, duties, and opportunities. His was not the limited, pragmatic view of feminism that Yeats deplores in his poem "Why Should Not Old Men Be Bad?" where he sees with horror,

> A Helen of social welfare dream,
> Climb on a wagonette to scream.

Instead, he longed to see women set free to develop that capacity for action in the service of peace and reconciliation that has been celebrated by authors as disparate as Aristophanes, whose *Lysistrata*, a bawdy and mischievous vision of Athens's ingenious collaboration with their sisters in the warring states of Greece to bring a weary conflict to an end encapsulates a genuine and moving plea for peace, and Schiller, whose poem *Würde der Frauen* (The Dignity of Women) contrasts the aggressive and active endeavours of men with the subtle workings of women who, by their gentle persuasion,

> *Lehren die Kräfte, die feindlich sich hassen,*
> *Sich in der lieblichen Form zu umfassen,*
> *Und vereinen, was ewig sich flieht,*

teaching hostile forces to embrace each other, and uniting those in constant flight from one another.

Gibran's views on the question of women's rights were further strengthened when, in 1912, he heard 'Abdul-Bahá head of the Bahá'i Faith, speaking during a visit to New York:

> The world of humanity is possessed of two wings: the male and the female. So long as these two wings are not equivalent in strength, the bird will not fly. Until womankind reaches the same degree as man, until she enjoys the same arena of activity, extraordinary attainment for humanity will not be realized; humanity cannot wing its way to heights of real attainment. When the two wings or parts become equivalent in strength, enjoying the same prerogatives, the flight of man will be exceedingly lofty and extraordinary. Therefore, woman must receive the same education as man and all inequality will be adjusted. Thus, imbued with the same virtues as man, rising through all the degrees of human attainment, women will become the peers of men, and until this equality is established, true progress and attainment for the human race will not be facilitated. (Talk delivered by 'Abdul-Bahá, Oct. 25, 1912).

This was not the only aspect of the teachings of Bahá'u'lláh which appealed to Gibran, who was equally attracted to his doctrines of the harmony of science and religion, the need for universal education and a universal language, the independent investigation of truth, the oneness of God, the oneness and continuity of the prophets of God, the oneness of the human race, and the elimination of all forms of prejudice and discrimination. The impression of Christ which he received from these addresses was in tune with his own vision, to which he gave lasting form when, in 1926, he embarked on his most ambitious work in English, *Jesus, the Son of Man*, where he once more expressed his rejection of the mawkish portrayal of Christ in other sources: "He was far from being lowly and meek. Lowliness is something I detest; while meekness to me is but a phase of weakness"—a phrase with a markedly Nietzschean ring.

Gibran shared with Nietzsche a deep reverence for nature; the symbol of the forest, for example, was important to both as a metaphor for the unspoilt source of primeval wisdom, as in Gibran's Arabic poem *al-Mawakib* (*The Procession*), published in March 1919, a dialogue between a youth and an old man on the border of a forest, which represents the wholeness which the world has lost through mistaken perceptions of duality. The landscapes of his native Lebanon were the source of many of the happiest memories of his early years, and the devastation of his homeland afflicted him deeply. As time passed, he became increasingly aware of the calamitous consequences of heedless misuse of the earth's resources, both in physical and spiritual terms; he was convinced that the terrible famine in Lebanon for which he helped to organise relief in 1916 had been deliberately caused by the Turks, for example. On a different plane, he declared in *The Forerunner* (21): "1 am afraid that tomorrow there will be no more earth to eat and no more sea to drink," a prophecy of the dangers of environmental degradation on a global scale. Elsewhere in the same book he frequently uses images and parables from nature (birds, fish, and eagles fighting over a lamb who prays for peace between its "winged brothers'—a symbol of great powers fighting over a small nation), emphasising the unity between man and nature and the dire consequences of destroying it in a consciousness of ecological issues far in advance of his time.

We have examined several areas in which Gibran attempts to make peace between conflicting interests, factions, and belief systems. As we enter the 21st century, it is sadly obvious that the work of peacemaking is still far from complete. Yet like all great poets, Gibran strives to show how opposites can be reconciled: good and evil are inseparable, as are joy and sorrow, body and soul, life and death. In the poet himself east and west, pagan and Christian, Ancient and modern join to reaffirm his faith in the "Unity of Being," as expressed in his masterpiece *The Prophet*, where, in striking at the root of the "old corrupt tree of civilization," he attacked the source of the psychological malaise responsible for the violation of human rights in East and West, whether through poverty or war, and made accessible a message of hope and inspiration, neither glib nor facile, but imbued with a deep sense of the unity of creation and a belief in all embracing love. With his growing recognition from China to New Zealand, from the Philippines-to Russia, and his acceptance as Gibran of America as well as of Lebanon, a voice of global consciousness and ever-growing resonance, he would surely rejoice, not in vainglory at his ever-increasing fame, but in the chance which it offers for bonds of mutual interest, compassion, and understanding, linking one nation to another so that, to use his symbolism of the trees, one branch may stoop a little lower and one stretch higher so that they may speak to each other in truth and peace.

□□□

The Flow of Civilisation

•

Lokesh Chandra

Dr. Lokesh Chandra, former Member of Indian Parliament and also a former Vice-Chairman of the Indian Council of Cultural Relations, is among the most respected scholars of oriental cultures, specially the South Asian cultures.

"When social, political, economic and ethical structures face the onslaught of consumerism, narcotism, extremism and monocentrism, Dr. Karan Singh is ever on the wings to restore the humane symbols that embrace the mindscape of the profound depths. From the delicate frontiers of the perennial collective of India, he rains compassion and beauty to worship all living things and all divine epiphonies."

The century stands at civilisation's impasse, groping for direction, seeking symbols of consciousness, a pathway to wisdom, a quantum jump towards wholeness, a resonating integrity into the multiple. It summons us to a dialogue of timeless day, from thought to awakening awareness, from dogma to dialogue, from ideology to ideas, so that tiny pebbles gathered on the shoreline of life become fine like pearls, and when we carry these pebbles back home to our hearts, intertwined with them will be the Sea of Consciousness in our sleeves. Reflecting over dialogues that have failed us, and tortured our deeds to exhaustion, we seek renewing glistening waters in the rhythms of the universe, in flow of civilisation, evolving humans to a growing wholeness in an inner unity and constant change. At the peripheral point of the fading century with its accelerated technologies destroying resources of nature and nurture, materially accumulative, concerned only with outer man, oriented to pollution, the dawning century has to call a halt to this lash of inequity, so that our inner systems can offer better choices of all-round potential, a deep perception of the art of living, cosmic interplay overshadowing engineered constructs, to bring into being new value symbols that are non-additive and in service to humankind everywhere. We need an integrative catalyst of the creative process in the wholeness of value systems, and remember Hegel's words "Beware the cunning of reason".

Humankind seeks a harmonisation of material riches of life and the treasures of the ultraconscious, that is attainable in joy and rapture, triumph and grandeur, reverential awe and wonder of a depth. Humans envision the emergence of a new level of awareness which will make life harmonious within ourselves and outside with the world. He who holds to the Perennial of Nothingness, can manage human affairs without cultural, political, spiritual and social pollution. Moderation and slowing down is an antidote to Overgrowth, Rush and Exploitation of nature, humans and self. Are men empty vessels to be filled through development? Are they a solitary moon suspended in the empty blue? Humans have to wash their inkstone of its profane words, with their thoughts lost somewhere along the way and their hearts moved, defilements vanished, leaving body and soul transparently pure. The great poet of the Northern Sung dynasty, Su Shih (1037-1101) says,

Today as I travel along the mountain peaks
Self and world are once and for all forgotten.
The winds of the immortals seem to caress my head,
As, tying up my hair. I receive their secrets.

We have to wake the world with a lion's roar. It will resound from ideals translated into life. We have to open up levels of coming reality, points beyond themselves, symbols revealing a modality of the real that will some day become evident on the plane of immediate experience. Symbols have a sacred quality and one who understands them opens oneself to the objective world, but at the same time emerges from personal situations and reaches out to the universal. His is an experience of enraptured awe which is both lived and transcendant. Experience and symbols share root meanings of living. They are the diamond that cuts across explanation and analysis, and reaches the truly creative level. They are the *vajracchedika* of the Chinese translation by the renowned master Hsuan-tsang. Symbolisation and rational thinking need to shape tools, to adhere to values, to devise institutions in a continuum of experience and perception. Human society is a spider's web: touch it in one place and the vibrations are felt everywhere. With the post-classical paradigm of science phasing out along with the present century, Homo sapiens seeks values-sensitivity, futures-creativity and holism. A paradigm shift at the dawn of a new order has to provide culture-sensitive, participative attributes wherein rigidity becomes diversity, elitism becomes participation, and reductionist analysis becomes holism. We need the freedom, meaning and feeling that refuses to be subservient to a mechanistic way of life. Lord Buddha left a kingdom to seek the sublime springs of life. The Future, the nascent Buddhahood, is the perception of a 'plenum' to harmonise the planetary and extra-territorial spaces, to stabilise our inner selves, to enliven ecology, human societies and organisms. The inner values of human inheritance and the affluence of human creation are two worlds, out of balance and in deep conflict. At the hinge of the millennium at which we stand, we need to stretch our mind, and act to resolve the conflict. We cannot forget the anguished words of Cicero addressing the Roman Senate: "Catilina is at the gates of Rome, and you deliberate". The coming century, likewise, reminds us that it is time for action that stems from insight, vision and their intimate connection with truth.

Humans are in a unique position within the universe because of their ability to transmit cultural values from one generation to the next, so that we can keep out the, as yet, little perceived electromagnetic and microlevel pollutions of both affluence and effluence. The life and work of humankind wells up from the depths of the individual superconscious rooted in the collective Unconscious. In the irresistible march of history, overcoming the dragon of negative spiritual and social forces is the task of the youthful hero, who is ever being born, every year, every century, every millennium. He is the heart of the durable, gleaming diamond in a revitalising synthesis. Life is a continuing flow that ever moves along the two banks of indestructible vital energy and meaningful cosmic power. We have to tap, for the oncoming century, the continuous stream of life energy and its lyrical source in the universe. That inner self, that indwelling Being, is the realisation of the harmony underlying diversity as world consciousness achieves maturity.

In an infinitely intercommunicating universe, a given community perceives and lives with a selection of intercommunications. The infinite universe is a cathode and the perceiving consciousness of a person is the receiving anode. The receiving intelligence is a psychic filter. This psychic grid is a protection for us. It prevents over-information from reaching our consciousness, which the universe is bombarding us with. We cannot live in the totality of intercommunications of the universe. We have to live within a limited world. The nature of life is to continue growing, expanding, changing. We have not to allow our borders to calcify, we have to keep them supple. Continuous alteration is a sign of a living, healthy state of an evolving being, at the same time intensifying the community of shared consciousness. Nature seeks unity of heterogeneity that approaches uniqueness. Through the lattice of our psyche, we seek a dynamic of our consciousness. We evolve, we manipulate grids and metagrids of the contents of consciousness. We pass from grid to grid, to supergrid, to metagrid, never equalling the infinite universe. We move, advance, communicate, create, knowing that our quest is eternal, infinite, beyond time and space, and even beyond our within.

The catalytic fact of the twentieth century is uncontrollable development, consumerist society, political materialism, and spiritual devaluation. This inordinate development has led to the transcendental 'second reality' of sacred perception that biologically transcendance is a part of human life. As the century closes, it dawns with imperative vigour that the 'first reality' of enlightened rationalism and the 'second reality' of the Beyond have to be harmonised in a worthy state of man. The *de facto* values describe what we are, they portray the 'is' of our ethic, they are *est* values (Latin *est* means is). The ideal values tell us what we ought to be, they are *esto* values (Latin *esto* 'ought to be'). Both have to be in the ebb and flow of consciousness. The ever new science and technology and the ever-perennial faith are two modes of one certainty, that is the wholeness of man, his courage to be, his share in Being.

The materialistic foundations of classical physics have crumbled down. Science itself has proved that matter is energy, processes are as valid as facts, and affirmed the non-materiality of the universe. The encounter of the 'two cultures', the scientific and the humane, will restore the normal vision, and will be the bedrock of a 'science of understanding' in the new century. It will give new meaning to the ancient perception that quantity (measure) and quality (value) coexist at the root of nature. Human endeavours cannot afford to be humanistically irresponsible.

Complementarity of the way of time and the way of timelessness, of history and eternity, is a part of human comprehension of life. The surface of the conscious and the abyss of the subconscious are facts of a latent reality of our inward eye. The balance of nature is an essential ground for human values. It is a flux, an arrangement of changing forces. Natural communities find ways to return used energy back into Nature. Organisms play their part in sustaining the self-repairing constructive process of Nature. Green plants produce organic materials out of air, water and earth in food chains, return the components whence they came, to resume usable form sans end. Likewise humankind is a cosmic emergent, to be discovered and experienced. He is a kin to moss and grass that cover the soil, shrubs and trees that beautify the plains and the hills, the singing birds and buzzing insects, the crawling, running and flying animals. Man has gradually mastered the forces of energy and domesticated plants and animals. Conscious of his consciousness he is the tune binder. He has created a hierarchy of existents, layering them into three kingdoms of the mineral, vegetal and animal. Above them he stands observer and master. The long path of history is his stream of consciousness, his power and capacity to change the earth. The future art of life lies in working and growing together in a relation of loving unity of humans, humans and other sentients, humans and nature.

Modern science has looked deep into the atom and it has looked deeper into the human mind. This deeper understanding is what feeds the new mind. With this deeper insight the knowledge of nature has become a part of new humanism. Outdating the notion of 'two cultures' the whole of human knowledge fuses into a single, magnificent humane culture. Culture embraces all the values man has created, and gives meaning and content to life. In the words of President Ikeda, it is the revitalisation of each human being, a journey to the truth that we ourselves are Buddhas. Sri Aurobindo has said : "When we have passed beyond knowing, then we shall have Knowledge. Reason was the helper; Reason is the bar.....Transform reason into ordered intuition; let all thyself be light".

Man will continue to contribute new meanings, and discover ever larger possibilities for communicating with nature and with himself. Einstein affirms the harmony of nature and human insight: "The Cosmic Religious Experience is the strongest and noblest mainspring of scientific research. The most beautiful and most profound emotion we can experience is the sensation of the mystical. It is the source of all true science".

In the darkest night man searches for light. In his deepest need, he seeks a dawning consciousness. He aspires to repaint the world canvas, to revalue what is in the primal sources of the eternal process. Out of the real and the imagined is born the Realm of the Future wherein man rises above himself, as a dynamic bearer of culture. He crosses the River of Today and ferries across to the Other Shore of Unborn Tomorrows. Crossing frontiers is man's heritage, his Paramita, or in the chimes of the Heart Sutra: *gate gate paragate parasarngate bodhi svaha*.

Humans are a part of all other humans, of all life, of all matter, of all stars and the voids of eternity. They are eternal pilgrims in quest of a new *forma mentis*. In the words of poet Tagore:

> "The traveller has to knock at every alien door to come to his own,
> And one has to wander through all outer worlds to reach the innermost shrine at the end"

Pilgrims to the yonder shore, we live to have something to outlive.

☐☐☐

Evolution of Human Consciousness and Language

•

D.P. Chattopadhyaya

Professor D.P. Chattopadhyaya, Chairman, Centre for Studies in Civilizations, is guiding its project on History of Indian Science, Philosophy and Culture. He has shared many concerns and activities with Dr. Karan Singh.

"I have the pleasure of knowing Dr. Karan Singh for more than three decades. As a statesman and philosopher his works have earned him name and fame. His academic interests and pursuits overlap with mine in many respects. I am glad to contribute to his festchrift. It is a token of my respect and affection for my old friend."

The accounts of the relation between consciousness and language are numerous. For the sake of brevity one may refer to only two of them as relatively basic, — Spiritualist and Naturalist. Broadly speaking, the Spiritualist's view of language states that language is identical with the supreme Spiritual Reality, — Absolute or Brahman, which articulates itself in culturally identifiable different languages and their families. The Naturalist view, on the other hand, tries to show that from Nature or *Prakriti* all physical, biological, psychological, and epistemological phenomena, including the linguistic ones, evolve as *parinamas* differentiated transformations. These two views are available, both in the Indian and Euro-American thought, mainly in terms of evolutionism and structuralism. The traits of evolution and those of structure need not be construed necessarily in an antithetical manner. Often these two approaches are found to be primarily a matter of method and representation.

Language is said to be the *two-way* bridge between (a) non-linguistic real or imagined world, on the one hand, and (b) physical speech sounds, on the other. Language has three components in it, *viz.*, (i) Phonology (concerned with sounds), (ii) Grammar (concerned with relation between different parts of speech), and (iii) Semology (concerned with the real world through universal semantics). The said three sub-systems of language are also related in two ways, upward and downward. Besides, each of the three sub-systems of language—phonology, grammar and semology have their component units. But since I am not concerned here with comparative linguistics, I do not propose to go into its details. But how language, its sub-systems and their component units change over time and in culture specific ways are intrinsically interesting to the historical linguists. On the very question, what is the true nature of language, philosophers are badly divided.

Śabdādvaitavād or *Sphotovād* is found in the Vedic tradition and defended by philosophers like Bhartrihari (in *Vākyapadya*) and Mandana Misra (*Sphotasiddhi*). The Sanskrit word *Sphota* literally means expression or disclosure. Its nearest Greek cognate would be phenomenon (from *phainomai* or to appear and *phainein* to shine/form). Linguistic naturalism, in the Indian tradition, is traceable to the Epics, *Puranas* and, more clearly, in the works of Kapila, Asuri, Pancasikha and Isvarakrsna (S āmkhyak ārik ā).

In the Western tradition the Greek word *logos* figures prominently both for its ontological and linguistic significance. It is endowed with the spirit of bursting forth *sphutan*. From Plato and Aristotle to Husserl and Gadamar one comes across liberal use of this concept both in logico-epistemological and hermoneutico-linguistic contexts. The naturalist account of language as traceable in the West is evident from the writings of the pre-Socratic thinkers like Anaxagoras and Heracleitus *via* to those of Hobbes and the French Encyclopaedists like Diderot, to Quine and his followers. Another influential version of linguistic naturalism is to be found in the writings of Noam Chomsky and his colleagues who maintain that the mind should be studied like any other natural phenomenon. Languages, they say, are structured in the brains of individual speakers and its grammar, universal in scope, is hard-wired into the innate linguistic competence of human beings.

II

One very instructive route to a deeper understanding of the philosophical nature of language, as already indicated before, is etymological. It is illustrated by the work of *Yāska's Nirukta*. The Sanskrit word *sabda* means *sound* or *noise* as *word* or *term*. While the former is natural, at least primarily (not exclusively) nature, the latter primarily semantic, i.e. meaningful, and therefore, somewhat extra-natural. If one is committed to linguistic monism (*śabdādvaitavād*), one realizes both expressions are manifestation of the same *Absolute* or *Brahman*. *Brahman* literally means "growth", "expansion", "development", "evolution", "swelling of the spirit or soul" [Monier-Williams]. It is derived from *brh/ brhat*, the great and vast, and also it means pious effusion or utterance, outpouring of the heart in worshipping the gods. In Rgveda *vāk (vāc)* is deemed to be the same as Brahman.

Philology and etymology are said to be the parents of genetic linguistics. Philology serves as a means towards the understanding of a particular culture. Etymology is a particular branch of philology and it presents us as the scientifically controlled study of the histories of words. Etymology is much older than comparative linguistics which emerged first in Europe and expanded elsewhere during the last 250 years. Let us see how etymology can help us in having a deeper understanding of the philosophy of language.

Max Muller [in his book, *Vedanta Philosophy*, Cosmo Print, Delhi,1985, pp. 147-154] writes "... the ancient philosophers of India believed that the world was created by the Word". Word or Brahman had been eternally there, even before the composition of the Vedas. In this connection Max Muller refers to the *Satapatha Brāhmana*, VI, I,I,9 which may be read like this: `Prajapati, the Lord of all created things, desired, "May I be more than one, may I be reproduced...He created first of all *Brahmana*". Max Muller interprets it in this way: Prajapati created first of all the Word or Brahman and the rest, including *Vakaspati* or *Vrhaspati*, the Lord of speech proceeded thereafter. If it is remembered that Brahman is rooted in *Brh* or that which as *Bruh* or growth, then the whole world of multiplicity, of name (*nāma*) and form (*rupa*), can be deemed to be easily traceable to *Bramhan* as *Vāk (Vāc)* that which, as said before, bursts forth. *Nāma* and *rūpa* are the connecting link between Brahman and the World.

Max Muller thinks that the same line of thought is to be found in the languages rooted in Latin. He claims that *Brahman* is derived from the same root as *Verbum* and Word. *Verbum*, like *Brh* and *Brdh*, also carries the sense of growing or bursting forth.

Independently of Max Muller and taking another (*Vedic-Upanisadic*) route one can also arrive at this conclusion. The most important aspect in the understanding of the word *bhāsā* is not *bhāsā* as such which seems to be a post-vedic and vernacular part of speech, but *bha* which means to shine forth, to appear, to be splendid.

For the fuller meaning of *bhā* one is advised to turn to *Mundakopanisad*, 2/2/11. Even the sun which illumines everything does not find its expression there in Brahman but it is because of Bhahman itself that everything of the world is expressed : *tasyabhāsā sarvam-idam bibhāti*. One may hear in it echoes of *Nasadiya sukta* of the RV. The fuller meaning of this hymn is both linguistic and, deeply understood, cosmological [and evolutionary].

III

Neither evolution nor its different forms, particularly the spiritualist and the naturalist ones, already referred to, are new. For example, in the *Upanishad*. We read: *tapasā ciyate Brahma tatohannamạabhijāyate* I *annāt prāṇo manaḥ satyam lokāh karmasu cāmṛtam* II (Kath. 1/1/8.). In plain translation what it means is this: By reflective knowledge or self energizing creative consciousness Brahma expands; due to the expansion of Brahman evolves or emerges the world of matter; from the world of matter emerges the world of life, mind, five elements, seven spheres, actions of human beings and their imperishable results. In this hymn one gets an extremely succinct statement of spiritual evolution.

For the naturalist statement one may recall that Kant's famous utterance, "Give me Matter and I will build the World from it". The physicist, the chemist and the astronomer who looked into the Newtonian-Kantian matter during the post-Newtonian era found out many strength phenomena and numerous spheres like chemical nuclei, electricity, electro-magnetic field, X-Ray, atomic and sub-atomic particles, radio waves, Milky Way and the strife between gravity and nuclear forces, Black Holes and pulsars. But Physics, the basic science, could hardly evade new battles of the mind due to its encounter with matter and energy, giving rise to the living world.

That life emerges out of Matter or, to put it differently, that living beings come out of non-living things constituting the eco-system is not ordinarily disputed. The two features of the higher forms of life, increasing integration or complexification, on the one hand, and increasing differentiation or organization, on the other, are also evident. But the missing link in the *metaphor* of evolutionary change is the emergence of *human* consciousness in a great chain of being. Admittedly, there is a continuum from one form of life to another, but to extend this continuum from animate matter to human consciousness seems to be a matter of faith rather than of scientific knowledge. The latest affirmation that a complete genetic code will soon be in place to remove this talked of mystery also seems to be a matter of *hope* rather than of scientific prediction.

At its lowest level, *life* means the deterministic and blind chemical reactions through which an organism, simple or complex, transmits its distinct traits to its descendants and reacts adaptively to its environment. At its highest level, *life* involves man's consciousness and free will and refers to a bottomless subjectivity marked by the individuality of self, irrespective of the external world. But it seems to me that, till date, there is no scientific way to link the said two extremes and apparently incompatible expressions of life, biological determinism and human freedom. Man emerged, not on the bare planet, but only on the already ordered and well diversified *biological world*. Man's future does not depend either on the planet or its biological level but mainly on his conscious choice, thought and action. In enabling a living thing, rather a form of life, to be human, involves symbolization and concept formation, translation of the sensible into the understandable and here emerges the crucial role of language.

Before the idea of language is introduced it must be admitted that there are many non-linguistic modes of communication, for example, through sign, signal, noise, smell and dance. Some naturalists like David Hume have noted how birds successfully communicate their intentions and emotions to fellow birds or other animals. Many other animals, having no language of their own in the human sense, successfully communicate between themselves. Therefore, a line has to be drawn between the linguistic communication and non-linguistic communication. Also this fact brings to the fore the fuzziness of the line of demarcation often drawn between naturalism and spiritualism. Many naturalists like Adam Smith [*Moral Sentiment* and *the Wealth of Nations*] and Charles Darwin [*Expressions of the Emotions in Man and Animals*] are found to have endowed animals having no language with communicative competence. On the other hand, linguists like Leibniz and Humboldt, deeply committed to the principle of spiritual consciousness, ascribe rudimentary consciousness even to the subhuman creatures communicative competence as well as performance.

Another point which deserves attention in the linguistic context is the untenability of the line of demarcation drawn between empiricism and rationalism. For example, when Quine's approach to language is described as *naturalist and empiricist*, Chomsky's one as *naturalist, innatist and rationalist*. The former's philosophical ancestry is traced to Hume and the latter's to Descartes. Interestingly enough, in spite of their clear difference, both Quine and Chomsky are reductionist in a strong scientific sense. In his studies in the formal nature of language Chomsky makes in-depth use of the concepts of universal grammar characterized by universal phonetics, universal semantics and universal syntax. The theory of universal grammar suggested by him, on his own admission, "will no doubt be proven incorrect in various respects." and "that its fundamental defect will be that it permits far too much latitude for the construction of grammars, and that the kinds of language that can be acquired by humans in the normal way actually are of a much more limited sort than [his] theory would suggest." [Chomsky's Index in E. Lenneberg, *Biological Foundations of Language*, pp. 438-39].

To impart logical elegance to his philosophical system Quine skirts many problems of the word-object relationship. He shifts his emphasis from talk of objects to talk of words. For he, like Carnap, does not believe in the existence of *external* world of objects which can give rise to world of words or language. In his discussion on "semantic ascent" he tries to show that the genuine question of philosophy is question of language and its base is what he calls stimulus meaning. From ordinary meaningful words to highly abstract entities like numbers and sets, it is claimed, are constructible out of irritation of neural endings. The common sense notion of externality between the word (*pada*) and object (*padartha*) is sought to be excluded from his way of speaking about the world. It is thus the naturalist-empiricist in Quine which paves the way for removing the so called third (scheme-content) dogma of empiricism. Neither Chomsky's structuralism nor Quine's naturalism seems to have succeeded in being fair to the complexity of natural language, still less to the richness, subtlety, pithiness and profundity of the idioms of fine arts, poetry and religious experience. In spite of Quine's claim that ordinary language and logical language are a connected fabric, one feels that his quest for logical elegance makes it difficult for ordinary mortals to see the connection of that also elusive fabric. It must be said here in fairness to Chomsky, that he is relatively modest in his pursuit and confesses its defect. It is to be noted that neither Chomsky nor Quine has anything to do with evolution. Their pictures of language are static.

IV

Chomsky mainly deals with constitution of linguistic knowledge, acquisition of language and how to use it. The answer to the first question is to be found in a particular generative grammar. Secondly, for an answer to the second question we have to look into the specification of Universal Grammar and the principles that take the initial state of the language faculty to the knowledgeable state on exposure to Primary Linguistic Data. The answer to the third question is to be found by spelling out how linguistic knowledge interacts with other cognitive capacities like expression of thoughts and parsing incoming speech.

The epistemologist has raised the question whether knowing language (in a general way) enables one to grasp epistemical issues, for example, of quantum mechanics and molecular biology. Chomsky does not go into these questions. But one can well infer his possible response from his basic position. He is likely to say that humans have in them science-forming capacity of different domains (like physics and biology).

Chomsky's criticism of Skinner and Quine is well known. He has consistently opposed empiricist prejudices like behaviourism, that is, empirically generated verbal behaviour and dispositions, the Quinean versions of underdetermination of theory by evidence and indeterminacy of the translation of the psychological language into the physical one. Chomsky points out that theory of Universal Grammar and Phonological Universals are by their very nature bound to remain underdetermined by empirical evidence. The Quinean criticism, it is pointed out, presupposes a world-object kind of evidential associationism. Chomsky rejects the primacy of the physical over the mental due to Newtonian causation and contrary to the Cartesian accent on consciousness. One is advised to remember, Chomskian notion of consciousness, unlike the Castesian or Kantian one, is not affiliated to any God-like transcendental principle, but rooted in brain. Yet its generative capacity is claimed to be infinite.

Chomsky's linguistic theory is clearly internal, intentional and individual as distinguished from external, social and extentional theory of language with very limited generative capacity. Empiricist critics like Dummett try to show that although individual's affiliation to speech-community may well account for the generation of almost quasi-universal linguist competence, but that capacity can never be really infinite and intensional. Chomsky refuses to accept the criticism that his internal, individual and intensional theory of language is pro-platonic in disguised character. He clearly affirms that his notion of language is not outside the mind/brain arena and has nothing to do with platonic reification of notions like language and community. Notwithstanding Chomsky's sustained defence of his notion of language, even his sympathetic critics are inclined to point out that there is no specific language like Hindi, English or Bengali which can be shown to be corresponding ("correspondence" in the strict sense) to his structural-grammatical notion of language. In other words, his theoretical move from grammar to language seems to be shaky, if not faulty. The price of high generality is missed specifity.

One of the main infirmities of the modern philosophy of language, *i.e.*, of theoretical linguistics, is its indifference to data-based (*i.e.*, factual) linguistics and applied linguistics, including phonetics. The positive aspect of contemporary philosophy of language is to be found in its increasing interest in interdisciplinary forms of linguistics, comprising psychology, biology and computer science. But the weakest point of the discipline seems to be its strange lack of interest in comparative linguistics. One cannot readily recall a famous Euro-American philosopher of language who is professionally familiar with the African (Aramic-Bantu), the Sinic-Mongolian or even the Indo-Iranian languages. I say "even" in the context of the Indo-Iranian languages like the Sanskrit and the Avestan mainly because of their close affinity with the Indo-European language family as a whole. The story of how the Greek, the Latin and the Slav languages phonologically branched off the proto-Indo European language family is extremely instructive both culturally and from an evolutionary point of view.

V

It is interesting to recall why the European thinkers familiar with the Sanskrit language felt so happy to discover its multi-layered relationship with the classical European languages like the Greek and the Latin. One cannot help recalling William Jones's informed observations (1786) at the Asiatic Society on this issue:

> The Sanskrit language... is of a wonderful structure; more perfect than the Greek, more copious than the Latin, and more exquisitely refined than either, yet bearing to both of them a stronger affinity both in the roots of verbs and in the forms of grammar, than could possibly have been produced by accident; so strong indeed, that no philologer could examine them, all three, without believing them to have sprung from some common source, which, perhaps, no longer exists: there is similar reason, though none so forcible, for supposing that both the Gothic and the Celtic, blended with a different idiom, had the same origin with the Sanskrit; and the old Persian might be added to the same family...

Those who like Sri Aurobindo had professional familiarity with the Greek, the Latin and the Sanskrit, naturally had been at an advantage to get to the roots of Indian culture through the linguistic routes.

The concept of evolution, broadly speaking, aims at narrowing the gap between the generics and specifics of the evolutionary context. In the Rgveda (IX. 86.42), we read: "His ecstasy, in one who holds it, sets into motion the births, the human self-expressions and the divine, and moves between them". Aristotle highlights the importance of teleology at all levels of Reality; physical, biological and psychological and beyond. He finds that natural bodies, free from *generality* developed into biological and the mental *particularity*. Everything in the universe seems to be *purposive* to him (*De An.* 1075a15, 1076a19). Interestingly enough, the naturalists like Lucretius and Auguste Comte, like the *Samkhya-Yoga* in India, maintain that all things, natural and living, develop in an orderly way towards perfection, marked by the process of differentiation and integration.

Similar ideas have been developed, among others, by Sri Aurobindo and Pierre Teilhard de Chardin from a distinctly *teleological* point of view. Man is the most self-complexified animal, capable of expressing himself in and through complex symbols. Both are of the view that humans are simultaneously natural and super-natural and, what is more, only semeotic being among the living creatures. While Sri Aurobindo speaks of the Super-mind, Chardin foresees inevitability of the (what he calls) Omega Point, the supreme end of evolution. The Super-man of these two thinkers is endowed with the capacity to create through symbols or languages without perceptual input. This suggests that humans at their highest level developed in them an innate capacity to create spontaneously or freely, and that experiential feed-back is dispensed with or completely internalized.

Sri Aurobindo has written extensively on the nature of *logical* language highlighting the inexactitude which is inherent in our conceptual thinking. He writes: "Our abstractions get fixed into differentiating concepts with sharp lines between them; but the Reality is not of that nature; its aspects are many but shade off into each other. Its truth could only be rendered by ideas and images metaphysical and yet living and concrete—images which might be taken by the Pure Reason as [mere] figures and symbols but [in fact] are more than that and mean more to the intuitive vision and feeling, for they are realities of a dynamic spiritual experience."

The word 'spiritual' is nothing mysterious or outlandish to Sri Aurobindo and Chardin. Spirit is what poesy is in the life of poetry and music in that of song. It is an enlivening impulse. Sri Aurobindo is perceptive enough to recognize the importance of logical language in our ordinary and scientific discourses. He writes, "Logical reasoning is useful and indispensable in its own field in order to give the mind a certain clearness, precision and subtlety in dealing with its own ideas and word-symbols...it is much more efficiently a guardian against errors than a discoverer of truth." For it fails to grasp simultaneously the main three features of all things, their *essentiality, commonality* and *individuality*. These limitations of all languages are substantially overcome by the language of poetry and music. But how? That is a matter of another and lengthy discourse encompassing, among others, the innate, biological and physiological conditions which make language and speech possible.

□□□

Questions for a New Millennium

•

Chungliang Al Huang

Professor Chungliang Al Huang is the President of the Living Tao Foundation with its headquarters in Urbana, Illinois, United States. An eminent scholar of Taoism and Buddhism his contribution includes an article presented at the Parliament of the World's Religions in 1999.

"At fifteen I was committed to learning. At thirty I took my right position. At forty I was of one mind. At fifty I understood the unfolding of my true nature. At sixty I was at ease with my contradictions. And at seventy, I may follow my hearts' desire without going astray".

I met Dr. Karan Singh during my first visit to India in 1982. Like Dr. Singh, I was one of the presenters for the International Transpersonal Association's conference held at the Hotel Oberoi in Bombay that year. It was a most memorable and consciousness altering experience for me. In addition to having to stand in last moment to open the conference in place of the ailing Dalai Lama, I had the privilege to share panel discussions with many old friends and to be in the presence of Mother Teresa, Swami Muktananda, Father Bede Griffith, and many other sagely and saintly teachers. But one of the most impressive and inspiring experiences was to be at a lecture by Dr. Singh. He combined superior intellect, infectious passion and spiritual exhaltation, with the highly mesmerizing and captivating skills of the poetic orator. I embraced him to show my appreciation and instantly we discovered many shared interests and mutual acquaintances. One of them was my mentor-friend, the scholar-mythologist Joseph Campbell, whom Dr. Singh met and hosted many years ago in India. I also told him of my childhood introduction to Indian culture through the poetry of Rabindranath Tagore when he visited China, and my fondness of embodying the symbolisms of the Shiva Nataraja statue through my Tai ji dancing. Immediately, Dr. Singh began dancing with me, moving through all the *mudras* and gestures of "The Lord of the Dance". From that moment on, I felt a deep kindred connection with him, pledging myself to relate to him and be accepted in true brotherhood in mind, body, heart and spirit.

After a brief tour of India, and before my departure, I was invited by Dr. and Mrs. Singh to be at their home in New Delhi, and was warmly welcomed and feasted at a most wonderful family dinner—still the best Indian meal I have ever tasted!

The crowning moment came when Dr. Singh took me into his personal shrine to perform his ritual and chanted a special *sutra* for me. He then presented me a precious silver statuette of Lord Ganesh—it has continued to hold a special place in my personal shrine at home where I mediate and pay tribute to my family and spiritual heritage.

Although we live oceans apart, pursuing seemingly very different lives, our shared, deeply committed endeavors in inter–faith spiritual work, and promoting inter-cultural exchange/understanding and global harmony, have frequently brought us together at gatherings around the world. We are always delighted to be in each other's company in many European and American cities; and at our most recent encounter in Cape Town, South Africa as assembly members at the 3rd Parliament for the Council of the World's Religions.

I feel very blessed to have found a kindred friend in Dr. Singh, and am honored to be regarded as such by him. I honor him and appreciate him deeply as a teacher, mentor, "elder brother", kindred friend. Most of all, I find him a very special human being, with all the cultivated qualities, so highly esteemed by the Chinese sages, *Confucius* and Lao Tze.

I congratulate him, on his 70th birthday. And I will quote and interpret, with this Chinese brush calligraphy from me, the illustrious saying by Confucius:

> "At fifteen, I was committed to learning.
> At thirty, I took my rightful position.
> At forty, I was of one mind.
> At fifty, I understood the unfolding of my true nature.
> At sixty, I was at ease with my contradictions.
> And, at seventy, I may follow my heart's desire without going astray.

So, my dear friend, may enjoy this sagely new beginnings of wisdom; and may follow his heart's wishes and be forever blissful and blessed!

With these wishes I add a few questions for a new Millennium.

I am responding to these questions, foremostly, as a human being, a world citizen who happens to come from a culture with more than 5,000 years of continuity in civilization. I am also a believer and practitioner of "Living Tao," who experiences the "ultimate reality" which is universally interrelated, and is shared by others in its essence, but may have various names such as Absolute, God, Tao, Brahman, Allah,or the Great Spirit. Since the "Tao can be Taoed is not the ultimate Tao" as stated by the sage, Lao Tzu, I am reluctant to call myself a Taoist, with "ism" attached, to attempt an explanation of the ineffable. Still, I represent those of us who are deeply immersed in learning the wisdom of the Tao for our everyday living. I will be using the term "Tao" for everyday living in a very broad sense, based on the essential teachings of the three pillars of Asian wisdom, hoping to synthesize a personal perspective from the scriptures, doctrinal principles, discourses, stories and musings of Taoist, Buddhist, and Confucian teachings.

Sustainability

Ancient Chinese believed in the separability of the unity. Heaven-Human-Earth, in the often quoted, "Heaven and Human are One." and "Heaven, Human and Earth co-exist." In Lao Tzu's Tao Te Ching, verse #67, one of the three treasures in frugality, teaching of the danger of overblown consumerism in the exploitation of the earth's resources. And, in verse #12, "The five colours blind the eye. The five tones deafen the ear. The five flavours dull the palate...," a warning of the madness of having too much, guiding us away from excess and toward the essential. Also, in #46," ...there is no greater curse than the lack of contentment, no greater sin than the greed for possession. Therefore, he who is contented with contentment shall be truly content."

On procreation and proper relationships between human species and others, Lao Tzu #42: "Tao gives birth to one, One to Two, Two to Three, Three to all myriad things. All things carry the Yin and embrace the Yang to harmonize the vital force of Life." It is in nature's perfect "Tai Ji-Yin/Yang" unity, a living being is created. For human beings, procreation is meant to become a sacred and spiritual act, not to be degraded in ignorance with gross biological urges only—a direct reflection in the current reality of the mindlessly unconscious over population in the world today. Tao also teaches us to learn from nature, from the animal kingdom and other living species, in the overall balancing act in natural habitats, in the food chain, and organically wise and scientifically sound, self-regulation and natural process of elimination.

And in verse #5, "Treating all things and people as sacrificial straw-dogs." Lao Tzu compared the human sage with "Heaven and Earth"—the Forces of Nature, as being non-sentimental and impartial to the prescribed superior and/or inferior species. Also, "How the universe is like a Bellows! It seems empty, and yet it never fails to supply. The more it is worked, the more it brings forth." To abide in the Tao, we learn to sustain life in moderation and not to exploit the illusory inexhaustible resources.

Progress

Verse #41 clearly contemplates on the idea of progress with this thoughtful aphorism: "Tao's progression seems like retrograde." Lao Tzu goes on to question the simplistic mind depending on the absolute answers with "who understands Tao seems vague and not sure of comprehending...who is advanced seems to slip backwards. Even those who move on the smooth and even path seem to go up and down in unpredictable variations." Indeed, progress is not a straight line to the top, or bulldozing one's way to the finish and be done with. It is a process to be experienced and to be reckoned with in all walks of life, in personal and collective ways, in society, and countries and in the world at large.

Ancient sages of the Tao looked at the rich and the poor with multi-dimensional views. To reflect on this perennial wisdom, we observe the materially rich countries so impoverished in the heart and in the spirit; and, let us not judge or treat the "under-developed" countries as being poor. Poverty is a concrete reality to be dealt with once the world is genuinely willing to share our collective wealth in resources. We all know that there ought to be enough food production to feed every mouth on earth. But, we also know that, what is preventing us from achieving the goal to end world hunger is often purely political, and can be most frustratingly impeded by human actions, as well as inactions.

Two of multiple symbols in Chinese for peace and harmony are simply a depiction of these two words "Ho Ping," meaning "putting food in every mouth to achieve peace and harmony." Also, another saying, "All shall be equal and just under the Heaven." Tao teaches the humans to be kind and fair, to be content and to share with others the basic needs in our lives.

To live the Tao in daily life is to cultivate some of these virtues and powers Chinese call Tc, the finer qualities of being a cultivated and civilized human being.

A pragmatic vision to live one's Tao is to be a realist knowing that in order to find peace and harmony in the world, one must begin from the self as an individual, cultivating the true human virtues as a model of integrity. So that the person as the basic single unit, is in true harmony with others and with the world. The individual who possesses this power within, can transform the world like a pebble dropped in the center of a clear pool. Its rippled effects will reach far and beyond.

Difference

Intrinsic in the Chinese language, which originated from ancient times with the symbol for humankind is "Jen Rei." This can be interpreted as an undifferentiated unit of "humans and others, or humans with other variations," implying a recognition and acceptance of other races, ethnicity, culture, class, politics and choices of worship. To acknowledge this Taoist wisdom in the true humanity as a multi-cultured, and multi-varied living species is not only an apt lesson for the Chinese today, it will be beneficial for the whole world as well.

Confucian teaching is based on the basic principle of learning about relationships. The key symbol for Confucian ethics is "Jen" (or Ren) — a depiction simply about what is happening "Between two human beings."

The gender distinction can be traced back to the original wisdom of the "Yin-Yang" balance of the Ultimate Reality—the Tai Ji harmony of the masculine and the feminine principles. In spite of the corruption and unfairness to women throughout the centuries in the patriachical society of China, the underlying wisdom for the elite and the enlightened is to find harmony and balance between men and women. To patch this gender gap, Mao Tse Dong even went as far as calling to the country to unify the male and female forces by emphasizing that "women held up half of the sky!"

Understanding

The core wisdom in the Tao is the understanding of Change and Transformation, deeply rooted in the teaching of the I Ching: The Ancient Book of Change.

All fixity creates decay, and the ultimate breakthrough in life is through the process of change and transformation.

Tao teaches us to look into alternative ways to achieve peace and harmony in the world. "To follow the way of the least resistance—in the Watercourse Way."

Wu Wei is the principal philosophy of learning not to interfere with the natural progression of things and affairs. Learning to harness the force of the wind in sailing, instead of insisting on using the muscle force of rowing to reach our destinations.

Beware of the contradiction in "fighting" for peace and justifying aggression in warfare to end war. Lao Tzu verse #31 clearly forewarns us, "Even the best weapon of war is an unfortunate tool, must be avoided with disgust. So the followers of Tao stay away from it... To enjoy using weapon is to enjoy the slaughter of mankind and to enjoy killing people is to lose your share of the Commonwealth of Man... It is only right that survivors of war must mourn for the murder of the defeated. Even a victory must be conducted as a funeral ceremony."

Tao teaches that the further we advance in science, the more perplexed and humbled we must become. From the first verse of Tao Te Ching, we learn to observe the obscure and the mysterious, to behold what has manifested in its outer aspects, and to marvel the hidden with its inner essence. And, to continue our search and research by entering into the "mystery within mystery, the gate of all mysteries." And, in verse #14, "looked at, but cannot be seen—that is called the invisible. Listened to, but cannot be heard—that is called the inaudible. Grasped at, but cannot be touched—that is called the intangible... Confront it and you do not see its face; follow it and you do not see its back. He who holds fast to the timeless Tao can manage the affairs of Now. To know the origins is to hold the thread of the eternal Tao."

On the wisdom of leadership and the ecology of the world, verses #17 and #60 are most enlightening: "Leaders are best when people scarcely know they exist...Good leaders have faith in the people. Talk little, honor promises. When their work is done, their tasks fulfilled, the people will all say: `we did this ourselves.' And, "Rule a big country as if cooking a small fish. Don't overdo it!"

The "Small is Beautiful" utopian vision is vivid here in "Ah, a small country with a small population. There are sophisticated mechanical contrivances, but people seldom have use for them. Let them be mindful of living and dying and decline to travel far. Boats and carriages, weapons and armors aplenty, but no occasion to utilize or display them. Let them fully enjoy their living simply, pleased with their home, thriving in their customs. Even though neighbouring countries are close by, there's no reason to mingle or interfere with one another." (verse #80)

□□□

Watching the Wheel Whirl Across Time and Space

Manoj Das

Manoj Das, eminent educationist, scholar and writer confesses that he has made his contribution with love and sincerity and hope and "this will give some of the readers an insight into a memorable work of our time, namely Dr. Karan Singh's Autobiography."

"What mystified me was, how could the sole heir to the throne of the fabulous Kashmir emerge as a scholar who never wore around him the airs of a pundit, as a musician, a poet and last but not the least, a student of mysticism who remained evergreen in his quest? How could he be so humble in his profundity and so un-imposing despite his fluency and oratory?"

That was early in the year 1982, in Singapore. A Press correspondent with whom I had some acquaintance called me in the morning.

"Can you please arrange for me an appointment with Dr. Karan Singh?"

The demand was unexpected and abrupt. However, I tried not to sound surprised and said, "Well, as correspondent for a reputed group you can surely explore better ways of seeking the appointment, but I believe I can help you too..."

"By the way, how do I address him - His Highness - His Excellency - Maharaja—or..."

"Were you to address his father, you could do even

more - Maharajadhiraj. But don't you worry at all. Address him as Dr. Karan Singh."

"Thanks. So, when do you think can I meet him?"

"Well, I do not know where he is now, in India or abroad."

"Are you that innocent?"

I was intrigued once again. "To look innocent in the eyes of a Press reporter, 1 believe, is not a mean merit..."

But he cut in, "Dr. Karan Singh is just a floor or two above your room—in the same hotel."

That was undoubtedly a most pleasant surprise for me and, I hope, to some extent for Dr. Karan Singh when I called him over the phone and he asked me to come up at once if I were free.

It was the massive Hotel Oberoi Imperial (since dismantled - something that characterizes the modern Singapore: even new buildings are blown out like bubbles for newer bubbles) and Dr. Karan Singh and Princess Asha-ji were put up in its finest suite, overlooking a line of green hillocks. After I had explained to him the purpose of my visit to that city-state — I was there at an invitation from the Ministry of Education of the Government of Singapore as a consultant for a certain project — he piloted our dialogue or discussion into several planes, pragmatic and mystic. He would often put a question and listen to me with the attention and humility of a seeker, but for me to realize before long that he knew the answer better than I. When he would fully agree with me, he would supplement my opinion with more arguments; if he disagreed — which he did with a charm that would never hurt one — he would still reinforce my point of view helping me with what I lacked. I had met him and talked to him several times since the mid-sixties, at Delhi, Pondicherry and also in mid-air, but that was the occasion when I had the longest ever talk with him, through a quiet exchange of mutual empathy.

The Press reporter who had contacted me of course did meet him and so did several others of that fraternity. Dr. Karan Singh addressed a meeting organized by an Indian association, but which attracted a large multinational audience and the spontaneous comments made by some non-Indians during the next few days had one subtle element in common: they had heard the most convincing exposition of the heritage of India, but with the wonderful feeling that it was *the human heritage.* The otherwise grim and rigidly edited *Straits Times* arranged Dr. Karan Singh's pictures projecting his different moods like a garland along the margins of a complete page circling a pleasant write-up on him.

Frankly, the making of Dr. Karan Singh had been an enigma for me, until I read his autobiography. And, reading his autobiography, I felt reassured of my conclusion. For me Kashmir was still Cashmere — as Thomas Moore presented it in his *Lalla Rookh* (early 19th century):

As the love-lighted eyes that hang over their wave?
Who has not heard of the vale of Cashmere
With the roses the brightest that earth ever gave,
Its temples and grottos, and fountains as clear.

What mystified me was, how could the sole heir to the throne of the fabulous Kashmir emerge as a scholar who never wore around him the airs of a pundit, as a musician, a poet and, last but not the least, a student of mysticism who remained evergreen in his quest? How could he be so humble in his profundity and so un-imposing despite his fluency and oratory? Year ago I had read what Winston Churchill wrote about the ex-Kaiser. No one should judge the strange character of the Kaiser, Churchill reminded us, without asking himself the question what he would have done himself in his position. "Imagine yourself brought up from childhood to believe that you were appointed by God to rule a mighty nation, and that the inherent virtue of your blood raised you far above ordinary mortals...You are to form a desire and it is granted. Limitless wealth and splendour attend your every step. Sixty palaces and castles await their owner; hundreds of glittering uniforms fill your wardrobes. Should you weary of the grosser forms of flattery, far more subtle methods will be applied.... "

And Churchill asks his readers, "Are you quite sure you would have remained a humble-minded man with no exaggerated idea of your own importance, with no undue reliance on your own opinion, practising the virtue of humility and striving always for peace?"

Those of our generation who had some knowledge of the Princely India, though that is fast fading in our memory, would appreciate how much of Churchill's observation held good for a number of Indian princes, for the quality of the paraphernalia and sycophancy was the same here, however different be the historical and political situations as well as the size and importance of their domains.

A number of factors contributing to the moulding of the Kashmir Prince, the Yuvaraj, into an uncommon personality can no doubt be identified. First and probably the foremost was the influence of his mother. Maharani by marriage, she came of non-feudal rural stock, and was evidently a highly mature character. The sudden change of luck, possible mostly in fairytales, hardly overwhelmed her. She remained faithful to her pre-royal culture of religious rituals and was never cowered down by her formidable husband. It is she who initiated the little prince into the realm of music — she would burst into her rustic rhymes in the company of her maids and friends herself playing the *dholki* before her deity - and what is more, indirectly initiated him into a reality beyond the mundane. In fact, an awareness of the mysteries of Nature as well as the mystique proper was brewing simultaneously in that impressionable mind: "Sometimes in the mellow Jammu evenings we would all assemble on the large veranda in Amar Mahal with its magnificent view of the Shivalik range, the triple-peaked mountains of Vaishno Devi dominating the skyline and the river Tawi winding down the plains. There, the small earthen lamps were lit, and with my mother in the lead we would all walk round the sacred *Tulasi* (basil) plant grown in an earthen pot, singing devotional songs in our lilting mother tongue, Dogri." (*Autobiography 1931-1967*)

It is significant that instead of accepting as natural the feudal way his birth had prescribed for him, the young prince found several traditions revolting to his sensibility. For example, it was easy for the authority of the royal household to find fault with the servants for any slight dissatisfaction caused to the lord of the house. "As I grew older these cruel inquisitions began to infuriate me and added to my growing alienation from the order into which I had been born. Here was authority without generosity; power without compassion." (*Ibid*)

In their *Lives of the Indian Princes*, Charles Alien and Sharada Dwivedi write, "The larger the state, the greater the status of its ruler and the less contact he had with his children. This was certainly true of the biggest of the Indian states, Jammu and Kashmir, where the Yuvaraj, Karan Singh, was born in 1931." The Yuvaraj rarely saw his father and that was a blessing in disguise. Had Maharaja Hari Singh been keen to bring up his scion in his own image, the flow of events over this sub-continent would have been twisted into yet another bizarre bend.

It was Providential that in his teens the prince happened to read Jawaharlal's *Autobiography* and *The Discovery of India*. I have a feeling that while these books had meant much to many, the single greatest channel through which these accounts of the past contributed to the practical shaping of the not-too-distant future was through Dr. Karan Singh. "I had of course a generalized pride in being Indian, but never before had the long and rich panorama of our history unrolled before me, nor had I appreciated the rich diversity and almost miraculous unity that had characterized India from the very dawn of human history. Reading Jawaharlal's two books gave me a new awareness, and strengthened the aversion to feudalism that had already been growing within me. I realized clearly that the old feudal structure was on the verge of collapse, and that , in any case, my father's life was not for me. What the alternative was I did not know, but inwardly I was ready for change." (*Autobiography: 1931-1967*)

If we find Dr. Karan Singh an irresistible conversationalist today - signs of an extrovert even in the best sense of the term - that should be a delightful surprise for any thorough reader of his autobiography. Situations had almost conspired to make an ideal introvert out of him. He had known what aloneness is and that too at epoch-making moments, as though Time was keen to spare him the trauma it had in store, but in the process causing him no less anguish. He found himself physically handicapped — probably the aftermath of a fall from a horse in his early teens — in that mighty historic year, 1947 itself. His father was yet to take a decision on the political fate of Kashmir when the impatient Pakistan engineered a tribal invasion of the land. Let us visualise the prince's condition then both physical and emotional:

"On that fateful day I was left virtually alone in the palace while my father and members of the staff were attending the Darbar in the beautiful hall at the city palace on the Jhelum with its richly decorated papier mache ceiling. Suddenly the lights went out—the invaders had captured and destroyed the only power house at that time which was at Mahura on the main road from Domel to Srinagar along which the invasion was proceeding. In the pitch darkness I sat alone in my room on the wheel chair. After a few minutes the eerie silence was broken by the sudden, blood-chilling howls of the jackals. Weirdly the cacophony rose and fell, then rose again into a mad crescendo. Death and destruction were fast approaching Srinagar, our smug world had collapsed around us, the wheels of destiny had turned full circle." (*Ibid*)

Aloneness dogged the Yuvaraj to New York where he had to be flown for surgery amidst the heaviest snowfall in sixty years in that city. It was the evening of the 31 December. "By the time I was transferred to my bed and the ambulance attendants departed it was getting on to midnight. They all had New Year parties to attend and were understandably in a hurry to get away...at last I found myself alone, with the picture of Durga and a photograph of my parents on the high table next to my hospital bed. I heard in the distance the sound of a great clock striking the midnight hour. A new year had begun and, for me, a new life."

Not quite comfortable with his father's old-world attitude to men and matters from his very childhood, he had to muster all his courage—the crisis demanded a very great exercise of freewill—when he decided to align himself with the changing times, put a higher value in his vision of a greater India transcending all the pulls of a powerful feudal and dynastic *Samskara* and the traditional duty of the heir-apparent, and belie the expectations of a stern and stubborn father. He decided to act in the best interest of the emerging new India and the best interest of Kashmir. He could not afford to sulk away from the stark realities as his father could.

And once again he was alone. This was in Delhi. "I was obviously embarking on a delicate assignment fraught with risk and even danger. My father made no secret of his unhappiness at the whole situation, and although he had bowed to the inevitable I realized that our relationship had soured in the process. My mother also was breaking away on her own, which added a new element of emotional instability to the situation. I had no one to rely on except Jawaharlal's support and such inner resources as I could summon at that critical juncture. 20 June 1949 was an important landmark in my life. My father, his staff and servants left by train early in the morning for Bombay. My mother, uncle and her maidservants left by car for Kasauli soon after. For half an hour I sat absolutely alone in my hotel room, poised between the weight of the past and the burdens of the future. It was one of those critical moments in life that remains forever embedded in one's memory."

In another hour or so his plane would take off for Kashmir - the valley so intimately familiar to him, yet which had grown unfamiliar in a weird way, passing from the sway of the dynasty founded by Maharaja Gulab Singh, into the clout of Sheikh Mohammed Abdullah, "an outstanding personality on the scene" and a trusted friend of Jawaharlal Nehru, but for the Prince-turned Regent a dark horse at best. The Sheikh was present with his entire cabinet to receive the son of his archenemy, Maharaja Hari Singh, little suspecting that this tender young man could one day shatter his ambitions when they would unexpectedly and unfortunately run amuck. Probably the Sheikh himself was not aware of the negative potency lurking within his own anti-Raj idealism. (How true Eric Hoffer was when he said in his *Temper of our Time* "Power is always charged with the impulse to eliminate human nature, the human variable, from the equation of action.")

The dramatic dismissal of Sheikh Abdullah in August 1953, it was then generally believed, could have been possible only with the prior approval of Jawaharlal Nehru, if not at his instruction. The fact that it was the courage and conscience of the twenty-two year old *Sadar-i-Riyasat*, unfolds an unsuspected aspect of Dr. Karan Singh's character.

Returning to the theme of the uncommonness of the character under focus, I have presented the external factors responsible for them — from the influence of his mother to that of the works of Jawaharlal Nehru. But do they fully explain the phenomenon? Don't we come across instances galore when outcomes of similar situations are quite dissimilar? I was sure and Dr. Karan Singh's life confirms my faith that how well the external factors would be helpful to one depends on an apparently inexplicable factor — a certain quality of consciousness. Dr. Karan Singh had his share of physical pain and suffering in ample measures - in his teens and later from an accident. But like his aloneness, his suffering, it seems, gave his inner self a boost which only the evolved can experience. Says Sri Aurobindo in his *Thoughts and Aphorisms*, "When thou art able to see how necessary is suffering to final delight, failure to utter effectiveness and retardation to the last rapidity, then thou mayst begin to understand something, however faintly or dimly, of God's workings." The poise with which Dr. Karan Singh passed through his suffering indicates as if this knowledge was imbedded in his psyche.

The prince had more than his share of embarrassments too. His father would make engagements for his marriage only to call them off. (The father's ultimate decision proved to be a marriage made in heavens is a different matter.) The prince was of course too small then to feel the impact of such imperious whims to any considerable degree. But imagine his father arresting Nehru in 1945 when the latter entered the State in order to meet his friend Sheikh Abdullah who was in jail. "I was stunned. Here was the most charismatic leader of the national movement for freedom, the author of the *Autobiography* and *The Discovery of India*, the declared future Prime Minister of the Indian Republic, and, instead of welcoming him and seeking his co-operation, we had arrested him." (*Autobiography 1931-1967*)

His embarrassment could not have been less when Lord Mountbatten visited them in order to impress upon the Maharaja the need for his acceding either to India or Pakistan, the Maharaja, after entertaining the guest lavishly and arranging for him a fishing trip quietly avoided sitting down for a discussion " on the plea that he had suddenly developed a severe attack of colic." (*Autobiography 1931-1967*)

Well, as a historian observes, "It was perhaps for the first time in the British Indian history that an Indian prince had refused to meet the King-Emperor's Viceroy visiting his domain." (Dr. M.N. Das: *Partition and Independence of India*)

It must have been a highly challenging task for Dr. Karan Singh to absorb such shocks and formulate his own directions and sustain an exemplary balance in his own conduct towards mutually antagonistic situations and elements. Despite the emotional and ideological discordance between them, Dr. Karan Singh was always respectful towards his father. Rushing back from the West at the news of the Maharaja's death, he performed the rites as had been desired by the departed as well as according to his own conscience. "All of Jammu had gathered for the last homage - endless crowds, crying and wailing for a man who had left them a dozen years earlier as their Maharaja. And I carried the urn in an open car through the milling crowds. Thirty years ago on the same route my father and mother had driven in an open carriage through cheering throngs in celebration of my birth. Twelve years ago my parents and I were taken out in a similar procession after my return from America. This time I was alone; my mother had donned the white clothes of the traditional Hindu widow and lay semiconscious in Amar Mahal surrounded by wailing women, and all that was left of my father's body was a handful of ashes in the urn that I gently cradled in my hands. How much, in the end, does a man weigh!" (*Autobiography 1931-1967*)

Soon thereafter his mother suffered a cerebral stroke. "It was heart-rending for me to see this once beautiful and vivacious woman, so fond of company and jewellery and colourful clothes, reduced to an invalid unable to leave her bed. We did all we could to comfort her, and as she loved to hear me sing I would render devotional songs every evening in her presence." (*Ibid*)

This is a plain picture of a mother and her son, not of a Maharani and a prince — a relationship that vibrates inside a million huts in rural India.

But Dr. Karan Singh's "uncommonness" does not emerge from his patriotism, courage, dutifulness, erudition and such qualities alone. It can be traced to a far subtler matter. At a time when the princes in general favoured the British rule, he chose for his doctoral thesis the political thoughts of a person who had been a legendary fighter against the British rule, an uncompromising revolutionary in the first decade of the twentieth century, Sri Aurobindo, whose genius, to quote from Dr. Pattabhi Sitasramayya's History of the Indian National Congress, "shot up like a meteor" and who, though "on the high skies only for a time, flooded the land from Cape to Mount with the effulgence of his light." While there are hundreds of theses on various aspects of the Aurobindonian lore today, Dr. Karan Singh was among the first few to choose that subject - and that too that aspect of it which should put off a prince at once. Nehru's preface to the work, *Prophet of Indian Nationalism*, unmistakably highlighted this: "It is significant to note that he should have devoted himself to his studies and, more particularly, to this analysis of the political thoughts of Sri Aurobindo during a crucial period of our history, instead of occupying himself with the normal activities of Indian princes, that is *shikar*, polo and high society."

If this speaks of an objective and a detached outlook on history, and it is far from easy to develop that kind of outlook in regard to recent history, no wonder that there should be an innate humility behind it. It is this quality that was Dr. Karan Singh's unfailing guide in his spiritual quest. It comes out once in a while in a reflex, for example when he recollects his meeting with Ronald Nixon-turned-Krishnaprem, in the latter's Himalayan abode: "I was lodged in a tiny cottage near the temple...*Aarati*, the evening prayer at the temple, was at seven. I stood as if in a trance while Sri Krishnaprem sang *bhajans* and did the *kirtan* in flawless Hindi, accompanied by Sri Madhava Ashish on a small double-sided drum. When the lamps were lit the third person there, a Rabindranath Banerjee, beat on the metal gong and the clear mountain air resounded with the sound of worship. I had never come across anything so simple and moving before. I just sat on the parapet, gazing at a distant star." (*Autobiography 1931-1967*)

I have been a fond reader of autobiographies and often I tend to agree with Hilaire Belloc: "Just as there is nothing between the admirable omelette and the intolerable, so with autobiography." For me, Dr. Karan Singh's *Autobiography 1931-1967* is not only among the admirable, but also the most absorbing one I have ever read. I know that a good deal of my uninterrupted interest in the work from the first word to the last was because, having failed to master any knack for speed-reading, I keep on pronouncing silently the text as I read it and being familiar with the author's euphonic voice, I had the pleasant illusion of hearing him speak throughout. But that apart, it is a treasure of valuable facts, a fascinating record of moments golden and tumultuous and an excellent work of literature where time and again decent prose plays host to shy poetry. And what is still more significant, often the author gives the impression of being a stranger from another world left on the banks of a whirlpool as a witness representing some mysterious authority. And that brings me to my mind a stanza from Sri Aurobindo's poem, *The Witness and the Wheel* :

Something watches behind, Spirit or Self or Soul,
Viewing Space and its toil, waiting the end of Time.
Witness, who then art thou, one with thee who am I,
Nameless, watching the Wheel whirl across Time and Space?

There are worthy scholars with deep studies in the vast spiritual lore of India. The past proves too absorbing and fascinating for them to let them look into the future. Four decades ago very few were there who, despite their devoted studies of the past and great love for it, could imbibe the futuristic and evolutionary vision of Sri Aurobindo. Dr. Karan Singh is one of them. His exposition of Sri Aurobindo, marked by a serene application of intellect and an offering of love, has been an experience for his audience as well as his readers. I have heard him in the recent past expressing genuine dismay over the state of affairs today, the predicament in which mankind has been caught, but never has his audience dispersed in a mood of gloom, for beneath his statements powerfully critical of the present, there runs a stream of subtle faith, a faith in Providence in general and in the future of man as envisioned by Sri Aurobindo in particular. As I conclude this piece—working which was a stretch of joy for me — a stanza from an early poem of Sri Aurobindo comes to me so forcefully that I feel obliged to put it down even though I cannot justify on the surface its relevance to my reflections on Dr. Karan Singh and his autobiography:

Rejoice and fear not for the waves that swell,
The storms that thunder, winds that sweep;
Always our Captain holds the rudder well
He does not sleep.

Kashmir: Yesterday, Today, Tomorrow

•

P.N. Dhar

Prof. P.N. Dhar can easily be described as one of the most eminent Indians of the 20th Century and a keen and close observer of the history of the Indian subcontinent. One of the major concerns he deeply shares with Dr. Karan Singh, is the continuing problem of Kashmir.

"Karan Singh is a name that conjures up many images for me. He is a writer, a poet, a persuasive orator, a Sanskrit scholar, a diplomat, an administrator and a warm friend. This is not all. He is a singer, a raconteur, and a man of great personal charm and wit. His interest in Vedantic philosophy and inter-religious understanding has had a wide influence within the country and abroad. However, the multiplicity of his talents has not turned out to be an embarrassment of riches for he has done well in all fields he has pursued."

Although born a prince, he never loses the common touch. He can easily outshine any commoner in an election campaign and does not mind rubbing shoulders with the unkempt and the unwashed. Everyone remembers that he was the first ruler of a princely state to voluntarily renounce his privy purse. He was one of the half dozen Congressmen who won in the Parliamentary elections of 1977 which turned out to be a total disaster for the Congress Party in northern India. When he became a Cabinet Minister, he continued to stay in his own house and worked honorarily on a salary of one rupee a month. Even though he is deeply involved in politics, he does not belong to the normal run of Indian politicians and has sometimes suffered precisely for that reason. One could say that Indian politics is lucky to have a person like Dr. Karan Singh in its fold.

Among his many concerns is the continuing problem of Kashmir a concern which I as a Kashmiri deeply share, and it is about this matter that I want to make a few observations in this volume of felicitations in his honour.

Kashmir Issue

Khishte awwal chun nehad memaar kaj
taa Suraiya mee ravad dewaar kaj
(If there is a slant in the laying of the first brick, the wall can never be straight, no matter how high it rises)

The roots of the Kashmir conflict lie deep in the two-nation theory, which was the basis of the Pakistan movement that led to the partition of India in 1947. Since then the conflict has undergone many contortions but the underlying cause remains unaltered. The basis of the formation of the two states was not only different but also quite incompatible with that of the other. The nature of this incompatibility and its relevance to what is called the Kashmir problem has been succinctly formulated by Joseph Korbel, a member of the United Nations Commission on India and Pakistan, in the following words : "The real cause of all the bitterness and bloodshed, all the venomed speech, the recalcitrance and the suspicion that have characterized the Kashmir dispute is the uncompromising and perhaps the uncompromisable struggle of two ways of life, two spiritual attitudes that find themselves locked in deadly conflict, a conflict in which Kashmir has become both symbol and battleground." In other words Kashmir has become an integral component in the self-definition of the two states since their birth . For Pakistan, a self-proclaimed Islamic state, it seems to be incomprehensible and unacceptable that a Muslim majority area like Kashmir should be outside its national frontiers despite its geographic proximity. For India, a multi-lingual, multi-ethnic secular state with its own Muslim community—as large as that living in Pakistan—Kashmir is equally if not more than vital for its statehood.

However, as it turned out, Pakistan was not able to sustain its viability as a nation on religion alone. It split in 1971 and Bangladesh emerged as an independent sovereign state. This was a death-blow to the two-nation theory according to which Hindus and Muslims are supposed to be two separate nations. It was assumed that after the secession of Bangladesh, Pakistan would become a normal territorial state and give up its claim, explicit or implicit, that it spoke on behalf of the Muslims of the subcontinent. In the changed circumstances it was also assumed that Pakistan's problems with India, including that of Kashmir, would get resolved peacefully through negotiations. That was the hope, particularly after the successful outcome of the Shimla Conference in the summer of 1972.

At Shimla, Zulfikar Ali Bhutto adopted a statesman-like attitude. He agreed with Indira Gandhi that durable peace and stability was a precondition for the removal of poverty and for economic development and social progress, the shared goals of the two countries. To achieve these goals both sides were agreed that they must bury the hatchet and explore ways and means to settle the Kashmir problem. And the most feasible proposal for this purpose seemed to be to convert the old cease-fire line which was renamed the line of control into what Bhutto called 'a line of peace'. This was to be achieved gradually by endowing it with the attributes of an international border in an environment of expanding economic co-operation and by first trying to start solving less emotionally charged problems.

The important feature of the proposal was that neither country was gaining or losing territory, nor did it involve any transfer of population from one side to the other. Kashmiris as an ethnic community were left undivided on the Indian side. The line of control was actually an ethnic and linguistic frontier. In fact in 1947, at the time of the partition, it was also an ideological frontier, being the limit of the political influence of the National Conference led by Sheikh Muhammad Abdullah. To be sure there were some anomalies in the line, but it was possible to smoothen them out to the mutual satisfaction of both parties.

It will be recalled that Sheikh Abdullah had fallen foul of India in 1953 on the question of greater autonomy for Kashmir. Indira Gandhi was keen to bridge the differences which had arisen. She initiated parallel but separate negotiations with Sheikh Abdullah to accommodate Kashmiri sentiment for greater autonomy even while negotiations with Bhutto were in progress. Bhutto was well aware of this. It was expected that a successful outcome of the talks between Indira Gandhi and the Sheikh would help people in the two countries to accept the understanding reached at Shimla.

India reached an accord with Sheikh Abdullah in 1975. The essence of the accord was acceptance of the fact that the State of Jammu and Kashmir had acceded to India and a reassurance that its special status as enshrined in Article 370 of the Indian Constitution would be further safeguarded. Mirza Afzal Beg, the protoganist of the Plebiscite Front declared soon after that the accord had rendered the demand for plebiscite irrelevant. This stand of his was overwhelmingly endorsed by the people of the state in the elections of 1977 which have been universally recognized as the most free and fair elections ever held in Kashmir. The Sheikh's electoral victory was expected to convert the Shimla understanding into the Kashmir solution to be finally formalized between India and Pakistan.

But this was not to be. The Shimla agreement got gradually eroded. Within months of its signing a major event with important economic and political implications took place. This was the sudden enrichment of Saudi Arabia and Gulf sheikhdoms as a result of the OPEC success in raising the price of oil fourfold in one blow, This resulted in an economic boom in these countries and made vast amounts of money available for Islamic causes as interpreted by the fundamentalists. The investment boom in West Asia opened opportunities for trade and employment which made Pakistan look away from economic co-operation with India. More ominously, Kashmir got added to the list of 'Islamic causes' for which petrodollars became available in plenty. The growth of Islamic fundamentalism, fuelled by petrodollars, started giving a religious edge to Kashmiriyat, a popular name for the ethno-cultural sub-nationalism of Kashmiri Muslims . Kashmiriyat was anathema to fundamentalists. Their local leader told a senior Indian journalist in 1973 that his organization, Jamaat-e-Islami, was going to create a new generation of "more devout and true" Muslims within fifteen years. This was no idle threat but a well-conceived plan. Numerous madrasas were set up in order to realize this goal.

Things went according to plan, no doubt partly assisted by the Government of India's high handed dismissal of Farooq Abdullah, Kashmir Chief Minister and his replacement by Ghulam Mohammad Shah who was pathetically dependent on the Jamatis for political support. Insurgency did start on target in 1989. Within days the entire community of Kashmiri Pandits was cleansed out through carefully contrived means of mass intimidation and selective murder. The cleansing of Pandits was followed by the elimination of secular JKLF activists who were betrayed to the Indian security forces by the Hizbul Mujahideen, the armed wing of the Jamaat. Finally, the Jamatis hope that the *coup de grace* will be delivered by the better trained and better armed and more fanatically, motivated non-Kashmiri mujahids under the direct control of the Pakistan government and its agencies.

The more serious onslaught of fundamentalism after the emergence of Afghanistan under the Taliban and the gradual Talibanization of Pakistan is resulting in large scale export of terrorism across the border of Kashmir. These developments have given a pronounced Islamic character to the original and indigenous movement for autonomy in Kashmir. The Talibanized groups, well organized and well equipped, project themselves as the proponents of a grand Islamic state stretching from Kashmir to Pakistan through Afghanistan and Central Asia. Their proclamations hint that they consider Kashmir just the beginning.

With Islamic extremists in control of Pakistan's policy in Kashmir and India's continued striving to be a pluralist society and a secular state, the conflict has taken on a dangerously increased military dimension. General Musharraf, the military dictator of Pakistan, has chosen to describe the terror let loose by his regime in the highly emotive idiom of *Jihad*.

Naturally India cannot accept all this visceral hostility which continues to be based on Pakistan's propagation of the two-nation theory. As a democratic state India cannot accept any theory that reduces its Muslim population to the status of second-class citizens. The question that faces Pakistan is a stark one : how many more wars should it fight, how many more innocent lives should be lost before it is able to erase its birthmark which makes it see itself as being in opposition to India and not as its neighbour. Pakistan is unmindful of these questions and continues to engage in a slow process of sapping both India and itself, ignoring more urgent and more productive tasks.

The Kashmir problem will be solved if the Kashmiri Muslims are able to and allowed to assert their Kashmiriyat and if the Government of India succeeds in persuading them that their legitimate aspirations of autonomy are safeguarded in law as well as in political and administrative practice. The Indian State has also to reassert its faith in secularism more convincingly. Such a development might convince Pakistanis that their concern about their co-religionists in Kashmir has been taken care of. In such a changed political and ideological environment, liberal and more forward looking leaders in the two countries may triumph and the Kashmir issue may cease to be a matter of life and death for them, thus enabling them to live in peace and amity.

At this moment this seems to be a utopian dream but history offers instances where such dreams have come true. To cite an instance, the Alsace-Lorraine region was a bone of contention between Germany and France and their rivalry over it lasted more than 75 years. The region became part of Germany in 1871 after the Franco-German war. It was ceded to France after the first World War, the region was returned to France without causing any heart-burning in Germany. This miracle could happen only because soon after the end of the war in 1945 France and Germany decided to bury their past animosity and co-operate with each other to build the larger and more prosperous European Economic Community. Alsace-Lorraine was easily dovetailed into the new economic community without either of the former contending parties being overly bothered about its exact constitutional status or local political hue. The chances of similar prospect in the Indian sub-continent seem very bleak, at least in the immediate future. Given the present intensity of its rivalry with India, Pakistan considers Indian proposals for economic co-operation as a camouflage for its hegemonic ambitions. With that misperception, Pakistan is determinedly following a beggar-thy-neighbour policy towards India, regardless of the fact that the policy is hurting it even more. Not merely that; its strategy of 'thousand cuts' is aimed at bleeding India to death. After the military and diplomatic setback that followed its Kargil misadventure, Pakistan has embarked on a policy of unprecedented terrorism in Kashmir which it sanctifies as *Jihad*. General Gul Hassan, a former director-general of Pakistan's Inter-Services Intelligence, addressing a seminar in Islamabad which was attended by several foreign diplomats, said openly, "It is our aim to weaken India from within—and we can do it." Even a modern minded and respected columnist like Ayaz Amir wrote in the prestigious daily Dawn, "If Kashmir was solved tomorrow, would Pakistan and India rush into each other's embrace and forget the atavistic memories of the past. Kashmir is not the core issue between us. *Size and geography are and will remain so 500 years from now*" (emphasis added). This was written after the peace initiative of *Hizbul mujahideen* was aborted under Pakistani pressure. This being the state of mind of the ruling elite of Pakistan, conflict with India will continue till Pakistan becomes a normal nation-state without any messianic pretensions. Mohammad Ali Jinnah who used the two nation theory to the hilt in his struggle for Pakistan realized the limitation of the theory as a basis for the state he had succeed in creating. In his inaugural address to the Constitution Assembly on August 11, 1947 he said "You are free; You are free to go to your temples, you are free to go to your mosques or to any other place of worship in the State of Pakistan... You may belong to any religion or caste or creed—that has nothing to do with the business of the State... you will find that in course of time Hindus would cease to be Hindus and Muslims would cease to be Muslims, not in the religious sense, because that is the personal faith of each individual, but in the political sense as citizens of the State..."

This may seem to be quite a *volte face* on Jinnah's part but he was side-stepping the two-nation theory in order to lay Constitutional foundation for a secular democratic Pakistan. Unfortunately he did not live long enough to implement his proposal and his successors lacked his stature and his farsighted vision to do so. Ironically, the *Mohajirs* who formulated the pernicious theory and led the movement for Islamic Pakistan are having second thoughts about it now, more than half a century later! Their current leader, Altaf Hussain denounced the Theory at a rally in far off London on 17th September, 2000, but it was a cry in the wilderness. Will real rulers of Pakistan, its power elite ever make a similar turn around and take their country closer to the vision its founder held out to them on the eve of its creation, or, will they like Ayaz Amir let the past bury the future? The peace and progress of the entire subcontinent will depend on their choice. ☐☐☐

Common Good and Good Governance

•

O.P. Dwivedi

Dr. O.P. Dwivedi is Professor of Public and Environmental Administration at the Department of Political Studies, University of Guelph (Canada). He was also formerly President, Canadian Political Science Association and Vice-President, International Association of Schools and Institutes of Administration, Brussels (Belgium).

"It is to the credit of India's constitution framers that they left a solid foundation for good governance and liberal democratic tradition, which although weakened, can be made resurgent. In this task, both the secular and spiritual institutions must work together for sustaining the common good... both are needed to serve the common good of the Loka and the fight for good governance."

The word 'good' is derived from the word God, and carries an innate sense of judgement and the word 'common' suggests "ordinary occurrence", "objects or values shared by the group or a community", or "the whole" rather than particular or individualistic. When combined, the term has come to mean several things such as "the good of the whole in which the parts share", "the greatest good of the greatest number", "the commonweal" or "the universal happiness". Perhaps in earlier times the term might have meant to embrace "all and everyone", but presently in the Western thinking, the term rarely encompasses universality. On the contrary, as will be explained later, the Hindu concept of 'common good' emphasises on *Sarva* (all and everyone) instead of *Bahut* (the greatest number), From the Indian perspective when we speak of this term, it means an action or a deed which is beneficial to all and everyone although such benefits or privileges may not be immediately attainable or available including whether or not everyone realises it. It should also be noted that while the benefits may be available to all, it does not mean that all the people are entitled to the same (identical or equal) benefits, instead the concept means that everyone should receive (or give) their individual and collective due share. Also to be appreciated is the Hindu concept of the "common good" which includes both receiving from others (including the community, State or other entities) as well as rendering to others whatever be their due share. Thus, both sides of the coin, the common good, encompass receiving and giving help.

Thinking in the West

It is important to distinguish between *a* common good and *the* common good. Examples can be cited about common goods which are exhibited by such special groups as a soccer team (for which winning a tournament is its ultimate common good), an interest group (for which securing a particular advantage to its members only is the sole purpose of its existence), or a political party (for which winning an election is its ultimate aim). Thus, the meaning of a common good shifts according to its context. On the other hand, according to Yves R. Simon: "the common good, however, refers to a comprehensive set of goods in which the entire civil society participates".[1] Those "comprehensive set of goods" relate to the material as well as spiritual goods and services of an entire society. Also, we should note that rarely anyone knows in advance how all the components of the common good can be made to fit together; the challenge is how to bring together the individual needs and aspirations within the over-arching domain of the common good. Further, the common good should not be perceived as some kind of a rigid or static declaration of values, rather it is a dynamic affirmation and promotion of values, beliefs, institutions, and cultural determinants which encourage pursuit of a common endeavour by a society, a nation, or a global community. The essence of the common good is in securing universal welfare by voluntary cooperation of community members. It also requires willingness of individuals in the society to sacrifice a part of their own advantages or privileges to the common good in the name of sustaining universal welfare. Thus, the common good is larger than any individual interest but it does derive its authority on the community voluntary cooperation.

There is no doubt that the term "common good" or "public interest" is vague; but this does not mean it is not a valid concept. Take the example of the term "beauty" about which perhaps every man considers himself an expert. But can someone define a beautiful woman for all the people in all places? There is yet to appear a well defined, and "operationally" or "procedurally" acceptable universal standards of beauty. Because even those who win the contest may not appear beautiful to each and everyone. Similarly, the definition of common good differs from place to place, and from culture to culture. But when the same concept is placed in a specific context, the vagueness disappears. Perhaps we can say that the common good is an action which is beneficial to everyone, if not immediately but at least in the long run, whether or not everyone realises it.

INDIAN VIEW

Concept of Dharma

How does the above perspective relate to the traditional Indian view of life? The prerequisite of understanding the concept in Hindu thinking is to accept the view that Brahman (the Supreme Being) is the ultimate source and cause of the universal common good not only of humans but also of all beings in the Creation. The common good for Hindus is the highest ethical standard which everyone ought to apply according to his or her *Dharma*. Further, the Hindu tradition requires that a common good takes precedence over a private good (including individual material good, personal or moral good, or special communal good); and it points towards the full realisation (development) of the potentialities of individuals as well as of the entire community. Under such a system, a virtuous (*Dharmic*) citizen will always be the common good by desiring towards fuller development of the potentials of his fellow citizens and of the community at large. In

Sanskrit, the term 'common good' can be related to such terms as *Sarva Loka Kalyankari Karma* (सर्वकल्याणकारी कर्म) *Sarva Hitey Ratah* (सर्वहिते रत:), or even *Sarva Loka Sangraha* (सर्व लोकसंग्रह). The first term *Sarva Kalyankari Karma* means an action or a deed done which results in the common good of all and everyone. The second term, *Santa Hitey Ratah*, on the other hand, relates to the action resulting in "caring for others", and includes duties which ought to be directed towards universal upliftment and welfare. For this to happen, mutual respect and cooperation must take place. The third term is *Santa Loka Sangraha* where the concept of *Sarva Loka* has a comprehensive meaning incorporating not only the entire humanity but the whole cosmos and other worlds (such as *Devaloka*, *Satyaloka*, and *Patal-loka*). Perhaps the word *Sangraha* should be explained further: it means, as explained by Bal Gangadhar Tilak, "maintaining, feeding, protecting, and defending it (*Loka*) in a proper way, without allowing it to be destroyed"[2]. The common good, as perceived by the ancient Indian thought requires people indulging in the *Purushartha* (duties), and striving towards the universal welfare. The scriptures mention *Dharma* as the foundation of that common good.

Dharma comes from the root *dhr* which means to hold or uphold; that by which people are held and sustained together is *Dharma*. In *Mahabharata* Rishi Utthya says to King Mandhata: *Prabhavartham hi bhutanam Dharmah srishtah syayambhuva* (प्रभावार्थ हि भूतानां धर्म: सृष्ट: स्वयम्भुवा). The All-Pervading One has instituted *Dharma* for the common good of all beings.[3]

Concept of Common Good

In order for us to provide a closer counterpart of the term "common good", let us revert to our previous discussion about those three terms suggested above. We need a synthesis among these three terms. Deriving on the concept of *Dharma*, we may need a concept which should be based on *Sarvajana Hitaya Sarvajana Sukhaya* cha (सर्वजन हिताय सर्वजन सुखाय च) for the universal welfare and happiness of all and everyone. As we know, Hindu religion decrees that we look after the welfare of all (not only the humanity but the entire Creation); it is here that the concept of *Sarva Loka Sangraha* becomes relevant to our discussion of the common good because this term assumes an action resulting in universal welfare based on mutual cooperation. Although the word *Sarva* has not been used in the following verse of *Gita*, nevertheless its purport is clear that it is the duty of people to engage in *Sarva Loksangraha*:

Loksangrahamevapi sanpasyan kartum arhasi

[*Gita*, Chapter 3, Verse 20]

लोकसंग्रहमेवापि संपश्यन्कर्तुमर्हसि!

(Keeping in mind the *loksangraha*, you must perform prescribed actions)

Let us return once more to our previous discussion on the term 'the common good'. It should be noted that the common good is larger than any individual person or a group of some individuals, and it remains incomplete unless it helps each and everyone to achieve their potency, their ends of life. Of course, it is not always possible to achieve full development of every single individual at the same time and in every situation. Although it may appear that the common good may be beyond human reach, yet it is crucial that everyone knows the purpose and meaning of that common good which they are exhorted to pursue. In that sense, the common good becomes an ideal to uphold, something akin to a universal truth. And it is here that the Indian concept of the common good, emphasis being on *Sarva Kalyankari Hitah* (सर्वकल्याणकारी हित:) or the Universal common good assumes a greater meaning; a meaning which relates to the fulfillment of their individual ends of life within the confines of *Dharma*.

To reiterate, the concept of common good encompasses not only the humanity but also the cosmos in its entirety. It recognises that each species has its distinct place in nature, and that each has its own ends of life and *Dharma* to perform. However, only humans (but not other species) have been entrusted with the obligation to look after the "happiness for all" (*Sarve Bhavantu Sukhinnh* (सर्वे भवन्तु सुखिन:). Furthermore, common good is not static in the sense that it changes and shifts with human development and our understanding of what the humanity can positively create.[4] In essence, the common good also means "caring for the other". It resides in the conscience of a person. A person who is conscious of his or her duties and obligations (*Dharma*) sustains the common good just as the common good persuades people to attain that consciousness and to reach for that common good. However, that common good may not appear to be the same for everyone, everywhere, and for all the time, despite omnipresence of its central thread of 'caring for the other'. For example, it is said that when the nuclear scientist Robert Oppenheimer witnessed the first testing (explosion) of an atomic bomb in 1945, he cited *Bhagavad Gita* to illustrate what he saw (*Divi surya sahastrasya bhave—dyugapad uttishthta* दिवि सुर्य सहस्त्रस्य भवेघुगपदुत्थिता—*Gita*, chapter 11, verse 12), and how he has become the destroyer of worlds. To him, that experimentation was a sure sign of the common good being destroyed.

Caring for Others

It is important that we shall come back to the question of *Sarva Hitey Ratah* (सर्वहिते रत:): caring and taking care of others by serving unto them. This notion is utterly intertwined with the general concept of common good. It is an obligation that human beings owe not only to each other but also to other beings as well as to the entire cosmos. But mere exhortations are not enough because most of the time it is hard for people to spontaneously and universally move in concert towards the fulfillment of the common good. In order for them to act, laws, governmental institutions and non-governmental organisations are needed as means to ensure a minimal system of taking care. To reiterate the example of environmental crisis, we know that until the 1960s people did not pay much attention to pollution problems with the result that a wholesale destruction of natural resources took place. Only when governing elites and the existing governmental system were forced to prevent pollution damage and to compel people acting as the trustees of nature, the common good pertaining to the conservation of nature and sustainable development could take roots. It is now accepted that a caring humanity not only concerns itself for the human rights but also equally cares about the environment rights.[5] Thus, caring sentiments when expressed in accord and unison become our collective sentiments which, in turn, relate to our main goal, the common interest.

Common Good and Public Interest

Is there a difference between the common good and public interest? While these two terms are used interchangeably, common good (*bonum commune*) could be seen aiming at creation of such socio-economic and political conditions under which individuals are able to pursue, with human dignity, their specific ends of life, individually and collectively. Public interest means, at the best, an aggregation of the interests of the many, but certainly not of all. Thus, the scope of public interest is not the same as we understand about the common good.

Good of Entire Society

In the classical usage of the term 'common good' the State has no other purpose than to serve the common good. The term became a symbol for the whole range of governmental actions; and in olden times, King became an embodiment of the common good for his people. And when King's divine right to rule was subsumed by a State, the government became an instrument to achieve ends related to promoting general human well-being, such as peace, order, prosperity, justice and human dignity.[6] Good governance meant when a government not only served the common good but also promoted the well-being of not only its own but of the entire society as well. As mentioned earlier, the common good embraced *everyone* because it consisted of not only an aggregation of individual 'goods' but the well-being of all; and in order to secure the well-being of all, it became important that all the individuals became willing partners in the enterprise. Both the parts and the whole became mutually dependent and reciprocal, each contributing to sustain the whole, while the whole in turn supported the existence of the parts. A King became duty bound to insure that the common good (*Dharma*) was protected. This did not mean a creation of the positive State as we have come to understand in the post World War II era, when King's intervention became essential only when people were unable to protect their individual goods. And when kings were replaced by a secular State, it is the government which assumed that role. Somehow, the common good got replaced by the public interest.

Public Interest

It is a long story to detail how the concept of 'public interest' came into being, it is suffice to say that in the Anglo-Saxon history, the common good became identified with private interests of a King: and later, the term common good became linked with negative connotation of royal desires, commands and demands which had to be met by his subjects. When the democratic and liberal revolt came against royalty, the term public interest gained currency. The word common was replaced by 'public' and the term good was changed into 'interest. Public interest became the interest of the majority, approximating the greatest happiness of the greatest number, something akin to the concept of *Bahujan Hitaya*.

It seems that the term common good which relates to the universalism (*Sarva*) is a better concept for good governance that the term public interest. This difference has been amply demonstrated by the environmental crisis of planetary proportion that the humanity is facing nowadays; because for decades, the prevailing public interest could not rise above the aggregation of some individual (private) interests who controlled the public agenda. In the process, the good of the environment (that is also the good of the humanity as well as nature and other living organisms) could not be permitted to take precedence over that of the private interest.[7] Between the two terms, only the common good as a concept can assume a 'divine' like sense because the public interest is unable to cover the good of the entire humanity if not the community of the whole in this world and beyond. In this respect, as Saint Thomas Aquinas states, "the common good of the whole is God himself in whom consists the happiness of all".[8] Although the common good of the whole is God Himself, nevertheless, the common good is not fixed once and for all simply because the will of God is interpreted by human beings who are limited in their vision and capacity. That is why the common good can be subject to interpretations given need, time and place to deliberate thereon. Nevertheless, that divinity in human beings has to but awakened so that it can become a foundation for universal welfare and upliftment which is facilitated by good governance.

DHARMA: THE FOUNDATION OF GOOD GOVERNANCE

View in Indian Scriptures

Let us now examine the foundations of good governance which is required to protect and sustain the common good, and the requisite duties and conduct of public officials as described in some scriptures and ancient writings of the Hindu religion and culture.[9] Among the main scriptures, let us start with the advice given to Arjuna by Lord Kirshna in *Gita*:

Tasmacchastram Pramanam te karyakaryevyavasthitau
Gyatva shastra vidhanoktam karma kartum iharhasi.

तस्माच्छास्त्रं प्रमाणं ते कार्याकार्ये व्यवस्थितौ।
ज्ञात्वा शास्त्र विधानोक्तकर्मकर्तुमिहार्हसि।।

[One ought to understand what is duty, and what is forbidden in the commands laid down by the scriptures (Shastras). Knowing such rules and regulations, one should behave as ordained by scriptures.] (*Gita*, Chapter XVI, Verse 24)

Lord Krishna further says:

Pravrittim cha nivrittim cha karyakarye bhayabhaye
Bandham moksham cha ya vetti buddhih sa Partha sattviki.

प्रवृत्तिं च निवृत्तिं च कार्याकार्ये भयाभये।
बन्धं मोक्षं च या वेत्ति बुद्धिः सा पार्थ सात्विकी।।

[O Partha! that understanding by which one knows what ought to be done and what ought not to be done, what is to be feared and what is not, what is obligatory and what is permitted, leads to the righteous path (SAttviki Pravritti).]

(*Gita*, Chapter XVIII, Verse 30)

That righteous path is called *Dharma*. But how does one know the righteous path for different people and for specific functions or duties? Hindu scriptures provide ample guidelines through *Dharma Shastras*. These guidelines or codes of conduct have been prescribed by great many seers which are spread all over in various scriptures of Hindu religion. But for our purpose, examples are drawn from the followings: (1) *Yajurveda*, (2) *Mahabharata*, (3) *Manusmriti*, and (4) *Kautilya's Arthasastra*.

Yajurveda

Dharma of rulers has been described in many places; at the same time, it is mentioned that such a ruler will be an elected one who will administer justice with the help of an elected assembly (Chapter VII, Verse 45). For example, in Chapter VIII, the good conduct as a prerequisite of the common good has been emphasised:

O virtuous and prosperous king, be knowledgeable about your conduct as protector of the learned, and impeller towards our progress and prosperity. Be in control of your passion, and conduct yourself in a righteous manner. Be a friend to us, Know the conduct as laid down by all sages.

(*Yajurveda*, Chapter VIII, Verse 50)

Such a conduct is funded on such virtues as humility, discipline, and voluntary conduct because the king is "elected" to undertake the duty of State. This is illustrated by the verse in Chapter 9, which describes the King follows:

> O King elected by the learned and wise for carrying out the duty of state, I accept thee who is knowledgeable, practices yoga, full of humility, leader among leaders, expert in science, and is kind. The administration is thy mainstay, I accept thee, Thou has been elected by the people, I accept thee...
>
> (*Yajurveda*, Chapter IX, Verse 2)

There are many examples from Yajurveda which are also full of similar advice to that elected ruler. Another example is the following verse from Chapter 20 *where* the King is asked to maintain the common good (righteousness) of his *Loka*:

> Assembly of Learned (*Vidya Sabha*), Assembly of Spiritual Leaders (*Dharma Sabha*), and the Assembly of the Administrators, (*Rajya Sabha*) are the three organs of government of a ruler. These should provide speedy justice and solution of problems, should consist of well-qualified persons, fully constituted to manage the affairs of state with prowess and skills, and to maintain the righteousness [common good] of government. (*Yajurveda*, Chapter XX, Verse 43)

Through these and similar verses, a Kings has been advised to preserve the common good by acting in a moral and virtuous way.

Mahabharata

In *Mahabharata*, after the Great War, King Yudhishthira approaches his wounded grandfather, asks him to give a discourse on the concept of common good, duties and morality of a King, his officials, and the public. Bhishma the grandfather, thus answers:

1. The eternal duties of kings are to make their subjects happy, to observe truth, and to act sincerely.

   (*Shanti Parva*, Chapter LVIII, Verse 11)

2. A King guided by conducting righteously (Vyavaharen Shuddham) and devoting his life in the service of his subjects acquires fame and immortality both here and hereafter. (*Shanti Parva*, Chapter, LXXXV, Verse 2)

3. The foundation of good governance is *Dharma* (righteousness). The King, his ministers and state employees who have taken the oath of their offices to uphold *Dharma* and to act in accordance with the common good, must not act unjustly or unethically so as to secure their private good through selfishness. If they don't behave appropriately, they all will surely go to hell along with destroying the moral basis of governance.
[*Shanti Parva*, Chapter LXXXV, Verses 16-17]
4. The main purpose of a King is to protect *Dharma* and to bolster righteousness and to be free from indolence and desires. One should know that a King is the defender of all (*Lokasya Rakshita*) (*Shanti Parva*, Chapter XC, Verse 3)
5. The Lord of Creation, Brahma, has devised *Dharma* for the care and well-being of all; it is the duty of a King to follow and advance the dictates of *Dharma*.
(*Shanti Parva*, Chapter XC, Verse 19).

These and various other verses contain advice for a righteous King.

Manusmriti

Among the all Hindu *Smrities*, Manusmriti is considered the most important and comprehensive codification of Hindu laws. It includes not only the precepts for the moral duties of all persons, but also the special rules regarding the conduct of kings, officials, and administration, of justice. The following two verses illustrate the basic thinking to symbolise duties for the King, his ministers and other officials:

1. Brahma has created the King to be the protector of the *Verna* and public order [common good] so that they discharge their several duties according to their *dharma* and rank. (*Manusmriti*, Book VII, Verse 35)
2. Thus conducting himself (and) ever intent on (discharging) his [prescribed] royal duties, a King shall order all his officials (to work) for the good of his subjects.
(*Manusmriti*, Book IX, Verse 324)

Through these and various other verses, moral tone has been set for the conduct of a King, and good governance of the kingdom.

Kautilya's Arthasastra

Although the book written by Kautilya (Prime Minister of King Chandragupta, 321 BC-296 BC) is not considered a part of *Dharma Shastras* (Scriptures), nevertheless, it s the greatest Indian treatise on the art of government and administration, the duties of Kings, ministers, officials and the art of diplomacy. For example, a King is expected to behave in a most righteous manner:

1. In the happiness of his subjects lies his happiness; in the their welfare his welfare; whatever pleases him (personally) he shall not consider as good, but whatever makes his subjects happy, he shall consider good.
   (*Arthasastra*, Book I, Chapter XIX, 39)
2. The King should look to the bodily comforts of his servants by providing such emoluments as can infuse in them the spirit of enthusiasm to work. He should not violate the course of righteousness and wealth... Thus, the King shall not only maintain his servants, but also increase their subsistence and wages in consideration of their learning and work. (*Arthasastra*, Book V, Chapter III, 247, 249)

The illustrations given, above denote a high moral tone assigned to those who govern and act as stewards of governance. For them, there is ample spiritual guidance for good behaviour. People who govern have been advised that good governance is sustained by adhering to a trinity of moral duties ultimately resulting in *Sarva Kalyankari Karma*, maintaining *Sarva Loka Sangraha* and aiming for the *Sarva Hitey Ratah*. These three dictums emanate from certain religious foundations which have been examined above, and which support the contention that governance is a moral endeavour.

SUSTAINING THE COMMON GOOD OF THE GOVERNED

Government, in a liberal-democratic State, is assumed to exist for the common good. This is achieved through certain institutions of the State whose actions and decisions the public accepts. The purpose of such institutions, and of the State itself, is to perform certain duties and fulfil acquired obligations. The justifications for the State to pursue the common good is actually the justification of its own existence. The basic thrust of the concept is to motivate people in government so that they can make full contribution of their capabilities in serving their nation and the community. The objective of good governance is to create an environment so that public servants as well as politicians in government are able to respond to the challenge of good governance. That challenge involves a notion of duty, vocations, and service to the public, as well as the caring responsibility for their welfare, And, it strengthens the values of liberal democracy. That ideal, based on vocation, duty and service also draws upon the concept of sacrifice—a concept which rises above self-interest, placing individualism over collective good, and greed. The concept of service (*Sarva Hita*) also creates a shared feeling or spirit of public duty among those who govern. This author has been advocating for some time that an emphasis has to be placed on the *service* or vocation as the main tenet of governing. Lately, this dimension appears to have been accepted by some governments; for example, the Canadian government in its Report: *Public Service 2000: The Renewal of the Public Service of Canada*, the Federal Government stated:

> ...the Government believes that public service is an ideal that should be fostered and that those who serve the public out of conviction and duty are making an important contribution to the maintenance of democracy.[10]

"Public service as an ideal" has been the classical view of good governance. That classical view also included such values as: probity, applying objective standards universally, willingness to speak truth to Ministers but a readiness to carry out instructions to the contrary if overridden, an appreciation of the wider common good which is over and above the public-interest, equity, and a constant concern for democratic ideals. Because, confidence and trust in the democratic system can be safeguarded only when the governing process demonstrates a higher moral, tone, keeping in view the upholding of common good. Because we get a moral government by creating and sustaining certain conditions within which *Dharma* and *Loka Sangraha* can survive. Such is the duty of those who wish to be involved in the difficult and complex world of governance. This is the essence and basis of good governance.[11]

That essence and basis of the moral State, as per ancient Indian thinking, depends on the triangle of those actions for governance which are undertaken for universal welfare (*Sarva Loka Kalyankari*

Karma), maintaining and protection to each and everyone in the Creation (*Sarva Loksangrahamevapi*), and securing universal care for all and everyone (*Sarva Hitey Ratah*). But that triangle has a centre point, the common-most good which is denoted by the term "happiness for all" (*Sarve Bhavantu Sukhinah*). However, these prerequisites as enunciated in ancient times in India are sadly missing among the stewards and practitioners of governance. There is a need to operationalise this ancient wisdom through the re-arrangement of socio-economic and political institutions; however, first a country like India would have to formulate a set of realistic indicators for achieving such a common good. It is to the credit of India's constitutional framers and freedom fighters that they left a solid foundation for good governance and liberal democratic tradition which although weakened, can be made resurgent. In this task, both the secular and spiritual institutions must work together rather than fencing out, in the name of secularism, the spiritual domain from contributing to good governance. There is a need to bring both together for sustaining the common good. Although they have different perspectives and objectives (one dealing with the welfare and care of life here and now, while the other striving for the life hereafter); nevertheless, both are needed to serve the common good of the *Loka* and the fight for good governance.

NOTES

1. Yves R. Simon, *Philosophy of Democratic Government, Notre Dame*, University of Notre Dame Press, 1993 [quoted by Thomas R. Rourke in "Michel Novak and Yves R. Simon on the Common Good and Capitalism", *The Review of Politic*, Vol. 58, Spring 1996, p. 237.]
2. Bal Gangadhar Tilak, *Shri Bhagavad-Gita Rahasya*, Poona, Tilak Brothers, 1902, p. 927.
3. *Mahabharata* (published by Gita Press Gorakhpur, India, 1988), *Shanti Parva*, Chapter 90, verse 19. All references in this essay pertaining to *Mahabharata* are from this publication.
4. Marcus G. Raskin, *The Common Good: Its Politic, Policies and Philosophy*, New York, Routledge & Kegan Paul, 1986, p. 27.

5. On this issue, see O.P. Dwivedi, "Human Rights and Environmental Rights: Their Compatibility in the Context of Sustainable Development", in Reeta C. Tremblay et. al., (eds). *Interfacing Nations: Indo/Pakistani/ Canadian Reflections on the 50th Anniversary of India's Independence,* Delhi, B. R. Publishing, 1998, pp. 363-76.
6. Bruce Douglas, "The Common Good and the Public Interest", Political Theory, Vol. 8, No. 1, February 1980, p. 104.
7. See, on this matter, this author's following publications : *"Man and Nature: A Holistic Approach to a Theory of Ecology". The Environmental Professional,* Vol. 10, No. 1, 1988, pp. 8-15; and *Development Administration: From Underdevelopment to Sustainable Development,* London, Macmillan Press, 1994.
8. St. Thomas Aquinas, *De Perfectione Vitae Spirituals* quoted by Michael A. Smith, *"The Common Advantage and Common Good", Laval Theologique et Philosophique,* Vol. 51, No. 1 February 1995, p. 121.
9. For further details, see O.P. Dwivedi, *"Administrative Theology: Dharma of Public Officials", Indian Journal of Public Administration,* Vol. 36, No. 3, July-September, 1990, pp. 406-19.
10. Canada, Privy Council Office, *Public Service 2000: The Renewal of the Public Service of Canada, Ottawa,* Government of Canada, Department of Supply and Services, 1990, p. 14.
11. O.P. Dwivedi, *"Conclusion: A Comparative Analysis of Ethics, Public and the Public Service",* in James S. Bowman and F. A. Elliston (eds.), *Ethics, Government and Public Policy,* New York, Greenwood Press, 1988, p. 318.

❏❏❏

The Good Genius of France-India Forum

•

Jean Francois-Poncet

Hon'ble Jean Francois-Poncet, President of the Commission of Economic Affairs and Planning of France was a Co-Chairman of the Indo-French Forum along with Dr. Karan Singh.

"His first words to me drew my attention to the fact that he was born in France, shortly before the Second World War, in Cannes, in one of the seafront palaces where his father, the Maharaja of Jammu and Kashmir, rented every summer an entire floor for his family and his attendants. He rejoiced at the fact that, by a happy twist of fate, he was called to preside over an institution devoted to the development of relations between his country and France."

In choosing Dr. Karan Singh to co-chair the Indo-French Forum, the Indian Government could not have made a better choice, nor could it have emphasised with more strength the importance it attaches to developing the relations between the two countries.

In my capacity as the Forum's French Co-President, I had the privilege to meet, for the first time, Dr. Karan Singh. His first words to me drew my attention to the fact that he was born in France, shortly before the Second World War, in Cannes, in one of the seafront palaces where his father, the

Maharaja of Jammu and Kashmir, rented every summer an entire floor for his family and his attendants. He rejoiced at the fact that, by a happy twist of fate, he was called to preside over an institution devoted to the development of relations between his country and France, which he visits nearly every year and whose history and culture, as a scholar, he knows well and likes.

The Franco-Indian Forum is a fascinating institution, which might also have been frustrating.It is fascinating because both governments have entrusted it with the ambitious task of looking after the development of Franco-Indian relations.But it might have been frustrating because they have not given it any financial means or any power of decision to enable the Forum to accomplish its task.The Forum thinks, suggests, proposes. But it is up to the governments, that is to say often their administrations, to decide and to act. And we all know the aversion of "bureaucrats" to new ideas and their skillfulness in burying them.Yet we are all pleased to recognize that the Forum has overcome this original handicap which could have reduced it to being a mere academic gathering, a "decorative structure", with no connection to reality, and has demonstrated its usefulness, proved its effectiveness. In two years, it has succeeded in imprinting on Franco-Indian relations a new dynamism. There are three reasons for this remarkable success.

Firstly it can be attributed to the Franco-Indian relations themselves. Their current substance, particularly economic and commercial, is weak when compared with the affinity and fellow feelings which unite the two countries. The people of France and India both have an old culture and a rich and troubled history ; they each defend zealously their independence and are deeply attached to life's spiritual dimension. So they are attracted to each other by shared hopes and by the same rejection of materialism which is invading our planet. One could say that the current inadequacy of their mutual relationship is a historical anomaly that, given a strong will, relying on intelligent proposals, can and must be corrected in a few years.

The Forum's success can be attributed also to its membership. It brings together quite an exceptional group of French and Indians who, in the most varied areas—from industry to banking, from art to the media and to science—play in their respective countries major roles and enjoy a wide influence. I will mention but one example, that of Mr. Cohen Tannoudji, a French member of the Forum who holds a Nobel Prize for Physics.

But besides these factors, it is certain that the personality of Mr. Karan Singh has been a decisive element in the fast growing success which the Forum is achieving. His natural authority, his great culture, his talent as a speaker, his generosity, and his personal aura have enthused the Forum and from the start enabled it to play a major role in establishing relations between the two countries.

Thanks to his superior but practical intellect, his overall vision of men and objects along with his concern with details and results, Dr. Karan Singh has been the "good genius" of the Forum.

In the overall tribute paid to him, the Franco-Indian Forum's Presidency might occupy only a minor position when compared with the tremendous services that he has given to his country as a Minister and to the world as a writer and a philosopher. But having been his colleague, I have to be witness to his eminent contribution to our work as well as to the development of relations between France and India.

The French members of the Forum will remember him as a statesman, a man of culture and of feeling, who has the elegance of mind and courtesy of a "grand seigneur".

□□□

Wonderfully Diverse and Distinguished Man

•

John Kenneth Galbraith

Prof. John Kenneth Galbraith, distinguished friend of India and Dr. Karan Singh, wrote from Harvard University in the United States that he indeed felt honoured by the invitation to contribute to the Birthday volume for Dr. Karan Singh. He wrote, "My pleasure is enhanced by the admiration I have always had for this most distinguished man. Anyone privileged by position in India must share my feelings."

"But I write with regret. Some six months ago I had a rather intricate heart operation followed by several months of invalidism. I am now making a recovery but I can under severe restraints as to any public effort, I could not write of anyone so distinguished as Dr. Karan Singh without some expenditure of real effort."

Alas, despite any recovery to date, which continues I cannot accept your invitation. I enclose a brief comment which you may wish to include in the volume underway.

It seems to me quite impossible that Dr. Karan Singh, a friend of many years and a greatly admired citizen and a leader in a greatly admired country, is now reaching his 70th birthday. I will always regard him as one of the most generous and effective and, needless to say, charming, citizens of my time. I have been invited, to my pleasure, to write a tribute to Dr. Karan Singh, along with an account of my own relation with him. This, for what I trust are some temporary health problems, I cannot do. But I can, with pleasure, tell of the great work of this wonderfully diverse and distinguished man. Nothing would give me more pleasure than to be present to make this tribute in person. That is not, for a variety of reasons, possible. Let my default leave no one in doubt as to my admiration for this charming, devoted and wonderfully remembered friend.

□□□

He Was Called Tiger by Jawaharlal Nehru

•

M.Y. Ghorpade

M.Y. Ghorpade, Karnataka Minister for Rural Development and Panchayati Raj has known Dr. Karan Singh for over three decades. He is fascinated by Dr. Karan Singh's many-splendoured personality and varied qualities. Among these is his facet as a conservationist and perfectionist.

"Whatever Dr. Karan Singh does, he does with good distinction. He is a perfectionist and a conservationist to the core, with finely developed artistic and aesthetic sensibilities. The genuine interest he evinced in my wildlife photography, which is my hobby, was really heart warming. He liked my tiger pictures. It may be recalled that he himself was called "tiger" by Jawaharlal Nehru years ago."

Dr. Karan Singh and I have known each other for over three decades. It has been more of a personal than a political relationship, though both ofus have been in public life for so long and, therefore, politics inevitably crept into our conversation whenever we met. India and the world has changed a great deal over past few decades, but our friendship has stood the test of time because it did not depend so much on external circumstances, as on our internal responses and perceptions of our own growing selves and a rapidly changing scenario.

Undoubtedly much has changed since Jawaharlal Nehru made Karan Singh the Governor of Kashmir at a crucial time in history, and Indira Gandhi utilised his services as a Minister in her Cabinet. But Dr. Karan Singh's attitude of doing any job entrusted to him with great competence and conscientiousness has remained the same, as that is a part of his inherent character and personality. He has not only studied the *Gita* in depth but tries to follow it to the best of his ability. That perhaps is the secret of his equanimity and calm under all circumstances.

I have alway been greatly impressed by his scholarship and erudition which flows freely in his speeches and writings. It is significant that he thought of working for his doctorate on a subject like the political philosophy of Sri. Aurobindo, so early in life and amidst the surrounding turmoil. The book still reads fresh and is clearly indicative of his deep insight into the fundamentals of our thought and culture. In more recent years I heard him speak on Sri Aurobindo at Baroda. It was a treat not only to the ear but to the intellect and the heart—a reflection of the soul of humanity.

Whatever Dr. Karan Singh does, he does with great distinction. He is a perfectionist and a conservationist to the core, with finely developed artistic and aesthetic sensibilities. The genuine interest he evinced in my wildlife photography, which is my hobby, was really heart warming. He liked my tiger pictures. It may be recalled that he himself was called 'tiger' by Jawaharlal Nehru long ago. More recently, Dr. Karan Singh was closely associated with the Tiger Project and the Indian Board for Wildlife, where he did a great deal for conservation and awareness of nature.

The spiritual side of his life always interested me. We discussed, to the extent possible, the spiritual nuances of precepts and practices. Ultimately, we both agreed, that it is the experience that matters and makes a real difference to the quality of life. He is a great *bhakta* of Shiva, but that name includes so much, the totality of experience, the heights to which our consciousness can grow and the great depth with which it can become one. I made it a point to send him whatever little I wrote on these aspects, like my "Human Quest and Experience" for instance. I could always look forward to a meaningful response from him. To me these were essential ingredients of our relationship.

At long last, Dr. Karan Singh visited Sandur, my home in Karnataka, to deliver the Adarsha lecture on 27 December 1997, on 50 years of Independence and inaugurate our Arogya Community Centre for eye care. As he himself said in his lecture: "This visit was first mooted a quarter of a century ago, and it took me 25 years to come all the way from Kashmir to Sandur. I am very glad that I am here at last and, particularly, to have been able to inaugurate the Arogya Community Centre. The Vedic prayer, '*Tamasoma Jyothirgamaya*' has of course a spiritual importance, but it has also a physical importance. If you cannot see and your eyesight is restored, it is a very great boon".

Dr. Karan Singh chose to speak on 50 years of Independence as we were observing the 50th Anniversary of our Independence. He held the audience spell bound, with many perceptive comments on the political, economic, social dimensions of our freedom. "15th August 1947 is a significant day in human history and is important not only because India became free but because we chose democracy", he said. He went on to talk about the democratization of India's political psyche, the dangers of political instability and corruption, the need to strengthen basic infrastructure and take a balanced view of economic development, which will have to fully take into account the needs of the poor and the vulnerable sections of society. "People are not expendable. They cannot be thrown away just because they happen to be poor. What we need is a coherent policy, and one of the weaknesses of our minority Governments is that there is no proper policy", he opined. He made a pointed reference to the disastrous consequence of uncontrolled population growth, wide spread desertification and deforestation, and recalled the National Population Policy he had submitted to Parliament in April 1976. "If that had been followed, the situation would have been much better today" he said. Then he talked of the empowerment of women as a key factor in family planning. "Wherever women are educated, take Kerala for example, Tamil Nadu and Karnataka, they are doing much better than the States in the North because the percentage of female literacy is much higher. Once you educate a woman, she becomes a co-equal partner in the process of development and not simply a passive object".

Dr. Karan Singh then went on to talk of how "India is a uniquely pluralistic society; all the great religions of the world thrive here. He mentioned the Temple of Understanding, an international organization of which he was the Chairman.

Secularism meant *'Sarvadharma Sambabhava"* equal respect to all religions and not "equal rejection or equal hostility to all religions". As the *Rig Veda* says, *'Ekam Sat Vipraha Bahudha Vadanti"*. The truth is one, the learned call it by many names.

He also expressed great concern about increasing caste conflicts and "casteism in reverse" as he put it. There is also inversion of values he regretted. "At the entrance to Parliament there is a beautiful *shloka* which ends with *'Vasudhaiva Kutumbakam'*, the world is our family. But what has it become, *'Kutumbaiva Vasudha'*, our family alone is the world, *'Ahimsa Pramodharma'*, non-violence is the highest dharma, said Lord Buddha, Lord Mahavira and Mahatma Gandhi. But now we find *'Himsa Paramokarma'*, violence everywhere in India. Finally, a beautiful Vedic ideal, *'Bhahujana Sukhaya, Bahujana Hithayacha'*—the welfare and happiness of the many, has become *'Swajana Sukhaya, Swajana Hitayacha* — the welfare only of our own kith and kin' ".

Though Dr. Karan Singh expressed at Sandur the anguish in his heart, he also expressed his heartfelt joy and concluded his lecture on an optimistic note. "We must recapture the vision of a great and resurgent India .... the vision of Vivekananda and Aurobindo", he said and made a moving appeal, especially to the younger generation: "The heart of India is still strong, our ideals are still there. You are the ones to achieve these ideals. The next five years are going to be crucial for Indian democracy. We must learn from the lessons of the past fifty years, move in a new direction, on a new trajectory, towards a stable, progressive India in which we can finally get rid of poverty and malnutrition, hunger and disease, and take our place among the great nations of the world." Thus ended Dr. Karan Singh's speech and his long awaited visit to Sandur, an ancient green valley which Mahatma Gandhi called an 'Oasis' when he visited it in 1934. Both these visits will be evergreen in the minds and hearts of the people of Sandur.

Dr. Karan Singh has completed 70 years. My mother tells me, from her historical memory, that Dr. Karan Singh is less than a year older to me. However, they say that the mind does not age as fast as the body, and the spirit does not age at all. All of us convey our heartfelt good wishes to Dr. Karan Singh and *'Bhabi'*, his gracious wife, who has been a great source of strength and solace to him all these exciting and eventful years.

❑❑❑

A Lifetime of Compassionate Vision

•

Vaclav Havel

President Vaclav Havel of Czech Republic, one of the tallest intellectuals of the world today has highlighted Dr. Karan Singh's lifetime of compassionate vision, eloquent advocacy and devoted action.

"Over the course of the last decade, I have been especially fortunate to develop friendships with a number of extraordinary people from many different nations. Each of these individuals has not only accomplished amazing tasks, but they also have made incredibly gracious, selfless, and substantive contributions to our world. Even within this group of distinguished individuals, Dr. Karan Singh stands out as an exceptional example of someone whose lifelong service to the cause of humanity provides me with enormous inspiration and cause for admiration.

I have been particularly grateful for his participation in the Forum 2000 conferences in Prague, at which he will participate again this year. His insightful comments, probing questions, and stimulating conversation have contributed a valuable dimension to the conference proceedings. His keen insights into the problems we face in the modern world have strongly impacted the success of the Forum 2000 mission.

In his own country, Dr. Singh has set an example of good leadership. His devotion to civic causes, social reform, religious tolerance and other issues are a living testament to his selflessness and his desire for progressive change. His years of official public service are a further example of his belief that we all must be participants and not just mere observers.

I am honoured to have the opportunity to contribute to a volume of work which acknowledges the work of Dr. Singh. I consider him an extremely valuable friend, and with great admiration and respect I wish for him an especially happy 70th birthday.

Culture of Peace and Buddhism

•

Daisaku Ikeda

Daisaku Ikeda, President of Soka Gakkai International, is among the tallest leaders of Buddhism, not only in Japan but all over the world.

"I wish to express my unchanging commitment to the creation of a human consciousness that sustains globalization. In this endeavour, I wholeheartedly join Dr. Karan Singh, for whom I hold much admiration for his invaluable contribution to world peace and who embodies the quintessence of the philosophy of India, the cradle of great spiritual heritage."

The Formation of a Sense of Humanity

In "The Way to Peace," Dr. Karan Singh shares a penetrating observation about the prospects of an emerging global civilization in the 21st century.

> While the movement towards globalization is gathering momentum, the global consciousness that is required to sustain the new civilization has still not emerged adequately. Thus, a most dangerous situation has arisen, caused by the lag between the growth of globalization and its acceptance by the vast masses of humanity, particularly political leaders. It is here that the great religious traditions of the world have a crucial and urgent role to play. (*Essays* 134)

For a short while it seemed globalization presented an optimistic forecast on the future of humanity. As events unfolded, however, we were struck by the eruption of regional conflicts of such intensity and magnitude that they entangled the entire world in a maelstrom of chaos and disorder. These have been the displacing events that present the rather stark reality we must confront at this turning point of the century.

As if prescient of such defining tragedies as befell Auschwitz and Hiroshima, Max Horkheimer (1895-1973) and Theodor Adorno (1903-69) sought to discover in 1944 "why mankind, instead of entering into a truly human condition, is sinking into a new kind of barbarism" (p. xi). It is a question that haunts us more than half a century later.

At this closing moment of an era, humanity finds itself squarely at a crossroad. That is, we have a critical choice before us. We can allow the downward spiral of this "new kind of barbarism," coupled with newer and better technologies, to cast its dark clouds over the entire 21st century. The viable alternative is to strive toward civilization that is woven of harmony and friendship, to create the environment for "a truly human condition."

According to Dr. Singh, the greatest impediment to peace in the coming century lies in our inability to grapple let alone keep pace with the sweeping changes of globalization. This is evident not only in global economy, the sciences, industry, and communications but also in world politics.

From globalization in the marketplace to information access, the ground covered is unattended by a similar growth in the landscape of human consciousness and culture. The imbalance appears only to fuel regional and communal conflicts. Yet unremittingly, Dr. Singh holds out hope for the great religious traditions of the world to nurture "a higher form of human consciousness" and a sense of humanity as a "single extended family."

The teachings of the Buddhist tradition originated in ancient India, from there spreading across the millennia throughout Asia. As a follower in this tradition, I believe the Buddhist perspective can contribute greatly to the development of the global consciousness that Dr. Singh calls for.

It is significant to note that the United Nations declared 2000, the turn of a new millennium, the International Year for the

Culture of Peace and 2001 the United Nations Year of Dialogue among Civilizations. In keeping with these themes, it is my intention to focus on the subject of culture in its broadest sense-religion, the arts, lifestyle, customs and those ideals which can contribute to the development of a higher sense of humanity. These, I feel, are brought to light through dialogue and are the hallmark of global civilization.

Transcending Cultural Relativism

Western thinkers have sought to analyse the post-cold war world. Their views and concerns range widely; for examples, Francis Fukuyarna in *The End of History and the Last Man* (1992), Benjamin R. Barber in *Jihad vs. McWorld: How Globalism and Tribalism Are Reshaping the World* (1996), and Samuel P. Huntington's *The Clash of Civilizations and the Remaking of World Order* (1996).

There is one admonition they do share: that the pivotal confrontation between the West and the rest of the world has led to progressive fragmentation and homogenization at every level of society, and it has uprooted the way of life for many people.

Global civilization calls out for a clear vision of unity in diversity to supplant the threat of isolation and divisiveness. From the elevated consciousness of humanity a symbiosis of cultures becomes possible, as a field of vegetation in vivid and varied bloom.

The term "culture" is an idiom comprised of two Japanese characters, "scholarship" and "martial arts." To Japanese understanding, it suggests the importance of balancing intellect with physical strength, as in the feudal example of a good warrior who is as well a good scholar. While we may euphemistically relate culture with peace, intercultural relations have not always engendered exchanges that are peaceful, and this is all too evident throughout the history of humanity.

In fact, can it not be said that the violence of imperialism and colonial expansion is the reality of culture that we have experienced in modern and contemporary times? This narrow bandwidth of cultural expression has left in its wake deeds so ominous that they serve nothing more than a prelude for more war and conflict.

Just as culture has its positive expression in the refinement of the intellect, it also has its negative expression in breeding the notion of cultural superiority. When a nation, group or community forcibly superimposes its cultural norms on another, friction and mutual hatred are inevitable results. Given the grounds and climate of history, it is but a short leap from culture to conflict. The 20th century has gained entry into the annals as the century of war and for giving birth to the culture of war.

This legacy can be traced to the domination of Western imperialism from the Age of Discovery to this century. The colonialist justified exploitation of other cultures by portraying them as uncivilized and savage.

How deeply embedded is this mentality of "racial" superiority it is not difficult to discern. One has only to take a cursory look at the unsavory statements left to us by such prominent thinkers as Alexis de Tocqueville, John Stuart Mill, George Wilhelm Friedrich Hegel, Karl Marx and Albert Schweitzer.

Out of post-colonial reflections, reparations and attempts at reconciliation emerged the notion of cultural relativism, an acceptance of value in all cultures. It offered a degree of objectivity in comparing cultures and was within reach for sympathetic understanding between people. In a way, cultural relativism proposed the acceptance of dignity and value in each culture by virtue of its existence.

An acknowledgement of cultural differences, however, directs us only to the periphery of progress, that is, to passive tolerance. Were we to place passive tolerance at "the center of global civilization, we would fall severely short of developing a higher sense of humanity to contend with globalizing trends.

Before us is a pressing need to transform the bedrock upon which the century of war was built, to effect a paradigm shift from a culture of war to a culture of peace. The foundation for global civilization must take shape from the mutually enriching interactions between cultures, and this means finding an elevated plane for engagement.

To build a culture of peace, I would offer that we must first agree on what we mean by culture and what our relationship to culture is. While interpretations of what determines culture vary from one field of inquiry to another, by culture we most commonly mean the lifestyle uniquely identifiable with a group of people, community or society and which is essential to their survival. There are several factors to be counted, including social knowledge, technology, tenets of belief, modes of communication, behavioural norms and received values from past generations.

Cultures occupy social and linguistic spaces that are perceived boundaries within which constituent members interact. As a result, we tend to think that over time culture, its norms and values remain unchanged.

For the observer and general populace alike, this static view ascribes a simplistic dimensionality to the activities within a culture. The isolation of one culture's activities from another can be counted as a primary factor leading to a sense of cultural superiority that excludes the claims of legitimacy from other cultures.

Given these misperceptions, creating a culture of peace requires a radical shift in perspective. In reality, culture does not remain static and inaccessible; it cannot be defined in terms of ethnic or genetic purity, homogeneity and invariability. Rather, culture must be seen as dynamic, receptive, multi-dimensional and transformative; in all, the viability of a culture must be viewed in terms of its ability to reinterpret itself. This calls to mind the derivation of the word "culture" from the Latin *cultura*, meaning "cultivation." It typifies the significance of culture as a continuing exercise in construction.

Without the stimulus of interacting with another culture or cultures, a culture does not come to bear the fruits of diversity or to explore fully its self-development. Out of cultural differences arises the opportunity, then, for both conflict and creativity.

Conditions for a Culture of Peace

Found within the Buddhist canon are a number of illustrations from which we may draw insights into the conditions for a culture of peace.

Let us focus on the illustrations found in the two most well-known of the *Mahayana sutras*, *The Flower Garland Sutra* (*Buddhavatamsaka-nama-mahavaipulya-sutra* or *Avatamsaka Sutra*) and the *Lotus Sutra* (*Saddharma-pundarika-sutra*).

A passage from *The Flower Garland Sutra* teaches that there is one vast land from which an innumerable variety of vegetation springs up, yet the land is but one land (cf. Cleary trans. 303). The earth is inseparable from the variegated life it nurtures. It stands as a metaphor for the principle of equality expounded by

Gautama Buddha, and the countless variety of vegetation for the countless people in the world, If we liken the seedling growth to all human behaviour and activities that comprise culture, the entire passage may be taken as a vision of co-existence and mutual benefit of diverse cultures.

One of the seven parables in the *Lotus Sutra* is The Parable of the Medicinal Herbs, which unfolds a spectacular scene of life's beauty. It describes the splendour of mother nature abounding in the plants and trees; some are large, some are small, "widely ranging in variety, each with its own name and hue" (Watson trans. 98). A dark spot appears in the boundless firmament, then gathers into a dense cloud and in one outburst showers all life below. This rain "accords with each particular species and nature.... Though all these plants and trees grow in the same earth and are moistened by the same rain, each has its differences and particulars" (Watson trans. 98).

Similarly, this passage conveys Gautama Buddha's teaching of equality and may be taken as a vivid description for a culture of peace. The variety of plants and trees are indicative of diverse human cultures while earth and rain from the heavens symbolize the supporting pillars of the great cosmos and the blessings of mother nature.

Nichiren, who lived in 13th-century Japan, analogized the diversity of life to the blooming of "the cherry, the plum, the peach, the damson ... without undergoing any change" (*Ongi Kuden* 784).

The invaluable lesson here is that each blossom, while nourished by the same great earth of life, manifests its unique brilliance of character. In the process described in Buddhism as "revealing one's intrinsic nature" or *jitai kensho* ("The Essentials for Attaining Buddhahood" 746), one is able to discover one's own meaning and mission. To live to one's fullest potential means to live in symbiosis with the great cosmos of life.

Thus, Buddhism leads us to the following insights into a culture of peace.

The first and foremost condition to establish is an appreciation for uniqueness and difference. We have only to look back to the culture of war to find egregious destruction wrought by sentiments of superiority.

Indeed, the 20th century has been an era of difference in which artificial boundaries of "race," ethnicity, religion, and mores have been the determinants of misery beyond description. Without question, all forms of discrimination must be eliminated. To do so, we must challenge the reigning notion that the solution to social ills lies in the conformity of all cultures to the standards of one.

The imperative of our challenge becomes all the greater when we consider the extent to which our hubris has reached. It is as if the world has donned a veil of worship at the altar of the gross national product to seek solace in the accumulation of wealth while it remains all but blind to the devastation it has done to precious nature as well as itself.

Those who warn against the encroachments of globalization see the outcome as a cultural standardization set by the United States because of its economic and technological lead. "McWorld" is one projected image. The problem, however, cannot be oversimplified as Americanization becoming the new expression of cultural superiority.

While each culture faces the imperative to enrich and refine itself by integrating elements of its contact with American culture into its own context, at the same time there is a reactionary outpouring of nationalism and fundamentalism in various parts of the world. We are seeing separations in the centrifugal mix of standardization and isolation .

As Dr. Singh clearly points out in his essay, "The Many Dimensions of Peace," the major impediment to peace is this chaos that has penetrated every dimension of living: the human psyche, the family, the society and its constituent communities, the modern state, and the entire planet.

Yet all cultures are sustained by the eternal life that drives the creative evolution of the great universe and nature. From this one source, each cultural tradition has nurtured its own unique spiritual heritage and identity. Each cultural identity has given rise to certain views of the universe and the world, value systems, moral sentiments and perspectives on life. We must approach these with the humility to appreciate and learn about what is different from our own. It is to acknowledge the eternal—the universe—from which cultural traditions draw wisdom and energy.

Cultural identity has the resilience to transform itself and generate creativity. Without efforts to respect, co-exist and learn from other cultures, a culture inevitably stagnates and its creative energy drains.

How are cultures to learn from one another and mutually benefit? It is through the pursuit of dialogue, which broadly includes conversation, the exchange of views and discourse.

I would propose adherence to dialogue as the second condition for a culture of peace.

While the past and present culture of war with its "me-first" mentality has had an insular effect on all cultures, a culture of peace embraces openness in all cultures. Dialogue exercises that openness toward others and is the means by which one gains respect for diversity, can transcend passive tolerance and develop modes of creative interaction.

Over the years, it has been my consistent path to choose to engage in a dialogue of civilizations in my encounters with leading thinkers from various world regions and religious backgrounds, including Hinduism, Christianity, Islam, and Judaism. Dr. Singh is one of the first persons with whom I engaged in such a dialogue. Through the experiences gained in the pursuit of dialogue, I believe I have come to be well versed in the vast potential of openness that emerges through dialogue.

For Socrates in ancient Greece, open dialogue meant heart-to-heart interaction, an act of exercising one's sincerity and integrity to the fullest, and a basis of respect for others.

From the annals of Buddhist history we find an apt example in the 2nd century B.C. of a dialogue between the Greek King Menander (also known as King Milinda of the Greek colony *Sagala*) and Nagasena, a brilliant Buddhist debater. This dialogue, to "converse in the speech of the learned," is recorded in *Milinda's Questions* and reveals the qualities of dialogue to which we must aspire.

To King Milinda's query about the way the learned converse, Nagasena responds:

> 'When the learned are conversing, sire, a turning over (of a subject) is made and an unravelling is made and a refutation is made and a redress is made and a specific point is made and a specific point is made against it, and the learned are not angry in consequence—it is thus, sire, that the learned converse,' (39)

In our present world, where parochial attitudes tend to exclude the interests of others and protract conflict, this demonstration of a critical mind and trust in others both at work is an important one.

The rapid advancements in communication technologies, from the internet to satellite transmissions, have not signaled generally better communication among civilizations. In this age of information, unless the content and quality of communication is enriched, we can never hope to create the kind of bonds among people that can transcend boundaries. It is, after all, human interaction made possible by technology that qualifies the nature of information conveyed.

An open-hearted dialogue between the learned, that is, a heart-to-heart human interaction and exchange, provides the hallmark of a dialogue of civilizations. It is, indeed, the key to opening human consciousness to global dimensions and to the possibility of global civilization.

The third condition for a culture of peace is insight into the universality of all life.

The extension of empathy and understanding towards other cultures leads to a deeper understanding and appreciation of one's own. Through contact and interaction between cultures, a collective consciousness takes shape over time. As we engage in dialogue with other cultures and attend to our own daily affairs, we discover stronger empathy toward others and a deepening mutual understanding. Often we find that despite apparent differences there is an underlying commonality.

The more contact and interaction externally, the more we can expand the reservoir of commonality internal to our own culture. The implications extend to the family, ethnic and social groups, the nation and to the entire civilization on our planet. The depths of this reservoir of commonality can be seen to extend even further to the oneness of human beings and nature if we take note of the fact that culture travels the four million years of human history and fuses with the global ecosystem.

When we return to the primal point of the human species, which is supported by and fused with the ecosystem, we gain sight of the universality that exists within all human beings and form an all- embracing consciousness of life.

Each cultural tradition, nurtured by the eternal life of the universe, represents a way of living centered on values drawn from a particular cosmology and world view. Thus, from each culture, human ethics is derived.

Only when a universal sense of ethics is made central to a culture of peace will there be a way of transcending cultural relativism and encouraging creative interaction among peoples, thus causing global civilization to flourish. Religious traditions provide spiritual energy to great cultures and civilizations, and they hold in common universal values that are embedded in the human consciousness. Leaders in religious faith are entrusted with the task of giving modern interpretation to these universal values that reveal their practical application.

Global Civilization and the Bodhisattva Way

Universal values that nurture global consciousness can be found in the quintessence of Indian spiritual tradition, which gave birth to Buddhism. Such moral qualities as not stealing and making diligent effort are taught in Hinduism, Jainism and Buddhism, and they are embodied in the basic principles of *satya* and non-violence (*ahimsa*) espoused by Mahatma Gandhi. It can be said that Mahatma Gandhi gave modern interpretation to human ethics.

Here, I would like to share a consonant Buddhist perspective on universal values and ethics necessary for establishing a global civilization in the 21st century.

The first universal value is the sanctity of life itself. The notion of "not to kill" is inspired from respect for the dignity of life. In Buddhist terms, it is described as the "precept forbidding the destruction of life."

Mahayana Buddhism teaches that all living beings are subject to salvation precisely because they inherently possess the supremely sacred state of Buddhahood. Therefore, efforts to share in the sufferings of all living beings and to resolve them together are lauded as the *Bodhisattva* way.

In modern society, a practical application of the culture of *ahimsa* is a world free of war, that is, it represents the right to peace. It is a culture thoroughly committed to non-violence, that denies all wars and conflicts, and that strives to find solutions through dialogue. A natural course for this culture would be towards, the abolition of nuclear weapons, arms reduction, and a shift in economic structure from one driven by military demand to one driven by civil demand. In the realm of education, too, the concepts of non-violence and compassion must be thoroughly incorporated.

From this Buddhist precept, we learn that all living beings inherently possess dignity and value that should be respected. Therefore it is essential for human beings to appreciate the benefits derived from the ecosystem and to pool all wisdom and resource to ensure symbiosis with the ecosystem. Scientific and technological progress in this vein can aid us to find new modes of sustainable living.

The second universal value is found in the precept "not to steal." The imperative of establishing a fair and equitable economic order is found in many religious traditions of the world.

The Buddhist precept is practiced as *dana* or selfless giving in the *bodhisattva* practice expounded in *Mahayana* Buddhism. The intent is the control of greed and encouragement of sharing in the fulfillment of basic needs. It is a precept in which one does not covet anything beyond the basic necessities of life.

This concept gave birth to a moral code prohibiting the exploitation of others that serves only greed. When industrialized nations and multinational corporations exploit the resources and labour of developing nations, they are committing the act of stealing. Likewise, when we deprive future generations of resources, we are committing the same crime. Given the accelerated globalization of the market economy, the ethical value of "not stealing from others" is all the more in demand.

Efforts to eradicate poverty while maintaining the best of the diverse cultural traditions of developing nations can also be considered adhering to the precept of not stealing.

The third universal value relates to ethnic, gender and cultural equality. It has as its basis the Buddhist precept "not to commit adultery." All human beings are equal and deserve to be respected, no matter what their circumstances. Everyone is equally entitled to the freedom of enjoying life.

From the times of Gautama Buddha, Buddhist philosophy has maintained equality of all people, transcending race, ethnicity, nationality and gender. This precept can be interpreted as the struggles against repressive structures, that is, structural violence, embedded in societies and cultures.

The fourth universal value is the establishment of faith. To serve this end, one must speak the truth. "Truth" in Sanskrit is *satya*, as in the term "*satyagraha*" populasized by Mahatma Gandhi. In order to speak the truth, Buddhism established the "precept against falsehood," which is cherished in other religious traditions of the world as well.

The "precept against falsehood" warns against the deliberate misrepresent-ations of falsehoods, flattery, slander, and equivocation. Contemporary times are replete with examples of deception in business, politics and mass media.

Trust between individuals begins with speaking the truth whether the mode of interaction is dialogue or participation in a larger group. All the more does this precept have application in efforts to build trust among ethnic groups and among people.

As we examine ethical values universally held, we can easily extract from them the qualities of non-violence and love; fair and equitable economic order; ethnic, gender and cultural equality; and the establishment of faith.

In Buddhism, the *Bodhisattva* way outlines the practice of these ethics, the means by which global consciousness can be aroused. In concrete terms, the *Bodhisattva* way aspires to fulfill the six *paramitas*.

The Sanskrit "*paramita*" means to have reached the opposite shore, that is, to arrive at the shore of enlightenment from the shore of delusion.

These practices by which *Bodhisattvas* are able to attain enlightenment have equal bearing in pursuing the ideals of global civilization.

The first is the practice of alms giving or donation: the giving of wealth, the giving of doctrine, and the giving of freedom from fear. In today's world, the giving of wealth can be observed in the financial aid given by developed countries to developing countries, and the giving of doctrine can be observed as providing technology, current knowledge, and education. Similarly, to give freedom from fear means empowerment, that is, providing people the material and spiritual resources with which to prevail courageously and confidently over their trials and tribulations. The compassionate practice of donation nurtures not only the freedom from fear but also the inner strength to control the heart of greed.

The second *paramita*, observance of the precepts, allows one to break through self-destructive tendencies and enhances one's moral strength. Universal ethics must be practiced diligently to the extent that they become convention.

The third practice is forbearance or *kshanti*. It means to endure all insults and hardships from a stance of patience, thus to control one's anger.

The qualities of non-violence and love require a strong commitment to forbearance. 'One Who Can Endure' is one of the names given to the Buddha. As the name suggests, the Buddha perseveres through all persecutions and relies on wisdom to save and liberate the people. Mahatma Gandhi's movement of non-violence and love was also the practice of forbearance, in essence, a struggle against the self that resorts to anger and consequent violence.

The fourth practice, assiduousness or *virya*, means to break away from negligence or *mora*. This is a practice required when one is hindered by obstacles or has grown inert and apathetic. The accumulation of assiduous efforts links the hearts of people in dialogue and sublimates the whole of humanity into the "single extended family" that Dr. Singh envisions.

The fifth is the practice of meditation or *dhyana*, which is to dispel from one's mind the elements that detract from spiritual progress. Whether in terms of the individual or group, it is to arrive at rational and piercing insight into a phenomenon or circumstance through probing deeply to its essence.

From such focused concentration, one's inner truth begins to shine outward like a clear, well-polished mirror that reflects the truth of others as they are. It is, according to Buddhism, to give up illusion and attain enlightenment.

The sixth is the practice of obtaining wisdom or *prajna*, to dispel the darkness of ignorance. This darkness means being ignorant of the true nature of existence, which is synonymous with the fundamental self. It can also be described as ignorance of the dependent origination of all things, or interdependence, expounded in Buddhism. The attainment of wisdom here is to discern the universal law of dependent origination.

It is through these six practices that *Bodhisattvas* are able to overcome shallow egoism. They are able to awaken to the true aspect of all phenomena in the universe, that all beings exist to mutually support one another. This then will lead to the creation of a global consciousness that views the whole of humanity as a "single extended family" and through which one perceives unity with all living beings.

Dr. Singh, a follower of Hindu philosophy, makes the lucid

point that "our spiritual quest must manifest not only in our internal spiritual practice but also in our external activity devoted to peace and human welfare" (*Essays on Hinduism* 135). This is the very point of resonance with Buddhism.

As one of the non-governmental organizations of the United Nations, the Soka Gakkai International (SGI) has been committed to movements for peace, culture and education based on the tenets of Buddhism, in order to create a truly global civilization through the solidarity of world citizens. The activities of the SGI are the modern emulation of the *Bodhisattva* way—more specifically, practice based on the six *paramitas*.

To conclude my message to the Felicitation Volume, I wish to express my unchanging commitment to the creation of a human consciousness that sustains globalization. In this endeavor I wholeheartedly join Dr. Karan Singh, for whom I hold much admiration for his invaluable contributions to world peace and who embodies the quintessence of the philosophy of India, the cradle of great spiritual heritage.

LIST OF WORKS CONSULTED

A Dictionary of Buddhist Terms and Concepts. Ist ed. Tokyo: NSIC, 1983.

Barber, Benjamin R. *Jihad vs. McWorld: How Globalism and Tribalism Are Reshaping the World*. New York: Ballantine Books, 1996.

Cleary, Thomas, trans. *The Flower Ornament Scripture: A Translation of the Avatamsaka Sutra*. vol. 1. Boulder and London: Shambala, 1984.

"Glossary." *The Writings of Nichiren Daishonin*. Ed. and trans. by The Gosho Translation Committee. Tokyo: Soka Gakkai, 1999.

Horkheimer, Max and Theodor W. Adorno. *Dialectic of Enlightenment*. Trans. by John Cumming. New York: Continuum, 1995.

Japanese-English Buddhist Dictionary. Rev. ed. Tokyo: Daito Shuppansha, 1991.

Milinda's Questions, vol. 1. Book 2: "The Distinguishing Marks." Trans. by I. B. Horner. 2 vols. Oxford: Fall Text. Society, 1990.

The Questions of Ring Milinda, vol. 1. Book 2 (Lakhana Panha); *"The Distinguishing Characteristics of Ethical Qualities."* Trans. by T. W. Rhys Davids. 2 vols. The Sacred Books of the East Series. Ed. by F. Max Müller. Delhi: Motilal Banarsidass, 1982.

Nichiren. "*Ongi Kuden*." *Nichiren Daishonin Gosho Zenshu*. Ed. by Nichiko Hori. Tokyo: Soka Gakkai, 1952.

——"The Essentials for Attaining Buddhahood." *The Writings of Nichiren Daishonin*. Ed. and trans. by The Gosho Translation Committee. Tokyo: Soka Gakkai, 1999.

——"The Four Debts of Gratitude." *The Writings of Nichiren Duishonin* Ed. and trans. by The Gosho Translation Committee. Tokyo: Soka Gakkai, 1999.

Singh, Karan. "*The Many Dimensions of Peace.*" Manuscript.

—— *Essays on Hinduism*. 2nd rev. ed. Delhi: Ratna Sagar, 1990. Watson, Burton, trans. *The Lotus Sutra*. New York: Columbia University Press, 1993.

Sustaining Development in the Developing Countries

•

T.N. Khoshoo

Dr. T.N. Khoshoo, Honorary Distinguished Fellow of the Tata Energy Research Institute and formerly Secretary to the Government of India, is one of the country's most eminent scientists. He presided over the 73rd Indian Science Congress Session as early as 1986 and was among the very first to speak and write on "Environmental Priorities in India and Sustainable Development."

"If humanity will follow Gandhiji, there would be no poverty but there would also be no stinking rich people. His life was a life of sacrifice. In national sense he was the poorest Indian, but in what he gave to the country and the world at large, he was indeed the biggest benefactor of the 20th Century. His was a life of sacrifice, charity and penance (yajna, dana and tapas). Unfortunately, twentieth century has seen more tormentors than benefactors like Gandhiji."

Sustainable development entered in the environmental agenda in the second half of the decade of eighties, more so when the book "*Our Common Future*" was published in 1987 by the World Commission on Environment and Development (1987). Today sustainable development is fast becoming a composite discipline and involves several major disciplines including science, technology, sociology, economics, ethics and law. But defining sustainability in exact terms has proved to be difficult. This does not mean that the concept of sustainability is not relevant. One of the easiest ways to comprehend sustainability is that the rate of harvest from a renewable system must never exceed the rate of annual increment. If it is within that limit, and, if there are no major environmental perturbations, the system can go on *ad infinitum*.

In 1992, that is five years after the publication of the above book, United Nations Conference on Environment and Development (UNCED) was held at Rio de Janerio with over 30,000 attendees. Thereafter, sustainable development became very popular all over the world. Most people thought that these two words constituted a panacea for all the environmental ills and problems facing the planet earth. Considerable euphoria was generated on this account, and, during the last decade, unusually large number of books and papers appeared on this subject. It became increasingly clear that sustainable development was not what it was supposed to be. Furthermore, it also became fashionable to prefix eco-or green-before every word or action so as to make such expressions (and sometimes even the tasks) ecologically respectable and thereby legitimise the same even when these are basically unsustainable. Much of it was only in words and little in deed. This was due to the tremendous amount of euphoria generated during the past few years. Thus in real terms, sustainable development still remains an enigma. For instance, what is sustainable development for resource-guzzling industrial world in its megacities, or an eskimo living in the arctic circle, or the ecosystem people in the dense tropical forests of Africa, Amazonia or Andamans or the very small hamlets in the Himalayan or Andean highlands, or people in deserts of Kalihari, or poor fishermen living in coastal areas, etc. The question arises that for such diverse situations, are there some common principles that would make development sustainable? Regrettably, so far the concept of sustainable development has been treated more as a socio-economic and political concept, but sustainable development would need tremendous inputs from science and technology. Another dimension of the problem is that sustainability in the ecological and economic systems has to be checked against a particular time-scale. It may vary between the life span of an individual, a species, or the earth itself.

The net result is that the concept of sustainability is becoming increasingly complex and amorphous. There is need for considerable thinking, debate, analyses and even modelling so as to define precisely the conditions and policies that help to confer sustainability in general, and in a specific ecological, socio-economic, scientific, technological and industrial situations. Reconciliation between economic and biological systems is also one of the central issues. For instance, what should be the population of human beings in a given time frame with a particular resource-base available in a particular habitat against a particular socio-economic, scientific and technological milieu. These are indeed difficult questions but need to be looked into in depth with a healthy and a positive approach and not with a doomsday approach. Thus, the euphoria generated earlier has of late been gradually (but perceptibly) subsiding and scientists, technologists, economists, sociologists and others have begun to grapple with hard facts.

One year before the publication of the report "*Our Common Future*", the present author (Khoshoo, 1986) while presiding over the 73rd Indian Science Congress Session (1986), was among the very first to speak and write on "*Environmental Priorities in India and Sustainable Development*" (Khoshoo, 1986). Perhaps this was among the very first documents to paraphrase the concept of sustainable development as applied to a large populous country like India which is reasonably rich in resources but not so rich in technology, and essentially a country of poor people. Twelve areas of work were identified that could help to confer sustainability in this country. This publication immediately became a teaching material in India and abroad. Today there are a large number of definitions of sustainable development (some think the number is over 100).

Originally the WCED (World Commission on Environment and Development) described sustainable development as development that ensures that it meets the needs of the present without compromising the ability of future generations to meet their own needs. It implies that the present generation has to impose voluntary limits on the use of resources as dictated by the present state of technology and socio-economics, and the resilience of biosphere to absorb the ill-effects of human activities. As a starting point this may be a reasonably good premise.

By the time Rio Conference was held in 1992, a good deal of literature was generated on the subject. During the subsequent five years (1992-1997), this concept was debated threadbare, and in 1997 the UN General Assembly held a special session to commemorate Rio+5(years). The concept of sustainable development got a big jolt on account of the stand taken by the Government of the United States of America by no less a person than the President himself. This was notwithstanding the fact that there is a UN Commission on Sustainable Development which reports through ECOSOC to the General Assembly of the United Nations.

The Indian Scene

India is a populous, fairly resource–rich and a reasonably science and technology-rich country. Even if India exercises strict population control, our population will still keep on increasing for the foreseeable future because prospective mothers and fathers are already with us. Can this demographic disadvantage be turned into an advantage? If so, how: This is true of most developing countries in Asia, Africa and Central and South America. So far, priorities have been dictated by industrial countries. The time has come for reversal of roles, because the industrial countries (Northern consumers) are using resources far in excess of their requirement and the rate of renewal of the renewable resources. Furthermore, the developing countries cannot afford a situation where machines replace people. This will be counter productive. They need, what has been called labour-intensive industrialization, or, should we say, *humanization of industrialization*. There is only a very general and a casual appreciation of economic evaluation of Nature's services; therefore, there is a need to evaluate such services in social and economic terms. This alone will bring home to the developing countries the scientific, technological and economic value of ecological assets and help in their proper conservation based on S and T principles.

The whole concept of sustainable development has been brought to a naught by western countries on account of their total indifference to making even modest alterations in their highly consumeristic lifestyles. They give the impression that the concept of sustainable development would be a drag on their development and, if implemented, it would involve a drastic reduction in their resource-guzzling lifestyles. On account of such indifference of industrial countries, the 1997 UN meeting on environment has been summed up in the famous equation: Rio+5=O. This equation conceals little and reveals a lot. The Kyoto Conference on Climate Change held in November 1997 and General Assembly of this Global Environmental Facility (April 1998) were not materially different. This is in line with the stance taken by industrial countries in several other conferences and meetings. The fact is that the industrial world is calling the shots and the developing world is watching helplessly. That is where the matter rests today. One doubts if there would at all be a real and lasting understanding between industrial and developing countries on this account.

Notwithstanding the stand taken by the industrial world in general, and the United States of America in particular, in the international fora the concept of sustainable development can still be a rallying point at least for the developing nations. There may not be total unanimity about the exact definition of the term, but its application can become widespread including in the industrial countries. The concept is indeed worthwhile, and one can hazard a reasonably good guess about the basic principles underlying such development which could confer sustainability no matter which habitat or which people are involved. With proper policies and programmes there is a possibility of ensuring good degree of sustainable development in developing countries which have large populations and face a science and technology crunch. This is possible only if these countries will decide to come to terms among themselves on these issues.

In India, there is yet another dimension to the problem of sustainability. Part of India's economic strength lies in the unusually large number of villages (5,76,000) and the habitations around the megacities. In terms of employment, the contribution of agriculture, animal husbandry, fisheries, village level small industry, vendors, rag and trash pickers, hawkers and the like of these is significant. Actually they are small-time producers who are unrecognized for their contribution to India's economy. No one has ever ventured to calculate in fiscal terms their contribution to GNP and the economy. Taken together they make a significant economic contribution. Though these are small vocations, yet these constitute the largest employment sector. With marginal technical and fiscal inputs, and with improved work and working conditions, their contribution to economic sustainability can become considerable. This is also clear from the fact that each and every megacity in India is indeed a twin city: the megacity proper and the slums around it . The two are interdependent in ways more than one, but at present both are inherently unsustainable. While it is difficult to bring sustainability to the megacity on account of its resource-guzzling nature, the slums can be made sustainable with marginal economic inputs, appropriate housing with sanitation and medicare. No longer this segment of India's population can be ignored in any consideration regarding over-all sustainability of the country.

Due to over population our environmental assets (land, soil, water, air, forests, biodiversity, fisheries etc.) are indeed highly stressed on account of over-extraction, over-utilization due to demand over stripping the mean annual increment or repairing capacity of these environmental assets. This indeed is not a healthy sign.

The Root Cause of Unsustainability

The present economic system is based on Keynesian Model. The basic philosophy on which this model rests is clear from the words by John Maynard Keynes himself enunciated by him in 1930:

> "*For at least another hundred years we must pretend to everyone that fair is foul and foul is fair;for foul is useful and fair is not. Avarice, usury and precaution must be our gods for a little longer still. For only they can lead us out of the tunnel of economic necessity and into daylight*".

There is now a need to say goodbye to the Keynesian economics and blend ecological and economic objectives into a mutually supportive and an integrated system. This is possible when we calculate the *real* economic value of our natural resources. For instance, what is the value of components of biosphere like fresh air, clean water against dirty and polluted air and water, fertile *vs* degraded land, forested *vs.* deforested areas, or what is the scientific and economic value of our rich biodiversity etc. Most environmental organizations do not take up work on innovative and relevant topics, but would like to flow with the current and take to very mundane aspects where considerable funds (both Indian and foreign) are available. There is a strong case for an annual National Ecological Survey and National Ecological Budget alongwith the National Economic Survey and National Economic Budget. The two have to be mutually reinforcing.

Ultimately we need methodology to calculate in realistic economic terms, both eco-decline and eco-regeneration, The two go hand in hand. This is only possible if we know how to cost natural resources realistically. We have today only a vague and a casual appreciation of Nature's services which now need to be costed realistically. It is here where involvement of considerable amount of science and technology and economics would be involved. This will bring home to less developed countries (LDC's) the value of their assets and build a climate for sound resource conservation based on sound S and T and economic principles. It is here that studies like the one undertaken by TERI (Pachauri and Sridharan, 1998) have become most relevant. Such studies are most timely and should become increasingly analytical with periodic updating. This has to be an on-going exercise, not only by TERI but several other organizations dealing with individual subject areas. With the publication of the TERI report, there is now a distinct need for encouraging many such studies at the national level.

The present economic system has evolved on a mistaken notion that natural resources are abundant, population is not so high, and there is relatively less pollution and eco-degradation, and ecosystem regenerability is higher than degradability. In addition it is also due to lack of strong S and T base in developing countries and its misuse in industrial countries. It is now abundantly clear that none of the foregoing assumptions are true. Therefore, there is now need to seriously ponder about it. The root cause for all these ills is the rising population and lack of S and T infrastructure in developing world and over-consumption and wrong use of S and T in the industrial world.

The Ground Reality

Roughly 40 per cent of the people in India live below the poverty line. They destroy the environment on account of dire need, while the rich destroy environment out of greed. To bring the former out of the present morass of poverty is one of the most important scientific, technological, economic and environmental challenges facing the country. For instance, firewood is still the only or the most important energy source in most if not all villages in India. This is so notwithstanding the fact that we have in this country all conceivable energy systems ranging from burning of cowdung/firewood/trash to atomic power with everything in between. The poor in the villages have still to sweat and toil for food, fodder, fuel and water. This is particularly true for village women who have to toil to make their ends meet with the added burden of acting as child-bearing machines. This is a reality, even when India has made good deal of progress in development during the last 50 years. The problems of the poor have not attracted the attention of scientific and technological community in India except in the agriculture sector.

In agriculture, India has made spectacular progress through the Green Revolution. Here was an area where commitment of the political system was total when it said that in India *Agriculture cannot wait*. Our agricultural scientists and technologists rose to the occasion. However, the tempo has not been kept up, and today there are signs of a *browning of the green revolution*. Given the wherewithal and the commitment of the agricultural scientific community, it should be possible to have successful Second Agricultural Revolution. It is within their competence and comprehension. Agricultural diversification and small scale industry are the answer to elimination of the abject poverty in the villages. People need technical support and facilities for credit and linkages with market. This would help marginal farmers and even landless labour.

The welfare of villages with development based on ecological and economic principles and gender equality together with access to education, health care, livelihoods, credit and decision making are critical to the success of such eco-development. This would make women, who constitute 50 per cent of the workforce, self-reliant by offering opportunities for education, better skills, livelihood security, right to make decisions (including the number of children they need to have), generate micro-enterprises, and have access to credit at the local level. They can then play an important role in alleviating poverty.

The local communities have to be adequately strengthened and empowered economically and socially. This would bring people into the mainstream of development. This applies particularly to the rural women. Not only their quality of life but also access to resources have to be improved. It can happen only when they participate in decision-making.

Any government howsoever strong and efficient cannot do everything all by itself. Sustainable development in India can be a reality only when proper linkages are built to sustain such development on a participatory basis and decentralized governance. The overwhelming number of villages in India cannot be governed, managed or served from Delhi or even from the state capitals. Centralization has not paid dividends as is clear from the past 50 years of experience. Communities have to come forward to take the challenge. Wherever decentralization has taken place in India (Khoshoo, 1995 & 1996), the results have been remarkable, because participatory management rests on decentralized governance, increased access to resources on a fairly equitable basis and generation of employment. Benefits in such cases have been reasonably equitable regardless of the social and economic status of the concerned community members. The net result has been that livelihood security of the rural communities has increased.

Communities have to come forward to take up such challenges. Decentralized governance has been the sheet anchor of such development. Any civil society has to guarantee a better future with long term security of its people. Therefore, in a developing country, sustainable development must generate economic and social growth that is equitable with no or manageable effect on environment. It must also lead to empowerment of people. Such growth and development will widen the range of choices and opportunities for the people.

What Will Confer Sustainability?

There is an urgent need to work out carrying capacity of different systems in terms of growth of population, resource availability and the technology used. These systems vary from the natural ecosystems where ecosystem people live, to agricultural systems (from subsistence to sustainable ones) and to variety of industrial economic systems, and from rural and small scale, to urban and large scale industry. The idea is to help developing countries to reach the goal of sustainability, a concept which at present is still eluding them.

For bringing sustainability in poverty-stricken villages of Bihar, Madhya Pradesh, Rajasthan, and eastern Uttar Pradesh (the so called *BIMARU* States) and Orissa, there exists not even an elementary study that is reliable. Also we hardly know anything about the way we can bring even a reasonable amount of sustainability in industrial areas in developing world let alone industrial countries. Most global environmental problems of the world actually emanate from the industrial countries. The latter have been over-taken by techno-optimists who care less and even advocate getting resources from other celestial bodies. Notwithstanding the inquisitiveness of human mind, the situation prevailing today shows little attachment to Mother Earth at least in industrial countries who having stripped the earth of its resources are now readying themselves to reach new pastures in our solar system. Even with all the uncertainities the concept of sustainability is still most useful to both developing and industrial countries.

For making sustainable development a reality under varied environmental conditions, deep thinking is needed about what will confer sustainability under a particular scientific, technological, social, economic and cultural milieu. As we go along, these studies can be increasingly refined and perfected. Obviously sustainable development is not a function of one or two or three or even more but a whole constellation of factors. As pointed out above, in 1986 the present author thought sustainability in India can be conferred by bringing an understanding of about 12 issues, but today with better understanding and a wider perspective, the list has to be enlarged to many interconnected, inter-related and interdependent issues. The list may expand further or even contract with better understanding about the complexity regarding paraphrasing sustainable development in specific scientific, technological, economic and social terms. We, therefore, need critical studies on the following issues which are grouped under five heads for convenience:

(i) Sustainable Management and Utilization of Natural Resources

Stabilization and control of population growth; Integrated land-use management; Conservation of water resources including its rational use; sustainable forestry for long-range ecological security and meeting rural, urban and industrial wood needs, from plantations, and helping in ecological revival/restoration; conservation and utilization of biodiversity and its linkages with cultural, economic, ethical and social diversities; Sustainable agriculture, horticulture, animal husbandry and fisheries;

protection of coastline and conservation of biowealth in the extended economic zone (EEZ); integrated and sustainable energy systems and augmentation of research, development and demonstration in solar and bioenergy systems with particular reference to rural areas; ecologically compatible housing and slum improvement; control of pollution of air, water (fresh and marine) and of land; waste and residue minimization (including hazardous wastes), and recycling of wastes so as to make industry environment-friendly; and sustainable development of island communities.

(ii) Improving Health and Access to Resources for Weaker Sections and Women

Primary health care in rural areas; updating health services and evolving strategies against disease-causing drug-fast microbes and AIDS epidemic; strengthening ecological, social and economic security of women and weaker sections of the society; free access to fertility control measures particularly to women of weaker societal sections and harnessing women's power; and sustainable livelihoods for the poor.

(iii) Economic and Ecological Efficiency and Security

Proper economic valuation of natural resources; transition from ecologically insensitive to ecologically-sensitive economy, and dovetailing economic, ecological and social goals; reducing and then eliminating poverty by strengthening ecological, social and economic security; environmental costing of projects; building environmental accounting system(s) by making ecology and economy mutually supportive; strengthening ecological security at national and regional levels; environmentally sustainable trade development; and generating employment and sustainable livelihoods.

(iv) Making Technologies Ecofriendly

Transition from eco-unfriendly and consumptive, to eco-friendly and conservation technologies including ecolabelling of products; strengthening micro-enterprises; improving environmental information technologies including collection and dissemination of data; environmental education and awareness; environmental rating of projects; environment friendly biotechnology; regional co-operation in environment; and strengthening scientific and technological bases of sustainable development.

(v) Participatory Management

Decentralising governance by appropriately blending top-down and bottom-up developmental patterns; encouraging participatory management; and periodic updating of legal support.

This is only an illustrative list of concerns which need to be updated and refined before taken up for implementation. By and large most of the foregoing issues are common to most developing countries because these countries are reasonably rich in resources but poor in technology. This group of countries need to take a hard look at abundant local technical knowledge and mini-local enterprises because many of these can confer sustainability at the local level, which would enliven the lives of this segment of the society. This would involve the use of science and technology, sociology, economics, ethics, law and other cognate subjects. It may be pointed out that each developing country will need to work out in depth its own pattern of sustainable development in relation to its social, cultural, economic and religious milieu and availability of resources and level of technology. For instance, what is true of United States of America may not be true for India because the former is about three times larger in area than India (1997), with 3.5 times less population (1997) *i.e.,* USA is in a 10.5 times advantageous situation as compared to India. *But USA is squandering this advantage by following the most unsustainable pathway of development and life styles.* It is technologically a very advanced country and cares less for sustainability.

Techno-optimists in USA have advocated that resources can be obtained even from neighbouring planets. Accordingly, the country is now racing to colonize moon and mars. It is not doing this only for scientific, technological and intellectual reasons but there appears to be a long-range covert agenda: once the resources of Mother Earth are depleted, perhaps they would get the same from moon and/or mars. Hence, USA is involved in geological prospecting (including water) of these celestial bodies. Furthermore, this programme also appears to be aimed at containing possible threat to USA from any country which may make itself bold to oppose USA. It is, therefore, a deep-seated economic, industrial and military agenda with a guaranteed long-range investment from the Government. This will ensure flow of resources which in turn will ensure a particular life style which is basically unsustainable. Thus, this exercise is not only an exercise of scientific exploration but also an exercise to control resources that may be available in the celestial bodies nearest to earth. History is repeating itself; only some five hundred years ago, Irish and other Europeans set out to colonize and subjugate indigenous people of the Americas, Africa, Australia, New Zealand and parts of Asia including India. They were enterprising people and wanted to explore new pastures. The reason was that the British Isles and Europe were over-full with people, new pastures and diseases were rampant.

On the other hand, the pursuit for sustainability by a developing country like India is going to be straight forward: for providing reasonably good liveable conditions to its teeming millions. Indians have nowhere else to go. In fact there are no uncolonized areas left on earth that are habitable. We have to ensure in perpetuity food, housing, energy, clothing, medi-care, education, vocations, etc. for our teeming millions. We have also to chalk out a realistic agenda for sustainable growth and development. Therefore, the foregoing list of items that are critical for sustainable development of a developing country like India, need to be understood in depth and steps taken to translate these into action.

There is a need to prepare State-of-the-Art papers, on the various areas listed above. This has to be done keeping in view the escalation in population. This task needs to be undertaken by organizations (government and non-government) which are conversant with the ground realities and adopt by-and-large a bottom-up approach. Some very good but isolated reports, such as the one on water by Centre for Science and Environment (New Delhi) (Agarwal and Narain, 1997) have been already prepared. The report is indeed very interesting.

The approach has to be realistic but incisive. A lesson has to be learnt from what were acclaimed as great success stories of the economic development in South Korea and Asian economic tigers (except Japan). These have now begun to show their covert unsustainable social and economic faces. Perhaps the story of Indonesia is an example of what not to do. The root cause is humankind's disregard for natural resources and economy. In this regard the recent forest fires in Mexico and Indonesia are only symptoms of an ecological and economic crises. These resulted in loss of virgin forests, and hot winds and smoke which covered even the parts of the adjoining countries. Initially these were the result of unsustainable slash and burn by Indonesians and Mexicans themselves and then Nature's wrath stepped in.

Opening a developing country's economy is good, as long as it follows a well thought out long-range policy, and avoids short-term populist measures. Our feet must be firmly on the ground all the time. Economic development is indeed a highly professional area and hard-headed economists and sociologists have to pool their intellectual resources to chart out a long-range path irrespective of which political party is in power. Sustainability in development (like policies on defence and foreign policy), has to be an all party agenda, no matter which party comes to power. A parallel exercise is needed for environmental threats facing the country taking advantage of our strengths while guarding against some inherent weaknesses. All these issues are basically national, therefore, above politics.

While no one would like to mix politics with sustainable development, it is but certain that at some stage politics will enter in its work and working. Developing countries have to be careful regarding their co-operation with industrial countries because now it is no longer necessary to *actually* subjugate a country militarily as was necessary in the bygone times. All that is needed is a covert economic agenda. Therefore, a developing country has to be clever enough to foresee and understand the after effects of such an agenda and guard against it. It is the small print of the agreements that has to be looked into very carefully. In this regard lessons have to be learnt from South-East Asia.

Green Technology

There is now world wide thinking that more importance should be given to conservation technologies rather than consumptive ones. Clear criteria are needed for declaring a technology green. Equally important is the question of the carrying capacity of natural habitats and those restored through eco-development.

The only answer to politics of development is self-sufficiency, self-reliance, complementarity and sustainable development:

where a country's resources are put to sustainable use with the help of technology relevant to the situation. Thus, from a unit of resource we should be able to get: maximum usable product with minimum use of energy and cost of production; generation of minimum pollution involving minimum cost of depollution and minimum damage to environment during manufacture, transport and use; generate minimum waste; and use packaging with a short life. Furthermore, development should not involve the use of resources that are from threatened/endangered species or from threatened habitats or cause cruelty to animals and destruction of flora and fauna, or affect other countries particularly the developing ones which are essentially poor and fragile. Also, development should not endanger the health of the user and the biosphere at large. To do this would involve abundant use of relevant high quality science and technology. Finally, there is the ethical dimension of sustainable development which cannot be ignored. In this regard the shining example before us is that of Gandhiji. His role and relevance has increased because he has been a path-finder for India and the world at large. A combination of ecological security, economic security, equity and social justice are going to be the bed rocks of the future technology. Therefore, scientists and technologists have to leave their ivory tower approach and add the foregoing dimensions to their work.

Major leaps will be needed for enhancing productivity of food with no or manageable damage to environment including land and soil. The same applies to health services, materials, transport, energy and information technology. Even in forestry there is needed a major jump to attain sustainability. Here basic orientation has to change from mere management of natural forests and harvesting mean annual increment, to *designer plantations* with high yield per unit of area and per unit of time. No longer we can afford to continue to over-extract wood from natural forests in perpetuity. A forestry revolution is needed most urgently where we leave natural forests only for long range ecological security, and meet all our wood needs from man-made plantations as we do in agriculture. Such a transition took place in agriculture long ago. Human race no longer depends on naturally growing plants and wild animals for its food and other needs. This change was associated with human race changing from a hunter and gatherer society to agricultural society. In this process man became wedded to the soil. In view of escalating population, there is need for a quantum jump in agricultural production per unit area/time because no new areas are available for cultivation. There is need for a Second Green Revolution which will have to be highly productive minus pollution, and labour displacement, and depend on biofertilizers and biopesticides that are non-polluting to land, water and air. Biotechnology will have to be used for enhancing production and productivity and storage.

There is thus an urgent need for high inputs of science and technology to make Green Revolution-II and Forestry Revolution-I a reality. The goal has to be designer agriculture for enhanced food production and designer forest plantations for meeting the needs of firewood, timber, veneer, pulp and paper etc.

Technologies that do not pollute land, water, and air and help in processing and storage will have to be developed. Special attention will have to be paid to human health. Disease control will have to be attempted on a very wide front and include drug-fast bacteria, AIDS epidemic/heart diseases and hypertension, etc. These will need special attention. India will need medicaments involving both high and low tech in a proper mix because we not only have disease of affluence but also disease of poverty. Technology whether in agriculture, forestry or industry has not to be labour-displacing but reasonably labour-intensive.

Energy scene in India is indeed very complex, we have all the conceivable forms of energy in use. With enhanced affluence there is going to be enhanced energy demand. We need to update, refine and enhance production of all forms of energy from low-tech (firewood and biomass burning) to high-tech use of atomic energy, and everything in between.

Lastly, there is another dimension to ecotechnology. When one buys firewood, fish, medicinal herbs or water (all these are collected from nature), we *only* pay for the cost of collection and delivery of these natural materials. Methods need to be evolved to calculate their intrinsic value so that we know the real cost of the natural materials. Thus, it is not enough to have Green technology but it has to be accompanied by Green-marketing.

Importance of Individual Action

One cannot minimize the importance of an individual in bringing about change towards sustainability. As individuals, we must think about our role and goal and the fact that in the ultimate analysis it is people as individuals who have to take decisions, and solve the problems of environment. The reason is that a community, a nation and the world at large, are, in the ultimate analysis, an extension of an individual. A sustainable community can spring from interdependence between well-informed individuals. Thus, sustainable lifestyles of the individuals can lead to sustainable communities, to sustainable nations and then to sustainable world. Similarly, key to the solution of global environmental problems lies in local action (Khoshoo, 1998).

An individual is the starting point of environmental degradation. If an individual believes in need and not greed, and in comfort and not in luxury and ponders about what is *enough* for a comfortable life style, most of the problems would be solved. We have reports of influential individuals owning 3000 pairs of shoes or over 700 sarees and what not. Regrettably, both these cases are from developing countries. What example do such individuals set for the society at large. Is it justifiable? One of the major root causes is undue thirst of resources which is particularly characteristic of the industrial world and the rich in the developing world.

Keeping the foregoing in mind, one can bring about sustainability in the poor families in Bihar, Madhya Pradesh, Rajasthan, Uttar Pradesh or Orissa, but equally important, if not more important, is to find ways to take to sustainability in the life of average resource-guzzling persons in the metropolitan cities in the developing countries and industrial world at large. Here each individual requires huge amount of materials and generates equally large amount of wastes. Major environmental problems are created during collection of raw materials, manufacture of finished goods and finally during their utilization and generation and disposal of wastes.

The most critical input for bringing about sustainability in a gamut of social, economic and cultural situations is education. The important point is that today an average human being in developing world is in socio-economic shackles, and follows value system(s) which leads to unsustainability. There is need to bring about a new value system that leads to sustainable development. The critical input for this change is also education, which gives us knowledge, information, understanding and above all stresses ethics and morality.

If one follows the history of human species, there have been two distinct but over-lapping phases. The species began as having *reverence towards nature*. At that stage human being looked at nature with awe and respect, something that he did not understand. Then, as time passed, understanding of nature increased, there came a phase of *subjugation of nature* which led to all manner of deforestation, ecodegradation and pollution and rampant abuse of natural resources. This has been the phase when human being got the erroneous feeling of being all powerful, and *looked* down upon nature to be exploited with vengeance. Today the world is in the latter phase. However, of late there is the beginning of a phase where there are many voices to be heard about *reintegration or a coalition with nature*. This change is the result of a phase in history when technology was used to the detriment of nature and ultimately to the detriment of human race itself. The reason is that everything on earth is interconnected, interrelated and interdependent. Our salvation lies in not approaching nature with arrogance but with humility and respect. Most biological scientists are of this view, because they have an inkling of the intricacies of and fascination for the web of life. This is what our scriptures in most religions teach. Science and technology need to be used for the good and the well-being of both the Planet Earth and all its inhabitants including human being.

Towards a Sarvodaya (or a Sustainable) Society

For convenience, we may consider four broad situations, two of which are unsustainable and the remaining two are sustainable (Fig. 1). Between and within each of these two extreme categories there are many intergrading situations. One of the two extremes of unsustainability is found among the Hunter-gatherers (lower left) who live in very harsh, fragile and unstable ecosystems such as deserts of Sahara. These people are essentially nomads with hardly any worthwhile assets. Here climatic conditions are very harsh and resource base is very poor, there is dire need and abject poverty. They follow local wildlife for their sustenance. Technology which is used to capture or kill the wildlife is very primitive e.g. stone tools or bows and arrows or traps. They make some use of fire. The other end of the unsustainable spectrum (upper left) is seen in the industrial societies of the world particularly in their metropolitan cities. Even in the latter (e.g. New York), the situation is uneven. Resources are abundant in oppulent sections while for people living in poorer sections of the city, resources are scarce. In the former there is the vulgar show of wealth and abuse of resources. They are rich in technology, which, by and large, is misused for the so called welfare of the rich. This is true of most industrial countries and megacities of those developing countries which have followed industrial route to development. Between these two extremes of unsustainable development there are many intergrading types. The two corners are assetless people with abject poverty on one side, and stinking rich on the other.

In the sustainable group (Table 1) one of the two extremes is constituted by the Hunter-gatherers (lower right) living in stable ecosystems. They are the *ecosystem people* like the original inhabitants of Andaman and Nicobar or many places in the Central and South Americas. Left to themselves, they have sustainable lifestyles because resources are abundant. There is no monetary economy *per se* but nature's economy prevails. They barter goods and services. There is need but no greed. Their technologies are primitive, but their lifestyle is sustainable.

Some of the best examples of sustainable development are seen in indigenous societies behind which is the time-tested robust common sense and local technical knowledge (LTK). Taking advantage of such knowledge, one could hazard a guess for sustainable society or what Gandhiji calls *Sarvodaya Society*. The success of such a society depends upon inputs of high science and relevant technology, and micro-enterprises based on local technical knowledge. These would give succor and bring them out of the morass of poverty and penury and transform the village communities.

At the other end of the sustainable group (upper right) would be a society where resources are sufficient, there is respect for nature, they believe in need and comfort but not in greed and luxury; they make good use of technology relevant to a situation. Their aim is to have welfare of the weakest (*antodaya*) which in the ultimate sense leads to welfare of all (*sarvodaya*). This is why one could call these as *Sarvodaya* or sustainable societies. The basic philosophy is to live and let live, and through frugality (*i.e.* more from less) and fraternity (getting in association with others). Herein lies the future of humankind. This is the society of the future. Today it may exist in bits and pieces but not in sufficient numbers and certainly not on large scale. There are several individual attempts in this direction like the work of Chandi Prashad Bhatt in Gopeshwar, R P Misra in Sukhomajari (Haryana) and Chakriya Vikas Pranali (Bihar), Anna Sahib Hazare in Raligan Siddi and A T Ariyaratne in Sri Lanka. Such attempts are being made even in the USA. Fig. 1 summarizes the broad characteristics and the relationships between the four societal patterns and their developmental concerns.

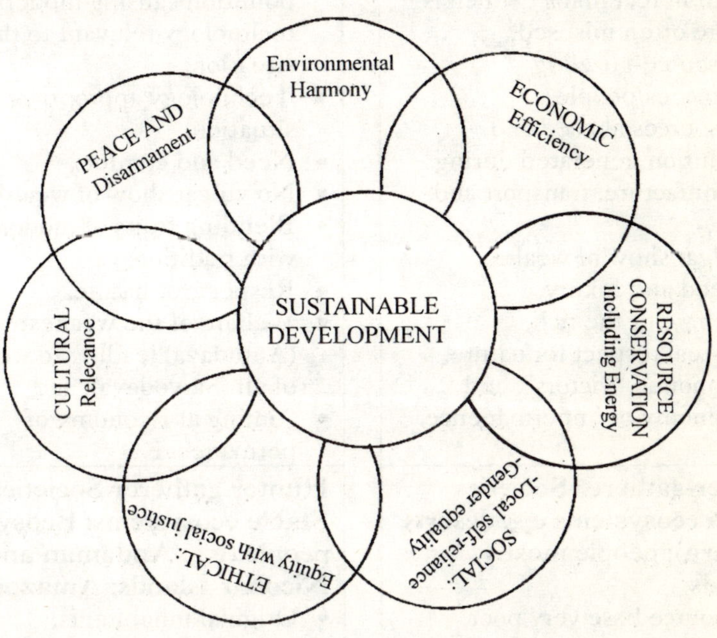

Fig. 1: Major Dimensions of Sustainable Development

Gandhian Development

Not withstanding the fact that Gandhiji earned India freedom with little bloodshed and became a Mahatma (a great soul) in his own life time; there is a growing opinion that the 20th century did not understand him. For some he was irrelevant and that he talked and believed in what was out-moded socially, economically

Table 1: Relationship between Societal Patterns and Eco-developmental Concerns

Unsustainable Development	Sustainable Development
Industrial Societies Metropolitan Cities • Resources abundant or obtained from less developed countries at nominal price, • Rich in technology which is more often misused, • Resource-guzzling countries/people, • Resources abused and pollution generated during manufacture, transport and use, • Vulgar show of wealth, • Greed and luxury, • Welfare of the rich, • No real respect for nature, • Economic "victors", and • Economy of impermanence.	**Sustainable (Sarvodaya) Societies At present largely an utopia** • Resources sufficient, • Essentially biomass-based (renewables) society using low pollution causing modern technology relevant to the situation, • Technology appropriate to the situation, • Need and comfort, • No vulgar show of wealth, • Blending fruits of modernity with tradition, • Respect for nature, • Welfare of the weakest (Antodaya) leading to welfare of all (Sarvodaya), and • Aiming at Economy of permanence.
Hunter-gatherer Societies Harsh ecosystems e.g. deserts (Sahara); people mostly nomads • Resource base very poor, • Access to resources limited, • Very primitive technology used, • Dire need, • No exposure to modernity, • Abject poverty and powerlessness, • Prevailing superstition, • No worthwhile economy, and • Ecological victims.	**Hunter-gatherer Societies Stable ecosystems: Ecosystem people (e.g. Andaman and Nicobar Islands; Amazonia)** • Original inhabitants, • Superstitious, • Indigenous age-old technologies, • Hardly any exposure to modernity, • Nature's (non-monetary) economy: Bartar system, • Need but not greed, • Respect for nature, and • Economy of permenance

and technologically. However, now there are many (all over the world) who believe that he was born at least a century ahead of his time and that 20th Century did not understand him. With his forethought and vision, he was actually a man of 21st Century.

When independence (*swaraj*) began to become a reality. Gandhiji was asked as to what pattern of development India would follow. At that point of time for a British Colony, such as India, the only model was the British Model. Gandhiji said: "*it took Britian the resources of half the planet to achieve this prosperity. How many planets will a country like India require*!" It is indeed a prophetic statement. He insisted on individual commitment because he felt *swaraj* (self rule) does not mean independence from all restrains. It means we take from earth what we *actually* need and no more. He stressed *non-violence* which means not to exploit anything including biosphere. Furthermore, one should not venture to take more than one's need. His thinking is contained in his very famous quote which has gone into the annals of environmental literature: "*The earth provides enough to satisfy everyman's need but not for everyman's greed.*" Obviously he felt that nature produces enough for our legitimate needs and comfort, but not for our greed, luxury and vulgar show of wealth. Such a mad rush for materialism is not only irreligious but also a criminal act against nature and humanity and all creations at large. It is unsustainable and a pernicious disease. It is untenable scientifically and technologically in the long run.

If humanity would follow Gandhiji, there would be no poverty but there would also be no stinking-rich people. His life was a life of sacrifice. In material sense he was the poorest Indian but, in what he gave to the country and the world at large, he was indeed the biggest benefactor of the 20th Century. His was a life of sacrifice, charity and penance (*yajna*, *dhana* and *tapas*). Unfortunately, twentieth century has seen more tormentors than benefactors like Gandhiji.

Sustainable development under conditions of a developing country should be people-centred and must lead to environmental harmony, economic efficiency, resource (including energy) conservation, local self-reliance, gender equality, equity with social justice, cultural relevance, and peace and disarmament. It should enable solving problems at the local level which will ultimately have impact at the national, regional and even global levels. It must aim at sensible, credible and implementable environmentalism and not ecofundamentalism. The biggest challenge is concretising sustainable development and translating it into *actual* action points so as to be in line with our social, economic, cultural, religious and ethical diversity. To make such development a reality, would involve considerable amount of relevant science and technology and inputs from economics, social sciences, ethics, law etc. Each item discussed in this paper needs to be enumerated in depth. The academies and non-government institutes dealing with science, technology, education, social sciences, economics, law and ethics need to take up such studies and prepare status papers for the benefit of the Government. Finally, such sectoral reports need to be integrated into one connected whole, to ensure the creation of credible and implementable option(s) that are relevant to the prevailing situation in India. We need to set our own house in order in the first instance. Only then we can confront the northern consumers who use resources far in excess of the renewal rate. Environment in general and sustainable development in particular have to be on our national agenda, but above politics like the foreign policy, defence, agriculture and economy.

NOTES

Agarwal, A. and Narain, S. 1997. *Dying Wisdom*: Centre for Science and Environment. New Delhi.

Human Development Report. 1997. United Nations Development Programme. Oxford University Press, Oxford, New York.

Khoshoo, T N. 1986. *Environmental Priorities in India and Sustainable Development*. Indian Science Congress Association, Calcutta pp. 1-224.

Khoshoo, T N. 1995. *Mahatma Gandhi: An Apostle of Applied Human Ecology*. Tata Energy Research Institute, New Delhi. 1995.

Khoshoo, T N. 1995. *Gandhian Environmentalism: The Unfinished Task*. IASSI, 16(1): 1-16.

Khoshoo, T N. 1996. *Gandhi and Environment*. World Wide Fund for Nature, New Delhi .

Khoshoo, T N. 1998. *Current Science*, 74: 914-15.

Pachauri, R K and Sridharan, P V. 1998. *Looking Back to Think Ahead*. GREEN India 2047, TERI, New Delhi.

Our Common Future. 1987. World Commission on Environment and Development. Oxford University Press, Oxford, New York.

The State of World Population. 1997. United Nations Population Fund.

□□□

I Knew Him As A Poet

•

P. Lal

P. Lal, well known poet, scholar, philosopher and cultural questor, in this very personal note calls Dr. Karan Singh 'Perhaps a twenty-first century Vivekananda. Why not?'

"After all, it was surely my friendship with Karan Singh that came to my rescue along with many others, when I passed through a near-death experience while on a lecture tour in the United States in 1989. My liver, kidneys, lungs and pancreas collapsed; and I was in an intensive care unit in Michigan for two months. Dialysis and other medical expenses totalled an incredible $400,000. Karan Singh arranged for a contribution from the Prime Minister's Emergency Fund during this fierce crisis, from which I recovered miraculously, awed, shaken and grateful."

It's a serendipitous coincidence. As I write this brief tribute to Karan Singh, I am also in the 44th session of my English '*sloka*-by-*sloka* transcreation of the Mahabharata of Vyasa in the library of Dharma and Culture of the Sanskriti Sagar in Calcutta. This is a Sunday morning 11 o'clock one-hour reading of the entire epic, to continue for ten years before a small audience, till the 100,000 odd '*slokas* are exhausted as I expect I will be too! The 44th session of the *Ādi Parva* deals with the friendship of Drona and Drupada. Drona is a Brahmin - and poor, Drupada is a *Khsatriya*, the prince of Kosala - and rich. Both studied in the ashram of Bharadvaja, and became friends in their boyhood. But when the adult *Drona* went to seek material help from Raja Drupada, what he received was a disturbing lecture:

न दरिद्रो वसुमतो
    नाविद्वान विदुष: सखा।
"There is no friendship
    between rich man and poor man,
between educated and unlettered,
    between hero and coward.
Forget this so-called friendship
    that never existed.
I was friends with you, O Brahmin,
    with a selfish motive.
You friends with me!~
    Only equally brave
or equally skilled
    inter-marry and are friends.
The poor and the rich
    neither inter-marry nor are friends."

[I : 131 : 8-10]

So how am I friends with Karan Singh, whose royal lineage is unquestioned? Playing card royalty apart, there are not many kings and queens left in our increasingly democratised and getting-to-be homogenised world. Could it be that Drupada was grossly overstating the case?

After all, it was surely my friendship with Karan Singh that came to my rescue, along with many others, when I passed through a near-death experience while on a lecture tour in the United States in 1989. My liver, kidneys, lungs and pancreas collapsed, and I was in an intensive care unit in Kalamazoo in Michigan for two months. Dialysis and other medical expenses totalled an incredible $ 400,000. Karan Singh arranged for a contribution from the Prime Minister's Emergency Fund during this fierce crisis, from which I recovered miraculously, awed and shaken and grateful.

Let me see. I never knew Karan Singh as *Yuvaraj* or *Maharaja*. I knew him as a poet. A very perplexing poet. On the one hand, he could write a fine tongue-in-cheek poem like "The Seminar" (which I included in the 700-page anthology titled *Modern Indian Poetry in English*, which I edited and which appeared under the writers workshop imprint in 1969):

THE SEMINAR

There sat the learned,
like rows of soda-water bottles
awaiting their turn to be drunk,
and one by one
they waddled to the mike and there unfurled
their private prejudices garbed in the robe of reason;
one, a jaunty little cockroach,
leapt to and fro while speaking,
another stood in solemn grandeur
like a statue carved with moving lips;
a third, bearded and grim and glaring like a hawk,
bore down in garrulous ferocity
upon the audience;
and thus it went until, in God's own time,
their words sloshed all around the crowded hall,
they mercifully left for lunch.

And, on the other hand, he admired and could recite by heart page after page after page of Sri Aurobindo's religious and mystical poems, from that incomparable "Savitri" to smaller pieces like the famous "Who?"

Recite? No, he chanted. He has this glorious sonorous bass; his style is hypnotic; his enthusiasm inspiring and infectious; his stresses and pauses and sense of rhythm just right. To listen to Karan Singh reciting English, Sanskrit or Hindi is pure pleasure, a rich learning experience. He is in the Indian *suta*-bard tradition. And an orator as well!

Poetry was our point of contact. A pity it wasn't Drupada's and Drona's. Had it been there would have been no humiliating face-off for Drona first and Drupada later.

Shelley was probably right when he wrote that poets were the unacknowledged legislators of mankind; for they sing of the Law that is at the root of all laws. And Karan Singh was both poet and legislator—and not only a member of the Lok Sabha but a Cabinet minister to boot!

I think he was not always easy in his parliamentary role. His heart was in literature and art and culture and the wonder that was and is India. A true humanist is never happy with authority and power. He wrote a fine romantic novel *The Mountain of Shiva* which he sent to me and which I published from Writers Workshop. We exchanged letters. I received inscribed copies of his autobiography—a fascinating record of our contemporary history and his maturing years in post-Independence India. I sent him my transcreations of the *Upanishads*, the *Gita* and fascicutles of the *Mahabharata* as they appeared in monthly instalments.

When I went to Delhi to receive the Padma Shri in 1971, I stayed at his residence at 3 Nyaya Marg. I think he and his lovely wife Asha Devi must be the only living royal couple in the world who take their royal status sensibly. This raja and this rani are so graceful and normal and informal that they have no hesitation in serving delicious dinner buffet-style in stainless steel canteen thalis! After all, it's the food and friendship that matters, not the *tamasha* of cutlery and crockery.

I remember the time Karan Singh came to Calcutta during the Emergency. He asked me over to tea at Firpo's.

"What do you think Purushottama?" he asked suddenly. "Should I remain in politics?"

"I don't know about that," I replied, "but I do know what you could do incomparably well."

"What's that?"

"You could be our twentieth century Vivekananda and spread the essential message of India to the rest of the world. Our roving Ambassador of Culture. Don't you think so?"

He looked at me, and did not answer.

Well, perhaps, a twenty-first century Vivekananda. Why not?

□□□

Human Survival: The Responsibility of Science and Religion

•

Ervin Laszlo

Ervin Laszlo, President of the Club of Budapest, of which Dr. Karan Singh is an active and eminent Honorary Member, takes a deep and balanced look at public awareness of threats to human survival which have emerged with significant strength since 1970.

"Creating the Holistic Alliance between science and religion is the best, and perhaps the only way to gather both the knowledge to tackle global problems and the motivation to act on the knowledge. If the alliance would extend to countries East and West, North and South, international cooperation among scientists and religious leaders could bring fruit. Expert and relevant ideas would be brought together and incentives to act on them would be mustered."

Public awareness of threats to human survival has emerged with significant strength since the 1970s. Recognition that growth cannot continue infinitely on a finite planet was triggered by the publication of the report to The Club of Rome, The Limits to Growth. The responsibility of science for human survival, in turn, has been widely debated at least since the detonation of the atomic bombs over Hiroshima and Nagasaki in 1945. But the conjunction of the two elements—of threats to human survival on the one hand, and scientific responsibility on the other—remained rather vague. Activities such as those of The Club of Budapest, of which Karan Singh is an active and eminent Honorary Member, insist on the clarification of the issue. That this clarification takes into account the role of religion is a significant step forward, since only through a creative alliance of science and religion can a satisfactory approach be found toward the resolution of the threats posed by global problems.

The global problems humanity faces are widely discussed and do not need detailed comment here. They include continued militarization in many parts of the world, the growth of the human population and its concentration in poor regions and in urban environments, the financial crisis of developing countries, the twin processes of deforestation and desertification and related environmental imbalances with serious human and social consequences. Even if humanity manages to avoid the ultimate catastrophy of a third world war, it still faces the possibility of depleting and overpopulating the global environment.

Scientists need to accept their share of the responsibility for this state of affairs. Greater self-discipline is needed among scientists regarding the selection of the fields and problems of research and the communication of the results. Researchers need to join forces through international scientific bodies to assure that a responsible flow of scientific knowledge reaches decision-makers, instead of the haphazard stream that includes whatever happens to catch the interest of funding sources and science-related public and private agencies.

The responsibility of science needs to be coupled with that of religion. The search for higher meaning and for genuine progress cannot be reduced either to natural science or to economics. The spiritual dimension of life remains essential both for the inspiration it can give to human initiative and for the integration it can provide for society. Religion, in the original sense of "religio", is as much a part of human existence as the material sphere of physical survival. Together, science and religion can create a basis for a new civilization, adapted to the global condition of humanity, a condition that cannot be reversed but can only be evolved and rendered humanly beneficial and meaningful.

The Responsibility of Science

Practically all the "high" technologies that make on impact on the survival and future development of humanity derive from research in the natural sciences. This is true in particular of nuclear and high-energy technologies, of information and communication technologies, and also of genetic engineering. Research in chemistry is the fountainhead of the estimated 70,000 synthetics that are currently in use.

Classically, scientists sought to engage in the search for knowledge without concern for the consequences. Basic research was said to be a search for truth pure and simple. But, because basic research produced many if not most of the global problems that now threaten human survival, the classical view has been increasingly questioned. Since the fateful nuclear explosions that ended World War II, scientists have become sensitized in regard to their social responsibility. In the 1980s many physicists, geneticists, and theoretical and experimental scientists posed ethical questions in regard to the various aspects of scientific activity, from basic research all the way to the publication of the findings.

Yet, by and large, contemporary scientists do not act in accordance with the fledgling waves of social responsibility. The main thrust of the contemporary science establishment is steadily centered on the armaments industry and the military. Worldwide, as many as one-fourth of all scientists in so-called "hard" science fields work on projects that have some, even if indirect, relevance to weapons technology and national security. Another large proportion of scientists converge on such highly funded fields of social priority as cancer and AIDS research. Natural scientists who are not in the weapons-and health-related fields tend to distance themselves from the concerns of society. In universities and academies, the teaching and researching of basic science are compartmentalized into specialized disciplines within which scientists concern themselves with abstract and esoteric questions. The majority of the natural, and many of the social, scientists have become super-specialists, encased in their laboratories, studies, and libraries.

If the problems unwittingly created by the short-sighted application of scientific results are to be effectively managed, and the mushrooming of similar problems in the future is to be avoided, as higher level of social problem-consciousness is needed in the mainstream science establishment. Further debates on possible applications and side-effects would have to take place before concentrated investigations get underway, leading to a more farsighted assessment of societal impacts. Impact assessment would have to keep in sight spatially as well as temporally distant effects: those that concern people in other lands and continents, and those that affect future generations. Since global problems call for worldwide cooperation, consultation and networking is needed among forsighted scientists in regard to the research, development, and diffusion of scientific knowledge. International organizations of scientists, in particular such bodies as UNESCO and the International Council of Scientific Unions, need to be entrusted with the relevant consultations and given effective mandates for carrying out the agreed results.

The responsibility of science does not end with the self-discipline of scientists. Responsibility lies equally with the institutions incharge of diffusing scientific knowledge, not only through direct application in technological innovation but through higher education. As H.G. Wells said, the history of the future will be a race between education and disaster. Contemporary science education would need to evolve as high a level of social consciousness as the scientific community itself. As it is, in most countries of the world standard curricula convey outmoded concepts of the "scientific view" of man and world. Teaching is fragmented along the fault-lines of the natural-scientific-technical, the social-scientific-political, and the artistic-spiritual-religious sub-cultures. Yet these divisions, as those between the hard sciences and the humanities, have now become obsolete. Within the advanced branches of the natural and social sciences, and especially within the transdisciplinary fields known as the "systems sciences" or "sciences of complexity," a more integrated concept is emerging. These sciences deal with the dynamics of the evolution of complex systems regardless of the domain in which the systems are found. The systems themselves can be natural or artificial, social or cultural, and even mathematical. Since a human being is one variety of complex system, the natural environment constitutes another, and modern artifacts yet a third, a coherent framework becomes available within which the mutual relations and dynamic interactions of the systems can be consistently analyzed and integrated.

Man, in the new transdisciplinary perspective, is an intrinsic part of nature, and both man and nature are intrinsic parts of the embracing system of the biosphere. Rigid separations between natural, human, and social structures and processes do not have legitimacy. If scientists would espouse and deepen the new understanding of man and world, and if educational systems would transfer and disseminate the emerging insights, a significant knowledge base could be created for tackling global problems and working toward human survival. Scientists and science educators cannot evade these twin components of the responsibility of contemporary science in today's crucial epoch.

The Responsibility of Religion

Science and science-education can only address human reason and intellect. Humanity, however, is both a rational and spiritual species; the human person has an intellective as well as an emotive faculty. If healthy and integrated societies are to be created following the present wave of transformation and restructuring, both sides of the mind, both aspects of human existence, must be addressed.

The great religions contribute to the fulfillment of individuals, and give guidance in their search for just and harmonious social relations. The social and humanistic element in the religious tradition is evident in the Judeo-Christian faith no less than in the belief Systems of the Orient. Judaism, for example, sees man as God's partner in the on-going work of creation and calls on the people of Israel to be "a light to the nations." At the heart of the Christain teaching is love for a universal God that must be reflected in love for one's fellows and service to one's neighbour. Islam, too, has a universal and ecumenical aspect. *Tawhid*, the affirmation of unity, means the religious witness "there is no god but *Allah*", and *Allah* is the symbol of divine presence and revelation for all people. Hinduism, unique among the great religions in not having an individual founder, perceives the essential oneness of mankind within the oneness of the universe, and Buddhism has as its central tenet the interrelatedness of all things in "dependent co-origination," interpreted by progressive Buddhists as a mandate for achieving higher forms of unity in today's world of interdependence.

The Chinese spiritual traditions revere harmony as a supreme principle of nature and society. In Confucianism, harmony applies to human relationships in ethical terms, while in Taoism harmony is an almost esthetic concept defining nature, and the relationship between man and nature. And the Baha'i faith, the newest of the world religions, sees the whole of mankind as an organic unit in process of evolution toward peace and unity—a condition that it esteems both desirable and inevitable.

These are significant elements of ecumenism and humanism in the world religions but, with few exceptions, they do not come sufficiently to the fore. They are overshadowed by parochial concerns, and the competition between particular faiths offering a unique path to fulfillment and salvation in exclusive possession of the truth. A new emphasis on the ecumenical, more valuable side of the coin would not do violence to the doctrines; it would only make them more relevant. The leaders and prophets of the great religions have claimed to be humanly and socially relevant to their time; their followers could not object to their teachings remaining relevant to *our* time.

If contemporary religions were to become truly relevant to our time, they would need not only to recover the humanism of their traditions but also to forge ahead to give new meaning to life and development in this period of restructuring and transformation. To achieve such a high objective, a return to fundaments, no matter how enlightened, is not enough. There must be a new elaboration, a creative extension of the ideas that have informed and inspired mankind's religions since the dawn of civilization.

The basic contours of this development can be already discerned. To begin with, an interpretation of the concept of God as external to man and to cosmos must be relegated to religious history. The concept of the divine, that is adequate to our times is that of an immanent spirit, inspiring the world from within, not commanding it from above. Then, the progressive self-creation of the world must be recognized, and indeed celebrated. The biblical tradition of the Occidental religions has not come to terms with an evolving reality. The Judeo-Christian religions, although they have a historical perspective when it comes to the spiritual development of the individual, do not have a corresponding perspective on the evolution of the world and of humanity as a whole. Yet such evolution occurred, and it continues to occur before our very eyes. We are now in the midst of a basic and irreversible process of societal and cultural evolution that affects all life on this planet. To remain relevant, the religions would have to convey a view not of an abiding and perhaps seasonally renewing world, but of a fundamentally and irreversibly evolving one.

The present period of societal transformation cannot be seen in an integrated perspective unless the world within which it occurs is likewise allowed to have an evolutionary aspect. This aspect need not be restricted to the physical basis of the cosmos: the totality of the universe can be perceived to have a spiritual dimension in addition to a physical one. It has been the historical task of the great religions to perceive and to proclaim this dimension, and to acquaint the faithful with its meaning.

The new knowledge of the cosmos, coming from the sciences, could be deepened and made humanly meaningful in the religions. Cosmic reality could become the personal reality of each human being. This development is not farfetched. Each of us bears, after all, within himself or herself the impress of every transformation through which the universe has ever passed. The elements out of which our bodies are composed have been created in the fiery process of stellar interiors and stellar supernova bursts. They passed through a phase of dispersion in interstellar space, to be brought together in the womb of the proto-stars of a new stellar generation. As elements on the surface of the planets born of these stars, they have participated in the original emergence of life in the rich mixture of molecules and protobionts in primeval seas. They entered and left living bodies for billions of years, cycling through the rich web of structured connections that make up the reality of "*Gaia*", the self-maintaining and self-evolving system of the earth's biosphere. The forces that brought forth the quarks and the photons in the early moments of the radiance-filled cosmos, that condensed galaxies and stars in expanding spacetime, and that created the complex molecules and systems on life-bearing planets—these forces inform our brain and infuse our mind, and come to self-recognition in each of us. As human beings evolve consciousness, *Gaia* is enriched and lifted to a new plateau. The biosphere becomes conscious: it becomes noosphere.

Religions could celebrate the world's evolutionary self-creation. They could celebrate the original flaming forth that gave birth to the known universe; the sudden synthesis of the quarks and of the wide diversity of microparticles as well as of atoms and molecules throughout the expanding reaches of cosmic space. They could celebrate the emergence of the macromolecules and protocells, the precursers and harbingers of life, on the surface of this planet and on countless if as yet unknown planets in this and in myriad other galaxies. They could celebrate the evolution of the noosphere on Earth as the next, especially significant, phase in the world's self-creations. They could recognize that the self-evolving cosmos is our larger self; that our journey as individuals, within the bio-noosphere reflects the evolutionary journey of cosmic reality from Big Bang to black hole. The cosmos is our primary sacred community.

Recognizing and celebrating the self-creation of the world, religious communities could recognize and celebrate the self-creation of life within the biosphere as the larger framework of the self-creation of humanity in the ionosphere. If they did, life, nature, and human mind and culture, would be re-sanctified: they would be seen as vital elements of the sacred community of the cosmos. And with the recovery of the sanctity of the natural world, humanity would also be impelled to reorient its attitude toward the natural enviroment. The great religions could become co-architects of the evolution of contemporary culture and society.

The Holistic Alliance

Religious renewal always came in the wake of civilizational crises. It was in the disastrous moments of the history of Israel that the prophets of Judea made their appearance; Christianity established itself in the chaos left by the moral weakening of the citizens of a declining Roman Empire. The Buddha appeared in a period of spiritual and social confusion in India: Mohammed proclaimed his mission in an epoch of disorder in Arabia; and Baha' Ullah wrote in confinement imposed by a moribund Ottoman Empire. Today, we are in the throes of the greatest and the deepest crisis our species has ever known; in an epoch when the very web of life on Earth is threatened. Will there be another great spiritual and religious renewal in our time? And will the renewed and re-invigorated religious communities enter into alliance with contemporary science and become a vital cultural force, illuminating and encouraging the next step in humanity's evolutionary self-creation?

The alliance between science and religion is now a historical imperative. Just as in the early 19th century after the Napoleonic wars, a "Holy Alliance" was created in Europe dedicated to creating a community of the Christain nations of the world, so today we need an alliance that is holistic even more than holy: an alliance between scientists and science educators on the one hand, and religious leaders and communities on the other—an alliance to join the artificially segmented rational and spiritual halves of our individual and collective psyche into integral unity.

Creating the holistic alliance between science and religion is the best, and perhaps the only, way to gather both the knowledge to tackle global problems and the motivation to act on the knowledge. If the alliance would extend to countries East and West, North and South, international cooperation among scientists and religious leaders could bring fruit. Expert and relevant ideas would be brought together, and incentives to act on them would be mustered. The epochal task of guiding the evolution of contemporary societies along physically sustainable as well as humanly meaningful lines could be tackled with improved chances of success.

❑❑❑

The Dynamics of Leadership and Clarity of His Vision

•

Clovis Maksoud

Dr. Maksoud served as the dynamic representative of the League of Arab States in New Delhi, later in the U.N. and is now a Professor at the Centre for Studies of Global South at the American University in Washington. He recalls his continuing interactions with Dr. Karan Singh in the Indo-Arab relationship perspective.

"Dr. Karan Singh found in the late Druz and socialist leader of Lebanon, Kamal Jumblatt, a close soul-mate. Jointly, they overweighed my emphatically more secular propensities. An on-going and delightful tension persisted in my relations with both and in our lighter moments their respective immersion with the spiritual dimension of India (Jumblatt in South India) catapulted me into a journey of discovery of how much I was missing! Dr. Karan Singh was always tempted to rub it in!"

Dr. Karan Singh's 70th birthday is a reminder to all of us that youth is not exclusively a social segment. It is also an attitude of mind, a projection of an inner realm and an on-going quest for consistency, relevance and coherence. These attributes of youthfulness have been, and remain associated with Dr. Karan Singh and explain the dynamics of his leadership and the clarity of his vision.

They further explain the steadiness of his policy involvements especially amidst the turbulent periods of his illustrious career. This steadiness in turn reinforced the affection and loyalty of those who shared his commitments and earned him the respect of most of those who disagreed or even disapproved of his opinions.

In a way, the philosopher and the politician in him continue to interact rendering Karan Singh's contribution a rare blend of principled consistency and pragmatic relevance. In periods of ideological polarization such a blend renders the likes of him the catalysts that heal, when healing is required and who empower the marginalized as a matter of commitment and conviction.

When we met for the first time in the very early sixties, our backgrounds were different, our experiences distinct and our politics definitely dissimilar. Yet as months passed by and our conversations became more intense, a subtle convergence kept creeping and as a result we discovered how many views are shared and how similar—and at times identical—our evaluation of developments were, and hopefully continue.

In retrospect, I think the convergence was expedited and rendered irreversible by the unbelievable sense of humour that engulfed his discourse. In a way, it demonstrated how comfortable and at ease Dr. Karan Singh is with himself. No wonder his wife Asha and family have made him always secure, creative, and affectionate. Asha's wisdom rendered his intellectual and political ventures precise and consequential. Timeliness was—and I believe remains—her forte. In their relationship there is a fascinating complementarity.

While the thrust of Dr. Karan Singh's cultural contribution remains in the realm of the spiritual it never was deemed as a separate category from the political and intellectual involvements that characterized his eventful career. In a way, this spiritual-cultural dimension explains the policy, administrative, and the diplomatic accomplishments associated with his public legacy.

My personal reminiscences are so many, and would require alone a chapter, if not a book! They are rich, interesting, funny, serious and in many instances can be considered 'bold' history footnotes if not historical. Suffice to say that as the Ambassador of the League of Arab States and he as *Maharaja* of Kashmir helped avoid many pitfalls and rendered anyhow manageable an endemic Arab-Indian contentious issue. Yet our clean association with Jawaharlal Nehru, each in his own way and circumstance, enriched our experience and allowed India-Arab understanding to sustain and even grow. This was maintained during Prime Minister Shastri's short tenure and further enhanced during the late Mrs. Gandhi's government.

Of course, the closeness of our friendship persisted when I left India and new political dynamics were introduced in both our respective patrimonies. The mutuality of our interests were further reinforced by the contacts we maintained with our common associates. Dr. Karan Singh found in the late Druze and socialist leader of Lebanon, Kamal Jumblatt a close soul mate. Jointly they outweighed my emphatically more secular propensities. An ongoing and delightful tension persisted in my relations with both and in our lighter moments their respective immersion with the spiritual dimension of India (Jumblatt in South India) catapulted me into a journey of discovery of how much I was missing! Dr. Karan Singh was always tempted to rub it in! While Karan Singh and Jumblatt's relationship was short and intermittent, my much longer and closer association with both opened up vistas that gave me access to areas of human experience that, as I grow older, come to appreciate more.

During the eighties, I became the Chief Representative of the League of Arab States in the UN and the US during which time Dr. Karan Singh acquired a third aspect of his career—Ambassador to the US! That we met again in Washington was an opportunity to reclaim our youth, refresh our memory, and update our agendas. What we discovered is that the gap in time suddenly evaporated as if the *years* of physical absence never affected the instant resumption of our conversation. It is this quality in Karan Singh that renders him ever present—that time never passes!

Again, at the age of 70, Dr. Karan Singh is a member of our Board (Center for the Global South) dealing with issues of environment, gender, habitat, human rights, food security, conflict prevention, sustainable development—issues that focus on bridging the gap between North–South. This is a living proof that youth is not a demagogical concept, but also an attitude of mind—and as he taught me, a projection of a vital enlightened and compassionate spirituality. ❑❑❑

Is Mutual Understanding Possible Between the Western and Indian Culture?

Vidya Nivas Mishra

Prof. Vidya Nivas Mishra, eminent Hindi scholar, philosopher and litterateur, presents his felicitation in the form of the transcript of a dialogue between him and the noted Spanish philosopher Prof. Rafael Argullol. The dialogue deals with the questions which are close to Dr. Karan Singh's heart.

ARGULLOL: Is it possible, a real dialogue between cultures beyond a mere exchange of formalities and good intentions that are politically correct? Is it desirable? On which ground? In which direction? Which of the two is stronger: The Global Village or the Metropolitan Tribe?
MYSELF: Yes, it is possible. There is a continuous stream of perennial philosophy in Indian thought. So its validity holds good in modern times as well as in ancient times..."

Argullol: *Religion, rite and myth. Is it possible a secularized representation of the world or 'the sacred' pervades each and every link of the relational net between man and the world?*

Myself: Secularism is a notion that can be better understood in juxtaposition with theocracy. Because the whole idea of secularism sprang out of a theocratic dominance in every sphere of life. We don't have any term corresponding to secular. The reason is that the absolute dichotomy between sacred and profane is conspicuously absent in Indian thought. Anything can be defined as divine, because divinity is latent in everything and vice versa: anything can be defined in absence of the divine.

The dichotomy present in Indian thought is one of purity versus impurity, but again the dichotomy is not absolute. To say that anything can be defined in absence of the divine is tantamount to accepting the presence of impurity in the world process. But that impurity is temporary and by definition impurities are terminable. It is like the impurity of a woman during her periods or the impurity of rivers during the rainy season. Such is the case with the universe and its recurrent impurities. The phenomena of impurity is not in the nature of things, but it is susceptible to come and disappear by itself. No external attempts are required to remove this impurity. Ritual is nothing but a self-purifying process or better a self-restoring process. It is in consonance with the idea of cosmic order, which ensures the adjustment of movements on the right path whenever there is a digression. The idea of such corrective measures is present in almost all the religions. The differences and variations in the nature of such corrective measures is perhaps the distinctive feature of Indian religions. Hinduism is such that there is not a final institution or an ultimate canon or authority to fix such corrective measures. And there is also a tacit understanding that the corrective measures can not be one and the same for different sets of people. Finally, it is the world of sacred experiences which has the potentiality to find out such corrective measures. That potentiality is acquired through contemplation and continuous practice. A priest or a preacher is only a helper. He is not a catalyst. The person concerned is himself a catalyzing agent in such a purifying process. The inherent idea is that purity is not generated, it is restored or revived. Purity is inherent in every being, sentient or insentient. Impurity is just a passing state. Therefore, one can conclude that according to the Indian worldview, or more specifically the Hindu worldview, the relationship between man and the universe is a natural and divine relationship. It is both mundane and non mundane. When you look at some relationships from a sensuous point of view it is mundane, when you look at it from a suprasensuous point of view it is not mundane. So it is both and none of them. It is an innate relationship, as between one part and another part of the same whole; each making the one and the other. All rites and archetypes are derived from this principle of mutual dependence between man and the universe.

One could object that how can the whole (the universe) be dependent on the part (man)? The answer is that even when the most insignificant part of the body is affected it sends a strain of pain throughout the body. So it is with the universe and vice versa. Even if a tiny branch of a tree is severed from its trunk, it will send a signal of terror in the entire body of the tree. Not only that, it does also affect the person who is cutting the branch from the tree. No matter how insignificant that modification might be from the surface. In India it is usually understood that a person's harmful intent towards a plant, sends a negative message which affects the mental equilibrium of the person concerned. This is in consonance with the general law of *karma* which states that all action produces a corresponding effect. What I have said regarding the results of a person's harmful intent towards a plant could be almost impossible to comprehend for a western man in the 19th century. But in an era full with the awareness that life depends on life, in an era that puts a special emphasis in eco-balance, that can be now easily understood and even applauded.

The Indian view is that the cosmos expands itself and that when the cosmic order is disturbed it contracts itself. So does man on a smaller scale during his life span and even beyond his life span. Therefore, there is nothing like annihilation or complete destruction. At the most there is a transformation at the cost of several things, body included. The physical body is transformed into a subtle one; the subtle into a causal one; the causal in course of time is transformed into an astral one. All these bodies are interrelated.

Coming back to rites. They are an attempt to rejuvenate a person through a re-enactment of the primordial act of creation. Every rite is a death and a rebirth. A death of the finite and a rebirth of the infinite. Such a re-enactment places man in the role of the first creator. By the end of the rite a person, transformed into the infinite, is restored to his role as a finite being. The restoration is a recharging of the finite with an experience of the infinite. This recharging is therefore not for one's good, but for the good of all beings.

When I earlier referred to a non–secular nature of all actions—what I meant was that every action is a micro process of the first act of creation. That first act, as told earlier, aims at finding the significance of one's own life in the other. Or in other words finding ourselves in the other. So that by going along with the other a fuller picture of being could be visualized which can not be visualized just by oneself. What I mean to say is that the very act of creation involve a total sacrifice of the first being for the multiplicity of the others. The other here is the most cherished one. This sacrifice as a total giving of our own being to the other is not an act of philanthropy, as said earlier. It is a total consumption and as such is an emptying out of a being in order to fill it again with the other being who is the counterpart of one's own. Fulfillment is then the complete merging of one self in the other. In other words, emptying out is the beginning of fulfillment and vice versa: fulfillment is a new start for another emptying out in order to obtain more fulfillment. This in certain aspects is quite akin to the idea of the dark night of the soul in St. John of the Cross or in other mystics for whom the ritual of the Mass has a similar significance.

I would like to give an illustration from a non-liturgical rite. Non-liturgical in the sense that the text used does not belong to the great scriptural tradition, but is an oral text which has variations from place to place. Even in that sort of rite we have a picture drawn of the entire cosmos on the floor, depicting day and night, sun and moon, benefit and malefic creatures, male and female. All these dichotomies are facing each other, so that they do stand in a position of mutual expectancy and dialogue. The whole picture appears to be a dramatic scene representing the act of multiform creation living in perfect harmony, although there are differences in some respects. When an invitation is sent to deities and ancestors prior to the marriage ceremony or some other ceremony, invitations are also sent to the so called evil or harmful beings like serpents, scorpions or wild animals; so that each one takes a share in the rejoicing and none bears any malice. This shows an all pervasive sense of well being in every act of rejoicing. We can construe it as a simple act of propitiation, but that means that one does not go deep into the feeling underlying such an act. The feeling is that of being charged with some divine intent. The divine intent is to ensure the share of every one, small or big. For a Hindu the essence of religion does not lie in believing in a particular deity or a particular code of conduct, like the Ten Commandments. The essence lies in the acceptance of the multiplicity not only of the object worship (deities, sacred scriptures, etc.), but also of the worshippers and the situations that induce such worship. Each one can choose his own deity, his own method of worship and stick to it without having any malice towards the other. This acceptance of multiplicity creates a very congenial atmosphere, unlike the situation obtained in the Greek pantheon. There, one can not afford to play jokes with the gods. Here instead there is intimacy with the divine and there is no fear or cause of alarm that the gods will be wrathful. Because we are a projection of their own beings and vice versa gods as objects of worship (*arcya*) are our own projections. That is why the deity is not what appears to be, but that which has been invoked through incantations according to a particular process. The outer form is just a cover symbol. It is not the symbolized. When you accept this the entire theory of rite takes a different shape. It is neither a primitive compulsion to do something out of fear nor the mere invoking of a potency in order to achieve something. Partially it may be so, but essentially it is not. It is also altogether different from the monotheistic temptation to subjugate all pagan gods in the name of God in capital letters. It is also different from the negation of the purity of gods. It is an intertwining of human and divine in a texture which calls for a complete absorption of all beings in a sublime act of creation. All arts, all crafts are an extension of the so called religious ritual. Even an ordinary and everyday act is a ritual. Taking a bath, for instance, is neither a luxury nor a necessity, but an ablution of the entire body. It is an immersion in the flow of life and an identification with the flowing waters of the Goddess Ganga, and ultimately with the ocean, the infinity.

Argullol: *Is it possible a real dialogue between cultures beyond a mere exchange of formalities and good intentions that are politically correct? Is it desirable? On which ground? In which direction? Which of the two is stronger: the Global Village or the Metropolitan Tribe?*

Myself: Yes, it is possible. There is a continuous stream of perennial philosophy in Indian thought. So its validity holds good in modern times as well as in ancient times. We can summarize under three headings the strains of perennial philosophy in Indian thought:

1) Awareness of the unity of life: while affirming this one has to include what we perceive through our senses, what we visualize in our minds and what we have in the inner layers of our consciousness. I want to emphasize that there is no physical matter which is not charged with spirit. And, whatever you may call it, spirit can not be manifested but in matter. So matter in each way holds the key to the understanding of the spirit. And the spirit in turn enlivens matter and activates it. It breaks its inertia. Having assumed this all what I have said before holds equally good for the so called present day realities of the modern world. The present world is no doubt the result of a complex set of phenomena and as whole is passing through an unsurpassed state of intellectual confusion. In spite of this the present world also pulsates and the pulsation can be felt by everybody commensurate with his/her ability to feel and describe it. Description alone gives validity to the feeling.

2) Secondly, the present world is still loaded with ideas that belong to the old-modern world. These old-modern world begins in the XVII century and terminates somewhere in the XX century. The termination point is still not very clear. Maybe the termination process is still on and the exact termination is still to come. But it seems to be true that many important notions that augured the advent of modern age are now on the wane. For example, the idea that man is the measure of all things and therefore he is entitled to enjoy the fruit of earth much more than any other living being. From this follows that man is the conqueror of nature. Often the taming of nature by man has been sung in glorious terms in this old-modern age. Another important notion, that is nowadays being revised is that the universe is mechanically arranged and determined, and consequently when one has the working knowledge of the world mechanism one can control the universe. This has prompted man to measure space, to send satellites, to land on the surface of other planets in the solar system.

3) Thirdly, all energy is drawn from a position of two harmonic forces. The theory of evolution has legitimised the disappearance of the weakest living beings and the right to survival of the fittest.

All these notions are getting falsified slowly. Some in physics, some in biological sciences, some in geopolitics. The retention of political power is becoming more and more difficult, if not impossible. And nothing to speak of other powers. Man is becoming aware of its failures as a citizen of the universe and he is now fully conscious of his commissions and onslaughts against nature, because the negative results of these failures are more conspicuous. It is man himself who has become more impoverished as a result. The interrelatedness of life is becoming more and more evident. And we see how all kind of institutions and societies are emerging to protect life that is understood to be in danger of extinction. The existence of plants and trees, of insects, of birds, of all kinds of animals is considered to be endangered. Man clearly understands that he has a role to play in maintaining the delicate balance of life cycles. Even the weakest has a right to life, not because of itself, but because it helps even the strongest to live better. When the weakest helps the stronger it is in no way subsidiary to the stronger. It is in fact in its own role of helping the stronger is stronger than the stronger. Right to live is not empowerment. It is rather fulfillment.

When I say this, I am fully aware that a typical western mind can not gulp it down, because it is conditioned by a different type of thinking, a different type of man-nature relation, a different type of subject-object dichotomy. I would qualify my statement by saying that there is a long way for the Western mind before it can be ready to accept the perennial ideas about life that belong to Indian thought. The only silver lining is that on one hand globalization is becoming synonymous with Americanization and is moving as a master roller levelling all elevations and all depths. On the other hand, because of speedier communications, ideas are fast intercepting each other. This has naturally created a sense of apprehension: Are we going in the right direction and is there any possibility of one to one relationship between the so called big and the so called small? Such apprehensions arise from a natural concern for some appropriate alternative for the well being of man and his environment. That concern is the silver lining.

Coming to the last part of the question. How can the modern European life fit into or harmonize with the Indian code of conduct which emanates from Indian thought? How can that be universally accepted? It is a valid question. There is an important reminder in the preamble to the famous *Manu Smriti* which says: "The laws enunciated in this book are subjected to modification according to time and space". And there is a second qualification that states: "All that follows in this book should be studied as a whole and should be scrutinized by the discerning eye of knowledge; and then only should be accepted as an applicable law". In spite of this, perennial laws hold good for all time and space. Taking a total look at those observations one could say that certain courses of conduct are culture-conditioned and certain faces of culture are conditioned by time and space. If the basic principles are not disturbed, alterations and modifications are in order. Even in India there are so many regional variations in rituals and rites and yet the basic principle of unity and totality of life is always kept in mind. The problem arises only when one questions the validity of all being one and also when one emphasizes the uniqueness of his own stand. Fortunately the present day situation is such that such an attitude is in the process of being rejected, because it does not hold water in a world of fast intermingling and intercommunication. So it can be hoped, perhaps hoping against hope, that prevalent rites and rituals specific to different regions in the world could get moulded by an all acceptable life principle.

I never think of an epoch when Hinduism will prevail over the world or for that matter any other-ism. But what I perceive is that the prevalent rigidity of stands, wherever they are or they come from, is going to crumble under the pressure applied by the need to come together and live in harmony in spite of differences. I can also see that they would be more occasions of intimate dialogues between cultures, not as an intellectual exercise, but as a human need. This is bound to bring change and instead of insisting for uniformity of norms one would begin to look for mutual understanding and acceptance of such differences which are products of history and products of geography.

□□□

The Absolute and Urgent Need for Proper Earth Government

•

Robert Muller

Dr. Muller is the Chancellor Emeritus of the UN University for Peace in Costa Rica and has been a former UN Assistant Secretary General. He is lifelong President of the Global Peoples' Assembly. The author of more than two dozen books in English, German, French, Italian, Spanish, Portuguese, Polish, Japanese and Dutch, he has been lecturing and promoting peace globally and his 'Two Thousand Ideas for a Better World' is considered a significant treatise in this direction throughout the world. Here, he has excerpted ideas from that visionary contribution.

"After my many years as a global servant I have come to believe that our future peace, justice, fulfillment, happiness and harmony on this planet will depend in the 21st century and third millennium, beyond proper Earth government, on divine or cosmic government, meaning that we must seek and apply the "natural", "evolutionary", "divine", "universal", "cosmic" laws which must rule our journey on this particular, miraculous planet in the vast universe."

During my fifty years of global service with the United Nations I was particularly struck by the following factors in the world situation:

Factor 1

The accelerated development of the human species into a global species through the multiplication and extension:

- of hands by machines
- of legs by transportation
- of eyesight by microscopes, telescopes, television
- of hearing by telephone
- of the nervous system by telecommunications
- of the brain through the birth of a global brain (science, global knowledge, the United Nations, the media, computers)

Still missing or underdeveloped are

- a global heart: love stops at the nation or at an ethnic group. Beginning of global love for peace, for nature and for the preservation of the Earth.
- a global soul: stops at a religion. Not yet a global spirituality in which all humans would be in tune with the universe and eternity.

Factor 2

From 1945 to the early 1970's: a comprehensive, unprecedented period of *Humanism* (avoid wars, prevent early childhood deaths, eradicate epidemics, increase the well-being of all humans, defend universal human rights, put an end to colonialism, apartheid and racism, increase literacy, longevity and good health, etc.)

1970's : while the agendas of the preceding period were still unfulfilled and mere overtaken by the world population explosion, as new major world concern came to the fore, namely the *Environment* (UNESCO's World Biosphere Conference in 1968 and the UN World Conference on the Environment in Stookholm in 1972, in other words: we humans on one side and the Earth and nature around us.

1980's: the new phenomenon of the depletion of the ozonosphere and menacing climate changes made *the Earth* priority No. 1 of our concerns and reduced economic development to "sustainable economic development".

This represents a fundamental change in the evolution of this planet. From now on the world will never be the same. This is why we should no longer speak of World Government, but of Earth

Government, the wise management, saving and preservation of our planetary home of which we are an integral part and whose further evolution now depends largely on us.

The UN Charter of 1945 does not use the words Earth, nature, natural resources and the environment. Why? Because at that time we considered the Earth to be unlimited in resources for a relatively small world population. The western countries also saw, and still see humanity as separate and superior to the natural world. This view has accomplished wonders for the human race. But humanity must now change its course, dominant objectives, values, institutions and laws if we want to prevent disasters in the further evolution of the Earth and of the human race.

Factor 3

- humanity rushed into economics (*oikos, nomos*) changing our home, before ecology (*oikos, logos*) the knowledge of that home;
- capitalism and business become the dominant ideals of the human society and not the environment and preservation of our Earth and nature;
- business globalized itself very rapidly and became the master of the world and of our lives, while governments, the entrusted defenders of justice, of the poor and the downtrodden, globalized themselves only timidly in the United Nations and even became the servants of business;
- religions did not globalize themselves at all.

There were excuses for the above:

- capitalism did wonders for humanity at the beginning when the world population was small and the resources of the Earth unexploited and seemingly unlimited;
- governments were still in the era of consolidating nations recently born from ethnic groups or provinces fighting each other;
- religions still believed that their truths were absolute, immortal and meant to spread to the entire world.

Today our objectives and efforts must be:

1. to see the religions globalize themselves into a global spiritual Renaissance in order to give us a universal, cosmic meaning of life on Earth and give birth to the first global, cosmic, universal civilization. The United Religions

Organization which is in the process of being created can do that;

2. national governments must absolutely globalize themselves significantly in a new, second generation United Nations with much more power, especially power of implementation, legislation and vastly increased resources commensurate with the tasks of the 21st century, or a United States of the World with proper balance of powers in a world democracy, or a World Union on the model of the recent European Union;
3. business must be put in its right place as a servant of the peoples' needs within a properly preserved Earth and renewed natural resources, and no longer be an instrument of unlimited power, profit and enrichment and the sole objective of life;
4. more generally we have come to the moment in evolution when we must give second place to the Darwinian theory of competition and survival of the fittest, and first place to a new ideology, science, strategy and methodology of cooperation for our evolutionary survival and continued progress on this perhaps unique, life-endowed planet in the universe.

Factor 4

During this period the rich countries and the rich in all countries became richer and the poor countries and the poor in all countries became poorer for the following reasons:*

The rich people, thanks to savings, inheritance and business can invest their money in banks, stockmarkets, mutual funds, retirement plans or in business ventures; many people do not have to work anymore to get richer;

The poor cannot save much or anything to put in banks, stock markets, mutual funds, retirement plans or to engage in business, and as a result remain poor.

The rich countries have the monopoly of inventions and

*The Secretary General of the UN reported to the 1997 UN General Assembly that 100 nations on this planet have become poorer in the last fifteen years and that 1.3 billion people of this Earth have a daily income of only one dollar.

patents, huge capitals accumulated over the years, sell highly elaborated, sophisticated goods at high prices to the poor countries from which they buy primary products at low prices. Investments, marketing techniques and advertisement are also used in the latter countries to make huge profits and gain new consumer markets for the rich countries.

Moreover poor countries and poor people have the highest number of children. Poverty elimination must therefore become a major factor in stemming the population explosion and vice versa.

SECTION 1
OUR NEW, OVERRIDING CONCERN: THE PRESERVATION OF THE EARTH

Since 1945 the needs, injustices and complaints of humanity, especially of the poor countries, have been high on the agenda of the United Nations. Recently the UN has held a World Social Summit on all these problems in Copenhagen and launched a United Nations Decade for the Eradication of Poverty, 1997-2006.

Regarding the newcomer in the age of global preoccupations, namely the Earth, we must listen to her too and respond to her complaints. If the Earth could speak she would say:

Why did I have to take all of a sudden a population increase from 2.5 billion people in 1952 to 5.9 billion today, more than a doubling in less than fifty years?

We could answer as an excuse: it happened out of sheer ignorance. After the war the rich countries and the United Nations wanted to prevent the early death of innumerable children in the poor countries. They died young because of epidemics, bad health conditions, malnutrition and hunger. But having no population statistics for the world and for most of these countries, we did not tell the parents that they would no longer need to give birth to an average of six children per family to have at least two left to till the land and to take care of their old age. Until 1952 we did not even know what the world population was! When the UN organized for the first time in human history decent global statistics and world censuses, we discovered that women did not have more children, but that children no longer died early (the mortality rate fell from 34 per thousand to 14 per thousand). When this was discovered it was too late, the children were born and a young population is highly reproductive. The UN warned nations and humanity by means of world population conferences and every other possible means that a world population explosion was upon us. But religions and other factors opposed it. Nevertheless, these efforts saved you from 2.2 billion more humans on your surface by the year 2000. Instead of 8.3 billion human beings in that year there will be only 6.1 billion.

The Earth:

Yes, but I hear that at the present rate you will be 9.3 billion in the year 2050 and stabilize only at 10.7 billion in the year 2200, which means 4.8 billion more people than today! You still increase by 80 million people every year. You will end by destroying me.

Our answer:

We continue to do our utmost. Each year the figure of population growth decreases by a few more millions. In October 1999 we will be 6 billion people. The increase during the preceding twelve months was 78 million. To change the course of global phenomena takes time. Humanity which is in the kindergarten of the global age has not learned it yet.*

The Earth:

You better learn it fast. I have another major complaint, namely while there is a population explosion in the poor countries you have also triggered off wild inventions, production, business, marketing, advertising and over consumption explosion in the rich countries. In these countries an individual consumes 30 times more of my resources than in the poor countries. From my point of view, namely the damages you do to my body, your population statistics are wrong: while the less developed countries count 4.7 billion people, the more developed countries' 1.2 billion should be multiplied by 30, *i.e.*, they represent in my eyes 36 billion people!

The Earth would have other complaints, she could ask for example:

---

*The UN's latest forecasts of the world population in 2050 are: a total world population of 8.91 billion, of which 1.16 billion (a decline of 40 million) in the rich countries and 7.75 billion (an increase of 3.05 billion) in the poor countries.

Why Each Minute

- do you destroy 21 hectares (52 acres) of my tropical forests (38 million acres a year) after having destroyed most of the forests in your "rich" countries?
- do you consume 35,725 barrels of oil to run around in cars and fly around me in airplanes?
- do you let 50 tons of fertile soil be blown off my cropland?
- do you add 12,000 tons of carbon dioxide to my atmosphere, to the air you breathe, a staggering total of 6.3 billion tons in 1997?

Why Each Hour

- do you let 685 hectares of productive dryland become desert?
- do you spend 120 million dollars on military expenditures, a trillion a year, which you could use for the good of your poor and for my preservation?
- are 55 people poisoned and 5 killed by pesticides?
- are 60 new cases of cancer diagnosed in the United States alone, over 5,000,000 cases each year with 20,000 cases leading to death, because of the thinning of my ozonosphere which protected you from the ultra-violet rays of the sun?

Why Each Five Hours

- do you let a species die out on this planet? This would mean a loss of 84,000 species in the next 50 years.

Why Each Day

- do 25,000 people die of water shortage and contamination?
- are 10 tons of nuclear waste produced by 437 and a constantly increasing number of nuclear plants? How can you let my body be reatomized when it took millions of years for me to loose the nuclear radiations I had when being born from the sun, and it was only when that atomized condition ended that I was able to give birth to life and to you?
- do 250,000 tons of sulfphuric acid fall and acid rain in the northern hemisphere, killing lakes and devastating remaining forests?

- are 60 tons of plastic packages and 372 tons of fishing nets dumped into the seas and oceans by commercial fishermen, killing fishes, sea birds and sea mammals?
- why each day are tens of thousands of men rushing to skyscrapers around the world to invent more, to produce more, to market more, to advertise more, to sell more, while only a few are concerned with my preservation? You cannot say, as you say for the population explosion, that each year that explosion diminishes somewhat. On the contrary I consider that it gets worse every day.

Why Since 1970

- have you destroyed more than thirty per cent of my nature and the destruction is accelerating, not decelerating as is the population explosion?

Why During A Human Lifetime

- do you dump so much garbage and waste on me: while the average is 150 times of the weight of a person in a poor country over a lifetime, why does the average American leave behind a mountain of waste 4,000 times his own weight?

And the Earth could go on. She could say:

"I regret to have no total figure on what you dump into the seas and oceans which cover 71 per cent of my body and contain the largest number of longest living of my species'. US industries and cities dump an estimated 6.4 trillion gallons of waste and sewage into the oceans every year:

I heard her also murmur:

"I almost wish that you humans would put colouring materials in the exhausts of your cars and airplanes to see what you add to the air which goes into your lungs and which I made so pure for you. Thank God, it begins to show in the form of smog over your cities."

The Earth would further say:

The UN Charter does not even mention me or my nature, natural resources, or the environment. But since the 1972 Stockholm Conference on the environment and the 1992 Rio de Janeiro Earth Summit you have begun to look into my miseries.

You have created a UN Environment Programme and an Earth Council, and you are drafting an Earth Charter, a Declaration of my rights. I hear that next you will take up the drafting of a universal declaration of human responsibilities. Ministries of Environment have sprung up in almost all countries. I thank you for that. But alas, the UN's recommendations have been often ignored and most poorly implemented, as was revealed by your 1997 Special General Assembly to review the situation. Why don't you transform the UN into an Earth Organization, in which humans and nature would cooperate for the optimum fulfillment and survival of both, and make me the most beautiful and flourishing planet in the whole universe?

She would add:

I have just read a statement by Mr. Mario Soares, the Prime Minister of Portugal and Chairman of a World Commission on the Oceans, who says: "the action taken for the seas and oceans since the Rio de Janeiro Earth Summit have been quite depressing." May I warn you: if the ultra-violet rays going through the vast hole in my ozonosphere (it has reached the size of continental China) kill the plankton and diatoms of my seas and oceans you might lose 2/3rds of your oxygen!

Yes, why, why, why...

It is to these fundamental global Earth challenges, in addition to the unresolved human ones, that the world community must address itself as we enter the 21st century and new millennium.

It is a vast subject which reaches from the individual to local, city, provincial, state, national, regional, continental and international, global levels, including the world's commons (the seas and oceans, the atmosphere, the ozonosphere, the moon and outer-space).

It is a vast subject also regarding the means of action: institutions, law, financial resources, taxation, human talent and resources, and the proper education and cooperation of 6 billion human individuals on this planet.

As requested, the present paper deals only with the subject: next development of the international system.

SECTION II
NEXT DEVELOPMENT OF THE INTERNATIONAL SYSTEM

Since globalization is the primary evolutionary phenomenon, challenge and opportunity of our time, it obviously raises the extremely important question of the type, role, structure, strength and resources of the international system.

And since the Earth is in peril and the greatest part of humanity is still in misery, the remedies must be audacious and strong, even if they seem unrealistic or difficult to accept by those in power. We must stretch our minds and hearts to the dimension of the problems. As President Roosevelt wrote in his own hand on the day before his death for the speech he was to deliver at the opening of the San Francisco Conference convened to give birth to the United Nations:

> "The only limit to our realization of tomorrow will be our doubts of today."

In my view, after fifty years of service in the United Nations system, all the above points to *the utmost urgency and absolute necessity for proper Earth Government.*

This should become the priority item on the agenda of world affairs for the year 2000. The poor countries who have been waiting so long for world justice should be the first to request it after 50 years of promises from the rich countries.

There is no shadow of doubt that the present political and economic systems—if systems they are—are no longer appropriate and will lead to the end of life evolution on this planet. We must therefore absolutely and urgently look for new ways. The less we loose time, the less species' and nature will be destroyed.

I would urge therefore that consideration be given to the following avenues:

I

To hold a *World Conference on Proper Earth Government through the Free Market System.*

Since business was the first to globalize itself world-wide, far beyond governments, and since corporations are now for all practical purposes ruling the world, we should give them the opportunity, even request them to assess their full responsibility for the future of all humanity, all living species and of the Earth itself and prove to us the validity of their claim that the free market can do it all.

The world corporate community should be asked to answer how they would take care of the above complaints of the Earth, how they would provide for a well-preserved planet and the well-being of all humanity, full employment, the renewal of natural resources, the long-term evolution of the planet and continuation of life on it, the real democracy of the consumers in a corporate power and wealth economy.

Such a conference would bring together the heads of the major world companies, banks and stock-exchanges, the World Bank, the IMF, the GATT, the new World Trade Organization, the International Chamber of Commerce and similar organizations.

II

To ensure *proper Earth government through a second generation United Nations for the 21st century.*

Since the United Nations is the only world-wide, universal organization at present available, since it had fifty years of valuable experience and many successes, since it paved the way to proper Earth government, instead of putting it on the defensive, unjustified attacks and criticism, reduction of resources and non-payment of obligatory contributions, governments should honestly ask themselves if a better way would not be to consider a second generation United Nations upgraded by a true quantum jump into a proper Earth preserving and human well-being and justice ensuring organization of our planet.

Such a conference would have at its disposal many proposals and ideas for the strengthening of the UN made by various UN bodies, governments, Secretaries General outside organizations and retired elders like myself. I have formulated many of them in my 2000 ideas and dreams for a better world. (*The author has added one thousand more ideas for the years 2001. Ed.*)

I recommend the urgent holding of a UN Charter Review Conference and second Bretton Woods Conference to assess the United Nations system's role, potentialities and substantial strengthening to cope with the critical issues and needs of the Earth and of humanity in the future. A Charter Review Conference would moreover give a voice to 134 governments of the present

189 members, which did not participate in the drafting of the Charter and creation of the UN.

The UN Secretary General, a member government or a group of governments should request the inscription of this item on the agenda of the next UN General Assembly.

There is no doubt that given the massive changes which have taken place since 1945, an Organization created 53 years ago can simply not be adequate to deal effectively with the mounting, unprecedented and massive world problems of a new century and new evolutionary phase of our planet.

III

A New Philadelphia World Convention for the Creation of the United States of the World.

The star-performance, often called "miracle" of the American States in the Constitutional Convention in Philadelphia 200 years ago which put an end to a similar political chaos in North America between numerous, sovereign independent states at the time, should be repeated.

Such a Convention of all nations would review the state of world democracy and would have to add to the system of balance of powers the new dominant power of business.

"Philadelphia II" is a project of US Senator Mike Gravel who proposes a convention for the writing of a Charter for a Global Constitution.

In this regard, we might well apply to the present world these words by George Washington concerning the political chaos which reigned in North America at his time:

"The primary cause of all disorders lies in the different state governments and in the tenacity of that power which pervades the whole of their systems."

A dear friend of mine, Captain Tom Hudgens who created in Washington after World War II the Association to Unite the Democracies, after laboring without success to get the governments of the NATO democracies to create a federal union was convening a Citizens' Constitutional Convention in Holland in 1998 to draft a Constitution for Democracies and to propose it to all democracies of the world.

IV

A *World Conference of all world federalist and world government associations and movements, to propose a federal constitution and system for the Earth*

An immense work has been accomplished by the World Federalist Association headed by Sir Peter Ustinov, by its national associations and many other world government movements. There exist already several draft World Constitutions. World philanthropists should sponsor a World Conference or other ways to come up with a world constitution for the 21st century. We may remember that during World War I, Andrew Carnegie brought over to the US two Belgian scholars who drafted the statutes of the League of Nations and earned the Nobel Prize for it. Contemporary philanthropists should be inspired by such examples. According to UNESCO only 15 per cent of philanthropy is international and most of it is bilateral. When the global world and the human family are in greatest need, they are the orphans of philanthropy.

And is it so inconceivable that two big federal countries like the United States and Russia might take the initiative of calling a world conference for the establishment of a global federal government in their image? After the cold war, what a warm spring, a spring of truly united nations this would be for our precious planet!

V

A *World Conference for the Creation of a World Union on the pattern of the European Union.*

The world has recently witnessed another political miracle, similar to the American miracle in Philadelphia: the miracle of Strasbourg, the birth of the European Union of 15 European countries which have finally put an end to their antagonisms and wars, decided to unite and cooperate and have abolished the borders between them. Every European can now settle anywhere in the Union, elect a European Parliament at the same time when electing his national Parliament, and can have his government condemned by a supra-national European Court of Human Rights when his rights are violated. Also, the European Union has its own European budget and tax system and is not dependent on national contributions as is the United Nations. In 1990 the European Economic Community had already a budget of 7.4 billion dollars, ten times the UN budget for all its world activities. This example is so hopeful, so powerful, so novel and inspiring that I recommend it as an outstanding guidelight for more regional communities and for the entire globe.

It is significant that the European Parliament has called for the setting up under the auspices of the United Nations, of an International Environmental Court and a World Environment Agency, of which the European Environment Agency would be a regional branch. It also wants that consideration be given to the setting up of a Parliamentary Consultative Assembly within the UN. We should wholeheartedly support these proposals.

I recommend that the European Union organize meetings and conferences with outside countries to show them how they can move towards regional unions and how a World Union can be established. This would render a great service to the world and to the UN General Assembly.

VI

A *World Conference of the planet's five continents for a Proper Earth Government through Continental Unions and a World Union.*

About ten years ago or more, I suggested to President Bush that in view of the creation of the European Union, the American countries from Alaska to Tierra del Fuego should create an all-American community or union. He listened to me but instead of creating that community in a common, joint effort of all American countries, as was done in Europe, the US negotiated separate trade agreements first with Canada, then with Mexico, and now the Latin American countries created their own Mercosur (the Southern Latin American market) and the future of an American Union is in doubt.

It might be noteworthy that indigenous people of the Americas believe in a prophecy according to which the Eagle and the Condor will meet on sacred Mount Rasur in Costa Rica from which a civilization of peace and nature will spread to the entire world. It is on that hill that the dream of the demilitarization of Costa Rica was born, and where the United Nations created the first University for Peace on this planet, as well as an International Radio for Peace. The Earth Council created by the Rio de Janeiro

Conference has also moved to it. Simon Bolivar, for his part, in his dreams, prophecized that someday the capital of the world will be located in Central America.

The continental approach to a world union remains an important avenue. One could conceive five continental unions: the European Union, an American, an African, an Asian, and an Australian Union. A World Union could be constructed as a superstructure and common political system of the five continents.

VII

A *World Conference on Earth and Human Government through new bio-political modes patterned on examples from nature.*

A very novel approach to the organization of humanity and its proper relations with the Earth and nature is to follow the biological models offered by the formation and admirable functioning of numerous colonies of cells, bacteria and living species observable in nature and now well studied. This is a very advanced science which opens up the most interesting and promising vistas. A bio-political science can and should now be rapidly developed on its basis. It would offer a very much needed bio-political revolution of the Earth' political system and science. Here the Earth and nature would come to their full pre-eminence and rights. All other world governmental avenues will sooner or later lead to it. First models are already the bio-regional approaches existing in certain areas of the world such as the Arctic Forum and the big river basins and mountain chains cooperative agreements.

Beyond this bio-regional vision and approach is the idea and proposal of Barbara Gaughen-Muller to create a United Nature, a transformed United Nations to respond to the fundamental unity of nature of which humans are a part. Humans would not dominate nature but cooperate with her and learn from her. It is probably the most advanced, timely and imaginative vision of the total, proper functioning of planet Earth.

The Natural Law Party created by British scientists, which exists already in 85 countries and has become the third largest party in the United States could be the spearhead of this new approach. See the book by the President of the US Natural Law Party, physicist Dr. John Hagelin: Manual for a Perfect Government. How to harness the laws of nature to bring maximum success to governmental administration, Maharishi University, Fairfield, Iowa 52557.

VIII

A World Conference on Proper Earth Government through what the world's religions have in common in terms of universal, global spirituality and world-wide human experience.

Last, but not least, humanity has reached a point when we must consider our human presence, past, present and future on this particular planet in the universe. We have now a tremendous information on the universe in which we live. In addition to our total consciousness of our Earth and its global evolution we are also now acquiring and developing a cosmic consciousness of the universe. This is one of the greatest advances in human history. But the mysteries of infinity and eternity will probably remain beyond human and scientific grasp. This has the result of bringing together the spirituality or basic "faiths" of all religions and science. God, the gods or the Great Spirit or Spirits and their emissaries, prophets and human incarnations like Jesus gave humanity at its early stages a cosmic, universal, all-encompassing faith or feeling for the mysteries of the cosmos, for the norms of love and for the miracle of life and norms of behaviour between all humans, other species and nature. These messages or "revelations" should not be neglected. They contain some of the profoundest answers to human behaviour, fulfillment and survival. Great was our astonishment in the environmental crisis to discover the wisdom and rules of behaviour towards nature dictated by the Great Spirit to the indigenous people of this planet, and towards Creation in practically all religions. The world's 5000 religions are filled with incredible wisdom regarding human morality, belief in life, environmental adaptations, survival and future evolution. This is strongly coming to the fore at this time in the following:

1. the dream and plan of my compatriot Robert Schuman from Alsace-Lorraine to see the European Union, which started with a coal and steel community followed by an economic community, followed by a political union, culminate in an all spiritual European Union including the Eastern European countries, especially "Holy Mother Russia". For him this was more important than the extension to these countries of a military union through NATO.
2. the San Francisco Initiative to create a United Religions Organization similar to the United Nations also born in

that city, where all religions of the world will cooperate, define what they have in common, provide their wisdom on human behaviour and morality, and right relations with nature, God's Creation and the universe thus ushering the world into a great Spiritual Renaissance. In the process they will hopefully reduce and progressively give up their fundamentalism in favor of a global spirituality, the same way as nations in the United Nations have reduced to some extent their national fundamentalism called sovereignty.

3. In August 1998, at the 20th World Congress on Philosophy in Boston, a World Commission on Global Consciousness and Spirituality was created. Mr. Karan Singh of India and I are its Co-Chairmen.
4. In December 1999, at the invitation of Nobel Peace Prize winner, Bishop Edmund Tutu, a third World Parliament of Religions convened in Pretoria, South Africa. The first such Parliament was held in 1893 and the second in 1993, both in Chicago.

Global religious cooperation towards a spiritual Renaissance is accelerating.

SECTION III
THE NEED FOR A CHANGE IN VALUES AND BASIC RETHINKING OF ALL PRINCIPAL SEGMENTS OF HUMAN LIFE

In recent years, Erika Erdmann, the research aide and Librarian of Nobel Prize winner Roger Sperry, and Professor Jean-Claude Leonide, a reputed French anthropologist undertook a survey of long-term evolutionary scientists which showed that scientists were becoming more optimistic as a result of the birth of a global consciousness which makes us humans aware of our mistakes and problems and helps us solve them by changing course and adapting to evolutionary requirements. Their survey revealed that the theory of "chaos" according to which the universe and human life make no sense is losing ground. The new theory is that on any planet having life in the cosmos one species sooner or later evolves to a point of gaining a total knowledge of the planet it lives on. It will then be in its power either to continue evolution or to bring it to an end. The first course will require that the former values of that species, values not respectful of the new phase of evolution, must be replaced by new ones which take evolution into account. These new values are a major new evolutionary imperative.

In my view and in theirs, humanity has reached that stage on Planet Earth: we must revise our basic values dating from the 19th and early twentieth century and acquire a new evolutionary wisdom which respects nature, the Earth and their basic laws. It nature has produced the incredible, sophisticated variety of innumerable living species around us, each one a true miracle, it is simply not possible that the human species is not a miracle too, perhaps the most advanced of all. We are no longer our own objective. We have become the caretakers, the trustees, the shapers of future evolution, the instruments of the cosmos, integral parts of it, as we have already recognized of late to be to of the Earth.

The future of the Earth will be bright and life will not become extinct if we decide so on the eve of a new century and millennium. We are entering a thrilling, transcending new global, cosmic phase of evolution in the line indicated by Teilhard de Chardin, the anthropologist, if the human species understands its suddenly momentous, incredibly important evolutionary role and responsibility.

The preceding requires that all basic segments of human life on Earth be reviewed and rethought from scratch as we march ahead in the 21st century. These are:

- a new political system for planet Earth
- a new economics
- a new education
- a new media and communications
- a new democracy
- a new global leadership
- a spiritual Renaissance and inter-religious cooperation
- a non-violent human society
- a well preserved planet
- a decent well-being for all humans
- a stabilization of the world population
- right human settlements on the planet
- the disarmament, demilitarization, denuclearization and global security of the planet
- a new science and technology

- a new anthropology, sociology and new ways of life
- a new human biology
- a new philosophy, cosmology and long-term view of evolution
- a new world ethics and justice
- a new world psychology
- a new science and art of planetary management
- an art and culture Renaissance

Such reconsideration is taking place currently in a whole series of institutions and conferences around the world. We can therefore be optimistic about our future as we enter a new century and millennium.

SECTION IV
THE NEED FOR FUTURIZATION OR EVOLUTIONARY FUTURISM

With our human concern for the phenomenon of globalization must also come a growing concern for the future, a long-term future, a new phenomenon which I would call "futurization" or evolutionary futurism.

Having recently attended as a member of an international advisory board, a conference on *Humanity and the Earth in the year 3000* by a new Foundation for the Future created in Bellevue, Washington by two firms of outer space satellite and stations construction, I was deeply impressed how all things earthly and human must be seen in their globality and interdependence when considered from a long-term point of view. Alas, political thinking today most of the time does not go beyond the next elections. We do not heed the Iroquois' custom not to take any decision without thinking of its effects on the seventh generation.

I, therefore recommend that all governments should create a Ministry of the Future and that the United Nations should create a main committee on the Future in the General Assembly to receive yearly reports from all UN specialized agencies and world programmes on the long-term future. The Foundation for the Future will hold in the year 2000 a meeting of 100 eminent long-term scientists and visionaries to provide a view of what the Earth and humanity are likely to be in the year 3000 under various conditions. Such long-term thinking and envisioning must become an important component of proper Earth government.

Also to be noted is the prestigious Millennium Project of the United Nations University in Tokyo designed to assist in organizing futurists', scholars and policy makers in 60 countries who work for UN organizations, corporations, governments, universities and non-governmental organizations.

******

"After my many years as a global servant I have come to believe that our future peace, justice, fulfillment, happiness and harmony on this planet will depend in the 21st century and third millennium, beyond proper Earth government, on divine or cosmic government, meaning that we must seek and apply the "natural", "evolutionary", "divine", "universal", "cosmic" laws which must rule our journey on this particular, miraculous planet in the vast universe." After global government, we will discover government according to the laws of nature, and will then discover that these are solar laws which themselves are the cosmic laws of the universe. We are on the threshold of an extraordinary, mind-boggling, new age of our human progress and evolution on planet Earth if we do not stick to obsolete beliefs, values, systems, institutions and laws.

As Leibniz said when the exact sciences were born: "Humanity will now be busy dissecting and analyzing reality for hundreds of years, but the time will come when it will be lost in so much detail and findings that it will have to acquire again a total, global view of reality." That "holistic" age has come.

CONCLUSION

I joined the United Nations world service in 1948 as a young man who had been in a German Gestapo prison, a French Resistance fighter and had seen the most horrible atrocities of war and destruction. I came from Alsace-Lorraine, a province of France bordering Germany, where my grandparents knew three wars and changed nationality five times between France and Germany, without leaving their village. I was a very pessimistic young man. If this had happened between two highly civilized white countries, how could I expect white and black countries, communists and capitalists, rich and poor nations, thousands of religious and ethnic groups to be able to live together in peace? Surely there would be an incident which would trigger off another world war within twenty years. Well, there was no third world war.

In the empty war factory in Lake Success where the United Nations was first located, a British delegate asked me what I was doing there. I answered: "I came here to work for peace, because I do not want my children and grandchildren to know the horrors I saw in the war." He answered, "I pity you, young man because you will lose your job. This organization will not last more than five years." Well, it celebrates this year its 53 birthday. Founded by 51 nations it has now a universal membership of 189 countries.

I was also told in Lake Success that decolonization was the priority item on the agenda of world affairs and that it would take the United Nations from one hundred to one hundred fifty years to solve the problem. Well, the UN did it in forty years. I was told the same about apartheid, women's rights, indigenous people, the cold war, and I could cite other examples.

I have been involved in the creation of several new UN specialized agencies and world programmes in the economic and social fields, including the world-wide United Nations Development Programme where I was the lonely first UN official working with Paul Hoffman, the former Administrator of the Marshall Plan. The UN listened to me when I suggested to channel the surplus food of the rich countries which burned them, to children and hungry people in the poor countries, and created the World Food Programme. The World Bank listened to my idea to give low-interest loans to infrastructure projects in the poor countries and created the International Development Agency. When I look at the list of 32 UN specialized agencies and the world programmes, I am astonished that I played a role in the creation of eleven of them!

I have seen the UN system assemble information on practically every aspect of our Earth and of the human family. Who remembers that until 1952 we did not even know what the world population was?

Through the United Nations I have seen the seas and oceans, the moon and outer space become legally the commons of humanity. I have seen the birth of the first concerns for the environment, a word coined in the UN when it convened the first World Conference on the Environment in Sweden in 1972. And the UN did the same for the world's waters, deserts, oceans, climate, atomic energy, children, women, the ageing, the handicapped, etc.

I entered the UN as an intern and was privileged to rise over the years to Assistant Secretary General working directly with three Secretaries General. When I look back, I thank the UN for a truly magical life.

And retirement was not the end. Three days before I retired from the UN in 1986, after 38 years of service, Rodrigo Carazo, the President of Costa Rica, a man whom I greatly admire, proposed that I should become the one-dollar-a-year Chancellor of the recently created University of Peace in Costa Rica. I accepted with delight to continue to work for a UN agency in a peaceful, demilitarized country to which I would give the highest mark for its initiatives and successes at the UN: the creation of the post of High Commissioner for Human Rights, the Nobel Peace Prize to President Oscar Aris, the celebration of the International Day of Peace and the world cease-fire proposed by Costa Rica for the week of the fiftieth anniversary of the UN. And how could I have ever dreamt that I would some day be appointed a member of a World Commission of Eminent Persons to prepare a better future for the UN? And that all the borders in western Europe would be suppressed, a European Union created, and that in 1994 I could, for the first time, cross without any controls the border between France and Germany in my hometown of Sarreguemines in Alsace-Lorraine? And that there would exist today in the world 34 schools bearing my name, using a new education which I derived from the United Nations.

In brief: from a very pessimistic young man after World War II, I have been transformed by the UN into an optimistic elder who deeply believes in humanity. I am infinitely grateful to the UN for having taught me that planet Earth is my home, that humanity is my family and that it was worthwhile to devote my life with enthusiasm and faith to the great objectives for which this Organization, a truly unprecedented ominous meta-biological organism of the Earth and of the human species was created. In the face of colossal obstacles and the shortsightedness of most nations, the UN has created many miracles.

After all these years, I asked myself the question: what would be my further expectations and dreams for the future? A host of answers and ideas upwelled in me. On July 11, 1994, there were 2000 days left to the year 2000, I began to write 2000 ideas for a better world as a countdown to the bi-millennium. I started with my Dream 2000 and the following agenda:

An Agenda for the Future

Our absolute priorities and objectives for the 21st century and the third millennium must be:

1. To make this planet a paradise
2. To eradicate from it all the nonsense and errors engendered by power, greed and egotism
3. To make out of all humans one family
4. To create a new social, political world order for the centuries to come
5. To attain a life of fulfillment and happiness for all humans
6. To achieve a human family in harmony with the Earth and the heavens
7. To be the ultimate cosmic success of the Universe and God

My most recent conviction is that the world's survival requires an enormously strengthened second generation United Nations, or a UN transformed progressively into a World Union on the model of the European Union, or a United States of the World on the great precedent of the United States or a United Nature without precedent. On the eve of a new century and millennium it is a matter of utmost urgency, of life or death.

Fifty years later we should remember these lines which Franklin Roosevelt wrote to the San Francisco Conference creating the United Nations.

"The work, my friends is peace: more than an end of this war—an end to the beginning of all wars. I ask you to keep up your faith. The only limit to our realization of tomorrow will be our doubts of today. Let us move forward with a strong and active faith."

ADDENDA

We should also bear in mind these statements by great visionaries.

- "With all my heart I believe that the world's present system of sovereign nations can lead only to barbarism, war and inhumanity." *Albert Einstein*
- "There is no salvation for civilization, or even the human race, other than the creation of a world government." *Albert Einstein*

- "Unless some effective supranational government can be set up and brought quickly into action, the prospects of peace and human progress are dark and doubtful."

Winston Churchill

- "I have long believed that the only way peace can be achieved is through world government."

Jawaharlal Nehru

- "...The point of a nation is not to draw a line in the sand and keep its members behind it, but to create world citizens who are secure enough to treat others equally."

Gloria Steinem

- "World Government is not an 'ultimate goal' but an immediate necessity. In fact, it has been overdue since 1914. The convulsions of the past decades are the clear symptoms of a dead and decaying political system."

Emery Reves

- "World Government is not only possible, it is inevitable; and when it comes, it will appeal to patriotism in its truest sense, in its only sense, the patriotism of humans who love their national heritages so deeply that they wish to preserve them in safety for the common good." *Peter Ustinov*
- "The age of nations have passed. Now unless we wish to perish, we must shake off our old prejudices and build the Earth. The more scientifically I regard the world, the less can I see any possible biological future for it except in the active consciousness of its unity." *Teilhard de Chardin*
- "Have I said clearly enough that the European Community we created is not an end in itself? It is a process of change, continuing in that same process which in an earlier period produced our national forms of life. The sovereign nations of the past can no longer solve the problems of the present: they cannot ensure their own progress or control their own future. And the Community itself is only a stage on the way of the organized world of tomorrow." *Jean Monnet*

Conceiver of the European Community,
now the European Union

- "When all humanity calls planet Earth our home, there is no alternative for the Earth but Global Government."

Barbara Gaughen Muller

□□□

Cosmic Puzzles and Speculations

•

Jayant V. Narlikar

Professor Jayant V. Narlikar, India's great man of science and music, is at present Director and Homi Bhabha Professor at the Inter-University Centre of Astronomy and Astrophysics, Pune. He touches upon the many mysteries of the universe which science is still investigating. It is a quest also close to Dr. Karan Singh's heart, he underlines.

"Clearly allusions to cosmic phenomena in the ancient Indian literature are in many respects similar to the present speculations about the cosmos. This in itself does not justify the claim that the ancients knew all about modern science. For testing such a claim one needs qualitative details about the cosmos in ancient literature, which are sadly lacking."

I recall a sunny morning in Delhi. I was sitting across the desk from Dr Karan Singh in his office in the India International Centre.

"So, what is the current puzzle in cosmology?" asked Karan Singhji.

I was at a loss for a definitive answer; for there were (and still are) so many puzzles about the universe. Still I recall mentioning 'dark matter'. Matter, which is believed to exist because of the powerful gravitational attraction it exercises, but which cannot be seen. It cannot be seen no matter what type of telescope one uses, optical, radio, infra-red,

X-rays,... As I came to the end of my brief reply, pat came the comment from across the desk:

"Asuryā nā m te lokā andhen tamas ā vrta"

The line means: "Those worlds are without any suns, being surrounded by blinding darkness."

"Where did you get this quote from?" I asked. Dr Karan Singh replied quoting chapter and verse from the *Isavasyopanishad*. And to substantiate it he wrote it down for me. On going home I looked up the relevant Upanishad, and of course it was there.

I cite this example as an indicative one showing the scholarly character of Dr Karan Singh, combining knowledge about our ancient heritage with interest in modern science. No doubt others who have had the privilege of coming in contact with him, have noted this particular aspect. In this article, dedicated to his *Festschrift*, I try to answer the question he asked me that day, in a more comprehensive way.

I begin by elaborating on the answer I gave Dr Karan Singh that day in his office.

Dark Matter

Till the early 1970s, most astronomers believed that aspects of the universe they saw through their telescopes contained most of what exists. And these telescopes, as I mentioned above, not only use the light our eyes respond to, but other wavelengths also, longer and shorter than the optical wavelengths. But these beliefs, however, began to receive blows as evidence began to pile up, of matter that cannot be seen, but which is believed to exist, if our understanding of the law of gravitation is correct.

Let us take an illustrative example. Our solar system has nine planets, ranging from Mercury to Pluto. Mercury, the nearest planet to the Sun takes about 88 days to make one round, while the farthest Pluto, takes about 248 years. If you calculate the speed with which these planets orbit the Sun, you will find that Pluto's speed is considerably less than Mercury's. This effect can be explained very well by Newton's law of gravitation. The force of attraction of the Sun on a distant planet being less than on a nearby planet, the former moves more slowly than the latter.

Now we can apply the same rule to clouds of neutral hydrogen gas which are known to circle our Galaxy and other similar spiral galaxies. The farther the cloud from the galaxy, the slower should it orbit round it. That was the expectation of astronomers as they used radio astronomy to measure the speeds of these clouds. But they were in for a shock. The speeds did not drop down as one looked at farther and farther clouds! And, this feature was not seen just in one galaxy, but seemed to be common for all galaxies. What do these observations mean? Why should the rotation speed stay constant for clouds at three times the distance of the visible periphery of the galaxy?

There were two options before the scientists. The harder option was to conclude that Newton's laws of motion and the inverse square law of gravitation, which had worked so well for astronomy, had at last failed and that some new laws were needed to explain these phenomena. The other, softer option, was to presume that the galaxies extend well beyond their visible boundaries, and so their gravitational effect also goes farther. This second option is generally favoured by astronomers who like to think that the extended region beyond the visible boundary involves masses that are extremely difficult, or impossible to see.

This dark matter is believed to exist on a much larger scale in large clusters of galaxies also. This belief is based on the fact that random motions of galaxies in a cluster are much more energetic than warranted by their mutual gravitational pull. Normally the greater the pull, the greater is the motion generated. Judging by the motions of galaxies observed in clusters, astronomers argue that substantial amount of dark matter must be present in a typical cluster. How much? In some cases the dark matter may be as much as ten times the visible matter.

And, most importantly, what is it made of ?

This is being discussed and speculated on. Mundane explanations could be that the dark matter is in the form of planets which are mostly non-luminous, or very faint stars, or objects that do not have sufficient mass to become stars and which therefore remain cold balls of matter. More fancy version could be black holes, made from huge stars that having spent all their energy sources, finally shrink and collapse to become black holes. However, the cosmologists who believe that the universe originated with a big bang cannot accept these alternatives, as they turn out to be inconsistent with the overall cosmological picture. For them the alternative has to be what is called 'nonbaryonic matter'. Baryons are what we are made of, particles like neutrons and protons found in the nuclei of atoms. Planets, stars, even black holes are made of baryons.

So what is this esoteric form of matter? Those who study the ultimate basic structure of matter believe that such matter may show up in interactions of extremely high energy particles. Unfortunately, these energies are a *thousand billion* times the energies that man-made accelerators could generate in their particles. The only way such particles could therefore have made their way into the universe was in the very early epoch, some billion-billion-billion-billionth part of a second after the big bang! Only at that stage was the universe able to accelerate particles to such energies.

So today astronomers do find such 'sunless regions surrounded by darkness' and would like to know what is their extent and what are they made of.

Black Holes

I am sure readers would like this tale...of course they must be aware of it!

The Indian scripture *Bhagvatam* has the following story about Brahma, the first of the trinity of Gods, who creates the universe. A king called Kukudmi had a beautiful daughter called Revati, who attracted a large number of suitors. Anxious to make the right choice of son-in-law, Kukudmi decided to consult no less an authority than Brahma. So he went to Brahma's abode along with his daughter. As he was occupied with some important matter of the universe, Brahma sent word to Kukudmi to wait for a moment.

Presently Brahma came out, and having greeted the King asked the reason for his visit. Kukudmi explained his problem and sought advice from the Great One. Brahma laughed and said: 'Let me explain. All those suitors on your list are no more. They are dead and gone. Although you waited for a moment in my abode, during that period, thousands of years have passed on the Earth.' The King was naturally dismayed. However, Brahma offered a solution: 'Never mind. Go back to your kingdom', he said.

'There you will find a suitable boy called Balarama for your daughter.' And Brahma gave Kukudmi details of this suitor-to-be.

This is one of the oldest stories that I know of wherein the concept of time passing at different rates for different people or places plays a key role.

Black holes are objects that have intrigued astronomers over the last four decades. The notion behind them, that of a massive compact object which is able to attract and pull back even light, so that it is never seen, was much older. For astronomers, there are several examples where they witness a huge output of radiation and even particles of matter, coming from a compact region. Paradoxically, they associate such regions with the existence of a black hole.

Typically a black hole is believed to arise when huge masses collapse under their own gravitational pull which always acts inward. Einstein's general relativity theory tells us that once the object has crossed a certain limit of size there is nothing that can stop its contraction. I will return to this aspect again later in this article.

Once an object has shrunk to a stage close to that of a black hole, it acts as an attractor of matter in its neighbourhood. The infalling matter may circle round the black hole and some of it may fall in while some could be ejected with great energy. In this way black holes are considered as 'energy machines' of the cosmos. The techniques of astronomy are becoming increasingly more efficient in identifying such an active region, usually close to the centre of a galaxy and placing observational constraints on speculations about what is going on there.

The episode of Brahma has a strange connection with black holes and the concept of what is known as 'time dilatation' in relativity. Imagine a massive star on which we station an observer *B* who is to communicate with a distant observer A, via light signals. The arrangement may be for each observer to send to the other signals at hourly intervals. What happens? *A* discovers that he is receiving *B*'s signals not every hour, but with a slight delay, say after every hour and ten minutes. Likewise, *B* finds that *A*'s signals arrive ahead of the stipulated time.

Why does this happen? Because, the rate at which the passage of time is measured by the respective observers is influenced by the strength of the gravity field in their neighbourhood. The stronger the effect of gravity, the slower is the clock. Near *B* the field is stronger than near *A*, as the latter is far away from the gravitating mass; and so *B*'s clock runs slower compared to A's. General relativity tells us how to estimate the magnitude of this effect

Using relativistic ideas, if we now imagine that the star has shrunk to a smaller size, then the gravity field near *B* will have become even stronger and correspondingly, the time dilatation of *B* relative to *A* longer than before. So at this stage *A* will have to wait even longer, say, for two hours between each of *B*'s signals. And the waiting period will progressively increase as the star further contracts. The black hole stage comes, when *no signal from B will ever reach A*. This happens when the star has shrunk to a size known as its gravitational radius, or its *Schwarzschild radius*. For the Sun this radius is only about 3 km., compared to its actual radius of 700,000 km. This illustrates the extent of compression an object of a few solar masses has to undergo in order to become a black hole.

Now let us identify *B* with Brahma. A few minutes in Brahma's neighbourhood may well have been equivalent to several thousands of mortal-years, if the time dilatation of the above kind were in operation! I am not suggesting this as an explanation; rather I wish to highlight the fact that our ancient literature quite comfortably accommodated ideas that are counter-intuitive, but are nevertheless justifiable by modern science.

Creation Events

In Chapter 9 of the *Gita*, Lord Krishna says:

Prak ṛ tim swāmava ṣ tabhya vis ṛ jāmi punah punah.

("Laying hold of my nature I create again and again.")

The idea of repeated creation is not therefore uncommon to the Hindu mythology. Unlike the concept of creation as a single event, as found in several different cultures round the Western world, here we have creation taking place again and again.

A significant question to ask today is: Do we see instances of creation of matter in the cosmos today? The evidence for creation of matter comes, I believe, in explosive fashion, such as in quasars, active nuclei of galaxies, gamma ray bursts, etc. These diverse events share one feature generally...namely the outpouring of dynamical energy from a relatively compact region. If these are not instances of creation of new matter in *mini-bangs*, what else could they be?

The standard way of looking at these events is to assume the existence of a black hole and let it play the role of an energy machine as discussed earlier. However, the difficulty with this explanation is that in a black hole scenario, we should be seeing matter from the surrounding region falling into the centre (where the black hole is presumed to be situated). *There is no evidence of this kind in any of the events observed to date.* It is conjectured that the infalling matter forms a disc which spins around the black hole and any infalling matter first gets into this disc and then falls into the black hole. While there are consistent arguments for such an assumption, there is no direct proof for it.

In recent years Fred Hoyle, Geoffrey Burbidge and I advanced a new theory of cosmology in which the expansion of the universe is driven by the explosive creation events, the *mini-bangs*. Such a universe shows a long term expansion superposed by oscillations (expansions and contractions), but has no beginning or no end. Known as the *quasi-steady state cosmology*, this model has been proposed as an alternative to the commonly accepted big bang model.

Did the universe originate in a single event, the *big bang*, or is it continually driven by mini-bangs? This is an interesting question for philosophers to speculate on. However, ultimately the observations will decide which picture, if any, conforms to reality.

The Scientific Attitude

Cosmology, the subject dealing with the origin, structure and evolution of the universe is certainly the most basic of all sciences. I have touched upon the present speculations relating to the big bang *vs* the quasi-steady state cosmology. These are *current* speculations. How do they compare with the past speculations thousands of years ago?

Science is characterized by a questioning attitude. The 'whats', 'hows', and 'whys' are essential for the scientific culture to take root and prosper. Going back to the Vedic times we do find evidence of this questioning attitude. I give an example from the *Nāsadīya – sūkta* :

> *Nasadaslnno sadaslt tadanlm nasldrajo no uyoma paro yat. Kimavarlvah kuha kasya sarmannambhah kimasld gahanam gabhlram. Na mrtyurasldamrtam na tarhi na ratrya ahna aslt praketah. Anldavatam svadhaya tadekam tasmadhanyanna parah kim canasa. Tama aslt tamasa gudhamagre praketam salilam sarvam a idam. Tucchynabhvapihitam yadaslt tapasatanmahina'-jayataikam. Kamastadagre samavartatadhi*

manaso retah prathamain vadasit. Sato bandhumasati niravindan hrdi pratisya kavayo manlsa. Tirasclno vitato rasmiresamadhah svidasldupari svidaslt. Retodha asanmahimana asantsvadha avastat prayatiah parastat. Ko addha veda ka iha pravocat kuta ajata kuta iyam visrstih. Arvagdeva asya visarjanenatha ko veda yata ababhuva. Iyam visrstir yata ababhuva yadi va dadhe yadi va na. Yo asyadhyaksah parame vyomantso anga veda yadi va na veda

(Rg—Veda, X, 129).

Loosely translated into English, this reads thus :

> 'At that time (when the universe was not born) there was no *sat* (being) nor was there *asat* (non-being). At that time there was no space nor was there the sky beyond it. Who (then) covered what, where and for whose welfare?, Was the dense fathomless water there? Then there was no death nor was there the immortal to be distinguished from it. There were no means available to distinguish between night and day. (Whatever existed) was unique and alone surviving on its own. There was nothing else or beyond. There was darkness and living forms covered by it and free of any distinction. The Brahma was covered by Maya and appeared later (in a different form) because of penance. The seed from its mind was *kama* (desire), the inspiration for creation, The wise have thought over it and decided that this was the (first) contact between *asat* and *sat*. 'This thread was spread between them below as well as above. (From these) some gave seeds that grew. Their power remained here and influence spread there. How did the spread of *sat* come about? Who can tell this in detail? Who knows definitely? Even gods came after the spread (of *sat*). So who can know where the creation came from? This spread (of *sat*), where it came from, whether created or not may or may not be known to him who presides over the great heavens (who can tell?).'

We also find evidence of this attitude in *Upanishads* and some of the *Puranas*. Unfortunately this attitude seems to have fizzled out, perhaps largely through the tradition of orally transmitting knowledge from one generation to another, with no critical discussion between the teacher and the pupil. Even in the *Bhagavad-Gita*, we find Arjuna asking critical questions in the early stages:

> Jy ā yasl cet karmaynaste mat ā buddhirjan ā rdana;
> Tat kim karmani ghore m ā m niyojayasi kesava.

Vy ā misreneva v ā kyena buddhim mohayaslva me;
Tadekam vada niscitya yena sreyo hamapnuyam. (III. 1, 2)
(If you hold, 'O' Janardana, that knowledge is superior to action, why, then, 'O' Kesava, do you engage me in this terrible action? With these apparently contradictory words you seem to confuse my understanding. Therefore tell me definitely that one thing by which 1 shall reach the highest goal.)

But later this critical attitude does not remain, although Lord Krishna Himself at the end does not insist that Arjuna follow his dictates : he says, *Yathecchasi tatha kuru* (Do as you please).

Our ancient tradition of accepting guru's sayings uncritically perhaps has not encouraged the scientific discipline. This may very well have been the reason why very few of our ancient manuscripts contain descriptions that would conform to the scientific discipline. I give an example.

As the late M.N. Saha pointed out, almost all the Hindu calendars are based on Vedic traditions, enunciated for example in the *Vedanga Jyotisa*. Various time scales are found in the *Puranas*, of which the time scale giving the day of Brahma as 4.32 billion years is intriguing. This duration is derived as made of 1,000 cycles of the four *yugas*, each cycle taking 12,000 divine years, with one divine year equal to 360 human years. The final answer of 4.32 billion years is amazingly close to the present geologically estimated age of the Earth, 4.6 billion years. Is this a coincidence? Or did the ancients know about dating the Earth and other astronomical objects whose ages are presently estimated in the 10-20 billion years range?

Unfortunately a scientific account is lacking and one must only conjecture. In this context an astronomical interpretation is given by S.R.N. Murthy in an article recently reproduced. Murthy points out that the above time scale and others, shorter and longer, were obtained in the *Suryasiddhanta* (one of the five *siddhantas* by Varahamihira) from the then available information on the rate of precession of the equinoxes. If so, the time scale of 4.32 billion years is related to celestial mechanics and not to the nuclear age determinations of the Earth and the Stars.

Clearly allusions to cosmic phenomena in the ancient Indian literature are in many respects similar to the present speculations about the cosmos. This in itself does not justify the claim that the ancients knew all about modern science. For testing such a claim one needs quantitative details about the cosmos in ancient literature, which are sadly lacking. What we have, however, gives us glimpses into the profundity of ancient thinking, Like Dr Karan Singh, I too like to speculate on how far the ancient thinking on the cosmos went. I wish him a long, happy and intellectually satisfying life ahead, and many fruitful speculations about the cosmos!

□□□

Politics, Religion and Interculturality

•

R. Panikkar

Professor R. Panikkar, Professor Emeritus at the University of California, U.S.A., has extensively researched and dealt with the subject of interculturality in his lectures and writings presented at various fora and institutions of learning around the world. He offers this presentation, "to the friend these reflections on a topic about which he has proved to be experienced both in theory and practice."

"Dr. Karan Singh is a politician. We should cease to give a pejorative meaning to this word. Politics is the art and science concerned with the welfare of the polis, the city, the human community. And for this one should not put aside spirituality and not even mysticism. On the contrary, the concern for society puts our spirituality in focus and the mystical insight makes of the political activity a sacred act."

Interculturality is not just cultural tourism —*i.e.*, becoming aware that other cultures more or less exotic also exist and also have something to say. [1]Knowledge of the other is important for self-knowledge, but it is not knowing my neighbour as an *other*, for the simple reason that my neighbour does not know himself as other, but as *self*. Our knowledge of the other is *our* knowledge *of* the other. It is not knowing *that* self which does not know itself as other. Briefly, interculturality is not to be confused with my knowledge of *other* cultures, nor it is simply a matter of absorbing within today's predominant culture all the riches present in other cultures: it is not of plundering the spiritual riches of others as in the past they were plundering material riches. We cannot ignore the fact that the dominating myth of the western culture has crept into the most hidden archetypes of modern thinking which may be well represented by the symbol of development. Interculturality is rather a process of mutual fecundation and of learning from other cultures without losing one's own identity.

2. *On the other hand, multiculturality does not exist.*

The moment I speak, I speak *a* language, thereby transmitting an entire culture, even if sometimes fragmented and still in the making.

Interculturality is not a matter of amplifying my sphere of knowledge, but of changing the very categories in which I think. I must learn to use the other's "categories" if I am to see his reality, and, ultimately, my own reality more deeply. It is therefore a change of lenses and not of perspective. It is not just that I need geographical or cultural broadening, it is a matter of trying to see with other people's eyes, in order to have a more complete vision of reality. We cannot remain closed in ourselves.

3. It is here that I introduce what I call *the metapolitical*. It is linked to the awareness of the inadequacy of our political categories. Not only are our categories inadequate, but the very modern notion of the political itself may be inadequate. This affirmation that politics, as it is commonly understood severed from religion, has failed, must be completed with the statement that religion too, as it is commonly understood, has failed.

Revelation is not *only* that of Mount Sinai, the Himalayas, the desert or somewhere else in the past. Ecology for instance reveals today something transcendent: there is no future for historical humanity if we continue to pursue present policies. This does not mean at all that we should break with tradition. On the contrary, only deepening the traditional wisdoms we shall be able to widen them.

I would like to offer one historical and one contemporary example of the metapolitical, by describing the failure of politics and religion when they constitute themselves as separate entities.

The historical example (simplified as much as possible) is the split between religion and politics in the West some fifteen centuries ago. For the ancients the fullness of Man included the political. Man is not an isolated individual. Without the *polis*, no truly human being can exist: there can be no salvation without politics. The *polis*, of course, has its Gods and temples. The metapolitical is not only power of making decisions, it is the art and science of finding possible ways for living the fullness of the human being, who is not satisfied with mere satisfaction of *laukika* (mundane) desires. *Aristotle's zoon politikon* means that Man is not complete without politics. This is why politics was not separate from religion and religion from politics. The Gods were the Gods of the city. When people displaced themselves, they took their Gods along, a piece of their land and founded a new city. There is no human identity without political and religious identity. It should be obvious that I take both religion and politics in their deeper and not sectarian sense.

The example that I would like to quote is that of Saint Augustinus. He believed, like everybody at that time, that Man cannot reach salvation without the *polis*, but the Roman empire was in the process of crumbling and Augustinus found that for an immense part of the population of the Roman empire (women, slaves, strangers, the poor) they had no possible full human life — that is, without political rights. It was then that Augustinus proposed his theory of the "two cities". It was the only way to instil hope in people. Heaven was well known before him, but he said that it is the question of citizenship, the *politeuma*, the human fullness lies elsewhere not in an apolitical heaven but in a heavenly *city*, the *civitas Dei*, as opposed to or at least distinct from the *civitas* of the political order of his time. This is the beginning of the cleavage that henceforward will manifest itself in the West: Politics only an earthly affair and religion for the other world. To be sure, when this was interpreted in the opposite direction, cæsaropapisms and totalitarianism of all sorts did arise, remedies that are worse than the evil that was being opposed. *Secularity* (not secularism) today means the effort at re-establishing anew the union between these two aspects of human life, which for centuries have schizophrenically gone their own way. This is the question of the non-dualistic relationship between religion and politics. We don't need to delve into the past. I am thinking of what will happen to the lakhs of villages of India, Brazil, etc. emigrating into slums of the modern *megalopolises* which are no longer *poleis*.

I am convinced that our categories, even when reformed, are

no longer of service. As an example I may give the modern cliche of "development." We seem not to have the courage to dispense with this word and so we qualify it by speaking of hard development, soft development, development of advanced technologies, sustainable, controllable, scientific, artistic and you name it.

We should ask ourselves, what are the anthropological presuppositions of the word? Is Man a developing animal? Does *purusa* or *homo* means that? What would happen if, instead of "development", we were to say "countries on the way to awakening" or "on the way to realization"?

I am criticising the extrapolation of the concept of development to other cultures. I oppose the universalization of that category. Besides, I fear that "development" is becoming a cancer, also in the developed world. When one loses homeostasis, to speak a medical language, then the cancerogenous proliferation of development begins.

Even the positive concept of development rests upon a perspective which is quite particular to our times. I am opposed to turning this word into a more or less universal symbol. I have spoken of awakening, of realization, I could have said growth, which is not necessarily development.

Dr. Karan Singh has been in political posts of great responsibility and knows how difficult it is to keep peace in the midst of the political tensions of our times — or of all times for that matter.

I offer to him here these *nava sûtrâni* on *Peace and Politics*

1. *Peace is human participation in the rhythm of reality.* This is why the dualistic separation between the *pax spiritualis* of so-called religious people, and the *pax civilis* of the socio-political milieu, is deadly. The relationship between these two aspects is an *ontonomic* one — an ontological harmony.

2. *Politics is the art and science of managing public life in order to make possible the bonum commune of citizens in view of the fullness of human life.* The problem here concerns the criteria and principles according to which this art and science are realized. For long millennia, the prevalent myth was that the ultimate principle that governs public life was a transcendental reality, person or system, that governs the common good — generally represented by the *râjâ*, the monarch, the emperor and the like. There has been an evolution of that myth, up to the present forms of democracy.

The mythical value of God has disappeared and instead the word People was installed and democracy was born. But in fact, nowadays we have a substitution of the *demo-cracy* by *techno-cracy*. What has the power (*kratos*) is not the people (*demos*) but technology. Democracy is substituted by technocracy. The *demos* knows nothing of the complexities of bioenergy, biochemistry, molecular biology, national defence, atomic armaments, the laws of modern agriculture—hence the people cannot make responsible decisions, it must rely on someone. And that someone, if he is a politician, is not a scientist, if he is a scientist, he is not a political scientist, so that finally one must rely on those structures that have their own autonomy, which is where the power of the present technology lies: in economy. I recall that a few years ago, during one of those recurring crises which endanger the present order, two presidents (of France and the United States), one chancellor (of Germany) and the head of the Kremlin, within a time span of 15 days, said that they would like to start a substantial disarmament but they *could* not. The majority of the people wanted it, but it would appear that technocracy makes democracy impossible.

3. *There is conflict between the common good of one tribe* (people, nation, state) *and that of another*, because of the plurality of cultures that I have mentioned. The common good of one need not be the common good of the other. We should not fall into idealisms, and hold that what is good for us is agreeable to all. True politics begins with the acknowledgement of conflict, of the tension between what is acceptable to me and what is acceptable to the other.

As long as cultural diversity (I mean culture, not folklore) was respected, there could be a creative polarity. But with a uniformized and homogeneous world the equilibrium is broken. A unique rational pattern of thinking and uniform "world order" cannot tolerate diversity. We cannot tolerate that 2 + 2 = 5.

Once the cosmic rhythms are broken by the continual acceleration of technology, there are no resources for all. We spend more energy than the earth can recycle.

This brings me to the formulation of a tragic law: within the present technocratical system: a *microsocial progress entails a macrosocial regression*. Any modern positive *technological* project in Kerala will have negative repercussions in some other part of the world. Once the limits are reached, and the earth is not the *Ersatz* for an infinite God, any "progress" somewhere will bring about a "regression" somewhere else. Since over thirty years we are witnessing that the rich people become richer and the poor poorer. And this is not question of good boys, bad boys: it is inbuilt in the system. One needs only to recall the technical fact that, the modern technological cultivation of one hectare of rice, uses 15 times more irrecoverable energy units than the numbers of calories that a hectare of rice will produce. Moreover, those who cultivate rice without having recourse to that infrastructure that impoverishes the earth fifteen times more, cannot sell their rice, because on the market the other one is cheaper. The Common European Market's subsidies to European agriculture are one of the causes of famine in other parts of the world — since the African agriculture, for instance, cannot compete in the world market, and Africa has even to import food .Once the rhythms are broken, it is not possible to re-establish a just equilibrium for all. We are paying heavily for the neglect of philosophy in schools and universities.

4. *This conflict is not only one of economics or power, it is also cultural, religious and cosmological.*

Taking interculturality seriously, not simply as a matter of recognizing the fact that Indians, Aztecs and Mayas have different *conceptions* of the world, but that they live in a truly other world. Theirs is not a different view of the world, but a different world. If we do not reach that awareness, we remain prisoners of our monistic perspectives or of our cryptokantianism that permeates the present modern and technocratic culture, and not only the western one. The epigones of Kant believe that there is "a thing in itself", a cosmos in our case, of which each has his own vision. This is a monocultural conception. There exist worlds that are different, This conflict of kosmologies (cosmology is only the scientific one) is the ultimate cause of the present crisis. One cannot deal with the present challenges with only a single conception of the universe and hence of Man. And here the religious contribution looms indispensable.

5. *The political can be, neither the sole nor the supreme instrument of peace.* Each political position is limited to a certain milieu and has no universal criteria. The theories of a universal market, a world bank, world government, of democracy for all, are simply well intentioned models of a colonialist mentality — the essence of colonialism being monoculturalism.

When I oppose a world government, 1 am not opposing a universal harmony or being against better communication between people.

We must seek together a middle way between solipsism, which means enclosure, and a world government that would put everything and everyone in the same bag. I am not envisaging a tower of Babel but small cottages where people could communicate on the human scale and eventually attain communion - which is always personal. This could begin to be realizable, if in one's approach to these enormous problems, we were not to rely only and exclusively on *logos*, and on that which orients us towards a rational world government, but at the same time on *mythos*, whose acceptance liberates us from the necessity of many controls and laws. Here is an example. One of the prevailing myths today is that human flesh is not to be eaten. It has become a myth — in the sense in which I use the word myth — and a world police is not required to ensure that in their apartments, people are not eating other people. Such a behaviour is not the fruit of a *logos*, but of an accepted *mythos*.

Naturally, each epoch has its myths. One should attain a myth that allows for a *respublica universalis* without a world government with its police control. This requires another kind of relationship between regions.

This requires again the recognition that what brings people together is not equality of opinions, but the acceptance of a superior instance. And here again religion appears.

6. *Neither religion nor politics can separately be the unique or supreme instrument of peace*; for the simple reason that Man is a unity and both politics and religion deal with the whole Man and not a part of it. In other words, *homo politicus* and *homo religiosus* are inseparable — although we must intellectually distinguish between religion and politics. The healthy separation between Church and State should not be confused with the apartheid between Religion and Life. An exclusively otherwordly religion becomes irrelevant for this world; and a solely worldly politics does not have any grasp on people and has no other alternative than to have recourse to the dictatorship (camouflaged as it may be) of those in power.

The *hieros gamos* or sacred marriage between the two (should I have said *maithuna*?) without dominion of the one over the other excludes any confusion (monism) and any separation (dualism). The wisdom of *advaita* is here paramount.

Religion entails the awareness of ultimacy, the dimension of depth, be transcendence or immanence, and the way to attain that goal. Now if we make a dichotomy between politics and religion, if we amputate the political from our humanness, from that belief that, in spite of everything, the other is worthy at least of interest, and maybe of love, and that he carries an aspect of reality which may seem quite negative to me, but which, however, exists and which I must accept, there is no peace possible on earth. That is why the relationship between religion and politics is not a dualistic one, as if each were on its own; this would convert religion into superstition and reduce the political to a sheer power of utilizing means within a particular dominant myth. This is a distortion of both religion and politics. The â*dhibhautika*, the â*dhidaivika* and the â*dhyâtmika* belong together, yet without confusion.

7. *Peace is the fruit of metapolitical-religious harmony*, which implies renouncing all sovereignty, political as well as religious, renouncing any world system, conceptual, political or religious. Harmony is not a concept, it is a symbol. Harmony is that non-dualistic relationship between various factors, elements or components of a whole. In harmony — and this presents a serious problem for the mind, but not for the heart—there is no monarch, no supreme principle, no monotheism, no chief. Harmony is contrary to every reduction of reality, or even of small realities to a supreme principle. This harmony (last *mantra* of the *Rig Veda*, incidentally) is what I would call trinitarian, cosmotheandric or advaitic spirituality.

8. *The proper instrument for peace is dialogue.* War begins with the rupture of dialogue. Dialogue can be used as a weapon or as appertaining to human nature. The former is dialectical, the latter dialogical, and that is why it needs a constant 'recreation', it is never finished, always open and provisional. Reality itself is polar. It is not a matter of dreaming about an idyllic paradise where everyone thinks the same thoughts and has the same convictions. The great challenge of our times is to pass from a culture of war to a culture of peace. The political instrument of this peace is dialogue, which is the wisdom of being constantly open to the dialogical dialogue as constitutive of reality itself. Reality is not a

thing.

A difficulty arises when trying to realize the dialogical dimension of the political we face the intolerant. This is where, echoing Gandhi, if I am not a saint, I am a bad politician. If, contrary to all dialectical laws, I do not leave the door open to the fanatic, the intolerant, the fundamentalist, I too entrench myself in my position and allow the alleged enemy to dictate the terms of our encounter in the battlefield. If a relationship is truly relational, it does not cease because one of the two closes up. Only the powerful can say: if he does not want to talk with me, let him go away. I have seen the reaction of thosc who havc no voice: how they suffer, endure exploitation, because they can survive only if they let others reject them. I remember many situations where the only way to survive for an exploited poor villager consists in accepting the injustice silently — and provisionally, otherwise he will be crushed . Here is where the politician should speak and act. The openness to dialogue means that we believe in the interconnectedness of everything with everything: *sarvam*, *sarvâtmakam*, *pratîtyasamutpâda*, *perichôrêsis*. It means the awareness, the *anubhava* I would say, of something that all traditions have seen, without the need of a television screens. What is the idea of the mystical body of Christ, of *dharmakâya*, of *sambogakaya*, of the body of *dharma*, of the body of Buddha: even of *karman* ?

9. *Peace requires the acknowledgement of pluralism.* Pluralism does not mean indifference to the claims of truth, but the awareness that the *satyasya satyam* transcends us. Pluralism means the experience of contingency. The relativity of pluralism has nothing to do with the relativism of the agnostic. Truth itself is pluralistic because it is relational and one of the poles of the relation touches the human shore.

Pluralism implies the insight that we are part and parcel of reality and not outside or above it. And even more, in the warp and woof of the real the I-Thou polarity is constitutive of reality itself — so I read the *tat tvam asi*, incidentally. Political pluralism may be easier than religious pluralism, but here is where these two factors of human existence could fecundate each other.

I remember well many years ago Karan Singh generously offering me a small place to live in the Dashâshamedh Ghât in Vâranâsi for my life of *tapasvin*, although I settled for years in a quieter Siva temple at Hanumanghât, until *Pûsan*, invited me to renounce renunciation as my *svadharma*. He understood, as not so many had, the next steps of my life and we kept an enduring friendship reinforced by our many meetings in India and abroad. We were all engaged in the interreligious dialogue for peace — which I called intrareligious, since we need to discover the religiousness of the others in our own hearts.

I met Karan Singh once by sheer chance at the entrance of the anthropological museum of Mexico City. With our long standing familiarity, and seeing him alone, I said "What are you doing here?", to which he smiling rebounded the same question to me. We felt as two guilty children: we both had "escaped", he from official and I academic "duties", not as tourists, not as scholars, but just as two human beings who knew that we have much to learn from the wisdom of other ancient cultures...

---

1. I have dealt extensively on this topic. I may refer to: "Non-dualistic Relations Between Religion and Politics". *Religion and Society,* Bangalore, XXV/3, Sept. 1978: "The Myth of Pluralism: The Tower of Babel—A Meditation on Non-Violence", *Cross-Currents,* New York, XXIX, 2, 1979, pp. 197-230; *Cultural Disarmament, The Way to Peace,* Louisville Kentucky, (Westminster John Knox), 1995: "Religion, Philosophy and Culutre", *Interculture,* Montreal, Oct. 1998, Issue 135; "The Pluralism of Truth", *World Faiths Insight* (New York & London), XXVI, Oct., pp. 7-16; "Nine Sutras on Peace", *Interculture,* Montreal, Winter 1991, Issue 110, pp. 49-56; "The Discovery of the Metapolitical", *Interculture,* Montreal, April 1999, Issue 136; *El espiritu de la politica,* Barcelone (Peninsula), 1999, and many others where I have expanded on the topic only indicated here.

The World in Transition 'Being' in the 'Making'

Aster Patel

Mrs. Aster Patel's is a voice from Auromadele, Auroville where the concept of a universal city is under evolution following the footsteps of Sri Aurobindo and the Mother, both close to Dr. Karan Singh's heart and mind.

"Among those who thus wait—in a conscious manner, aware of the singularity of the moment—is a personage in whose honour this volume is being brought out. In the depths of silence, together we anticipate......"

Our lives are a saga of 'beings in the making' We often speak of a world that is in transition—the world that is changing too fast, too rapidly. Not only in terms of technology, but of ideology—in the sense and meaning of life that we hold, as individuals, as nations, as a world community of people.

Not only is the pace of this change imbued with another kind of 'movement', but the fact of 'change' is in a process of re-defining itself. It has become 'radical' in its contours, in its direction towards different goals. Change appears to be leading towards something called 'transmutation'—with new possibilities emerging. But transmutation of what? Of the world? Of our surroundings, Of the means at our disposal? Or, of *ourselves*, as such?

Transmutation of ourselves, as beings! For everything is inextricably inter-twined. No longer can being and nature be seen as separate—as subject and object. All is laced together and functions or dis-functions as 'one'. But the centre seems to be in 'ourselves'—as 'beings'.

And this 'being' seems to be in a process of transmutation-not change, that is slowly wrought about by circumstance or otherwise. But a transmutation working itself out in the very stuff of what we know as ourselves. A being, *re*-moulded, cast a new! All its layers—the inner and upto the most outer—are sort of 'kneaded' together till the distinction and separateness between the inner and the outer no longer remains. A curious process—that blends all into one continuum.

Even 'life' and 'death'—or, all that is 'beyond' what we know as 'life'—merge into a strange cycle of experience, the experience of Reality. The many dimensions of the Real are like a stairway—one traverses them, one step or rather one 'field' leading into the other. There isn't a 'break'. There is a *piercing* through, a going through, different orders of 'densities', of lightneses, of hues—but there is a curious, inexplicable continuity. It is like travelling through many dimensions—all of them conscious, though in different ways. Till one reaches a kind of 'expanse'—Where all *is*.

And, then, one returns to what we know as the 'world'! The world of material moorings, of interactions, of necessities as we call them. The world of sensibilities, of ideas—if they are still around!—of technology, of our 'tools' of living.

But where is the 'fact' of livings in all this? They have to discover their relationship in this new experience. This re-discovery will possibly create the new being in us—the transmutation we talked about earlier. It is too soon to say with any definiteness—for the process is active and on-going. And the results are in the making but nowhere visible.

The 'absoluteness' present *in* things and wanting to reveal itself to our experience, the vast and the eternal merging with the small and the ephemeral—is this the burden this process carries?

The light that is on the heights seems to be also in the depths—the depths of our life *in* matter. A 'Whole' of existence given in experience? The Real given to us as one continuum? Is it from such experience that will emerge the new being?

Eternality in out moments—death revealing other dimensions of the experience of the One Reality....

One awaits-since all is in process. What is the being in the chrysalis going to be like?

Such are our times. Not repetitive of the old—but creating something totally new. Not known, altogether unforeseen.

Among those who thus wait—in a conscious manner, aware of the singularity of the moment—is a personage in whose honour this volume is being brought out.

In the depths of silence, together we anticipate. . .

❑❑❑

Truly A Prince Among Men

•

Syed Mir Qasim

Syed Mir Qasim, former Chief Minister of Jammu and Kashmir, really came into close contact with Dr. Karan Singh in 1953 when the Mir was inducted as a Cabinet Minister in the Ministry headed by Bakshi Ghulam Mohammad.

"Dr. Karan Singh firmly believes that Kashmir is the bone of contention between India and Pakistan and the dispute has caused immense distress and suffering for the people of Kashmir. In his opinion it has become a 'sore issue' for India though Pakistan prefers to call it a 'core issue'. The solution of the problem can be found only through a process of open-minded dialogue among all parties concerned."

Birthday greetings are customary. But occasion acquires a special quality when it marks the biblical stage of three score and ten. Even more special when those years represent a highly distinguished career and outstanding personal accomplishments.

To wish Dr. Karan Singh a happy 70th birthday and many more years of success and fulfillment I feel happy and proud. I feel the pride because we are sons of the same soil, the State of Jammu & Kashmir, and share the same kind of love for our countrymen and humanity at large. I have watched him for half a century during which he has been Regent of J&K then *Sadar-i-Riyasat* (elected by the J&K Constituent Assembly), later as Governor. Coming on the national scene he became a Cabinet Minister and later Indian Ambassador to the United States. I have no hesitation in saying that in every capacity he has acted with dignity and brought honour to every post he held.

Dr. Karan Singh is widely known and respected not only in India but also abroad. He is a rare combination of scholarship and spirituality. Not only has he drunk deep at the profound wisdom of Hindu scriptures but has also developed a keen sense of music and appreciation of various fine arts. He has written books on history of Kashmir. His books on religion reflect an approach intended to harmonize different beliefs as a measure of developing a civilized society.

I have known him closely since 1953 when I was inducted, for the first time, as a Cabinet Minister in the Ministry headed by Bakshi Ghulam Mohammad. I have found him a true gentleman, frank in opinion, candid in expression. His integrity is never in doubt. Even when one differs from his opinion, genuineness of his concern can never be suspect. His attachment to religion is more spiritual than community-centred which makes him totally free from any sectarian feelings. His deeply humane and realistic approach has won him respect of all sections of the diverse population of J & K State. If he has headed the management of Vaishno Devi Temple, Katra and Raghunath Temple of Jammu his respect and devotion for the Hazrat Bal Shrine in Srinagar and Dargah of Sheikh Nuruddin at Charar-e-Sharif is also well known. It was possible for him to visit the Hazrat Bal mosque in most complex and critical situations—at the time of the disappearance (or displacement) of the Prophet's hair in 1964 and later when the shrine had been intruded upon by militants. All this is a tribute to catholicity of his religious attitude.

His approach to the affairs of J&K is quite realistic. He feels proud that his fore-fathers brought together people of different religions and cultures, speaking different languages. At the same time he is aware of the problems and tensions that this diversity presents. He values the importance of maintaining the state's unity as in 1947 as a major contributory factor for developing a secular culture and for that he recommends genuine distribution of power among various regions of the state.

He is sometimes blamed for being partial to Jammu but I think the criticism is unfair. My impression is that he is generally in favour of a federal structure in the whole country in which there is equal devolution of powers to all regions. His advice had played a decisive role in the decision to appoint the Gajendragadkar Commission for distribution of powers among the various regions of J&K State. It is unfortunate that implementation of the Commission's recommendations did not proceed beyond some matters of immediate concern.

I have had many occasions to discuss the problems of the state and the country and found myself generally in agreement with his views. His anxiety to evolve an arrangement in the state to help people live in harmony is palpable. Though some of his suggestions in this context I found unrealistic I have never doubted that his concern is genuine. I recall a conversation at a dinner meeting with Mr. Chandra Shekhar when he was the Prime Minister. Dr. Karan Singh had pointed out the need for thoroughly going into the reasons for the resentment felt by Jammu and Ladakh regions since independence. I think he was factually correct.

In my opinion, he only faltered in deviating from just and constitutional path when he dismissed Sheikh Abdullah on the somewhat flimsy basis of differences of opinion in the Cabinet. We had not realized it then but realized soon after that it was damaging for the interests of the state and the nation as a whole. That he concurs with this opinion is evident from the wry comment that he light-heartedly makes of the use of national interest as an excuse for that unconstitutional act. "Was it in national interest that we first brought the Sheikh to power and then dismissed him? We then inducted Bakshi Ghulam Mohammad in his place and after a few years dismissed him too and put him in jail repeating the treatment we had meted out to Sheikh Abdullah earlier. Then we launched the process of reconciliation with him and brought him back as Chief Minister and subsequently withdrew support from him. After his demise we brought his son Dr. Farooq Abdullah to the helm of affairs and conspired to replace him with G.M. Shah. All this was supposed to have been done in national interest. I would like to understand what this national interest is." His query remains unanswered.

Dr. Karan Singh firmly believes that Kashmir is the bone of contention between India and Pakistan and the dispute has caused immense distress and suffering for the people of Kashmir. In his opinion it has become 'a sore issue' for India though Pakistan prefers to call it 'a core issue'. The solution of the problem can be found only through a process of open-minded dialogue among all parties concerned *i.e.*, Pakistan, India and all sections of the people of Kashmir including those in the POK areas.

As I have pointed out, his concern is not confined to any community or region of the state. Indeed he enjoys wide respect throughout the state among almost all sections. Such cross-border and cross-community regard for his person is evident from the announcement of J&K government-in-exile by JKLF President Amanullah Khan. In the announcement Dr. Karan Singh's name was mentioned as cabinet Minister in the proposed set-up.

He is highly sensitive to the suffering of people. I was struck by this trait of his when he responded frankly to my protest and dislike for the coercive methods used for family planning during the Emergency. He was the Health Minister and felt unhappiness at his helplessness in the matter as some chief ministers were damaging a nationally beneficial policy for exhibiting unwarranted zeal to show results, quite often fake.

□□□

West Must Relearn Spiritual Knowledge From the Orient

•

Kathleen Raine

Prof. Kathleen Raine of Temenos Academy, London, even at 92 is deeply involved in teaching the 'perennial philosophy', the Sanatana Dharma. She typed out her presentation personally.

"How fortunate I have been in meeting the elite of India's golden age, and how fortunate London has been in having Dr. L.M. Singhvi here as 'our' High Commissioner for six years. I hope that Karan Singh has many years before him and that his contribution to the spiritual well-being of the world—'the politics of eternity' as Yeats's friend, the mythical poet and painter A.E. called it. My own life entered at the age of seventy when I first set foot on the Indian soil, a new beginning."

I visited India for the first time when I was already over seventy (I was born in 1908) as the guest of the Government of India, in order to give the inaugural lecture of the Yeats Society founded in Delhi by Santosh Pall, of whose Doctorate thesis I had been the external examiner. Thus, from the first I was introduced into the company of India's finest minds—and in India the intellectual and the national elite are the same people. In the nineteen-eighties these were still the people who had seen, and participated in, the struggle for Independence and the afterglow of a Golden Age was still in the air, Gandhiji's memory was still a living presence, and his grandson Dr. Ramchandra Gandhi was one of the first friends I made in India. Kamaladevi Chattopadhyay, who had spent eight years of her life in prison under the British was one of the first people I met. Uncrowned queen as she was, she was the founder of the Indian Government's support of crafts, of women's organisations and founder of a museum for theatre artifacts of all kinds—puppets, and masks—where crafts-people still produce such things. She more than anyone has left her mark on modern India. I met Pupul Jayakar, founder of the fine craft centre in Delhi where, again, crafts-people are able to both make and sell their goods. The great scholar, Kapila Vatsyayan, creater of the Indira Gandhi National Centre for the Arts, now the world-centre and source of Indian studies, took the chair of my first lecture on Blake in the India International Centre.

Thus, plunged into India at the deep end I knew nothing of the recent history of modern India which had made Karan Singh one of the outstanding statesmen and thinkers of that distinguished world. I had been in India for less than a week, when Karan Singh invited me to visit him, and I met for the first time the hereditary heir to the throne of Kashmir whose striking presence lent credence to his family claim to descent from the Sun, whose warmth and radiance is outpoured over the Sub-continent. What I discovered at once was Karan Singh's great love and knowledge of poetry and the eloquence with which he quoted from memory the English Romantic poets, not least from Yeats. I knew nothing at that time of the recent events in Indian history which had made the young heir apparent of the Maharaja of Kashmir first a protege of Nehru, then at the age of eighteen Regent of Jammu and Kashmir, and thereafter Governor until 1965, when he entered Parliament, he has since held a number of important Cabinet posts, and become an eminent and honoured statesman of contemporary India, and a romantic presence in the world.

In his boyhood, Karan Singh suffered from a long-standing muscle atrophy of his right hip, which finally made it necessary for him to go to New york for treatment. Thus, he came to know the West, and his increasing concerns with aspects of global unity at a spiritual level. He has presented the Satchitanand Ashram for the study of Sri Aurobindo's 'integral yoga' at Buckingham, Virginia with a seven-foot statue of the Lord Shiva. He has in his house a puja-room in which symbols of the various world *i.e. faiths* are present. At a conference in Switzerland which we both attended Dr. Karan Singh's great charm and eloquence brought the presence of India to the heart of the West - one cannot but feel, when he rises to speak, that he speaks as 'India' in the Shakespearean sense in which a character speaks as 'Burgundy' or 'Kent' or some other name of his country. He has spoken, on visits to England, for my own Organization,, and on my last visit to India for a joint conference between Temenos and the IGNCA. None of us will forget the eloquence with which he described to us the significance of the symbols of Shiva Nataraj. It has given me great delight to receive a letter from him (dated July 17th 2000) in appreciation of my Millennial Hymn to the Lord Shiva published in *Vihangama,* the journal of the IGNCA.

Karan Singh has always been deeply supportive of our work, which is concerned with teaching the 'perennial philosophy' - the *sanatana dharma* - in its many forms, in accordance with Blake's teaching that 'all religions are one' - the religion of the Imagination. He as a Fellow of Temenos Academy has lectured for us, and several times contributed to our Journal. Believing as I do that the time has come when the materialist West must re-learn spiritual knowledge from the Orient (*ex oriente lux*) - and India has been, and remains, the mainstream of spiritual civilization, I value above all, our links with India. I know that no one shares this belief more sincerely than does Karan Singh, and on my many visits to Indian since that first memorable meeting, he and Asha have always welcomed me with warmth and supportive friendship

He invited me to visit Kashmir, and later offered my Organisation, the Temenos Academy, a place in Jammu for a conference. (He was for many years himself Chancellor of the University of Jammu and Kashmir.) sadly this was never to be, for those beautiful lands, from time immemorial scenes of India's epic poetry— and indirectly of Shelly's *Prometheus unbound* have been overtaken by the turmoil and torment of war, from which Karan has no power to save his beloved country.

I soon discovered that Karan Singh was a devotee of Lord Shiva whose symbolic trident headed his writing-paper, and he was already moving increasingly from participation in 'the politics of time' to the 'politics of eternity'. This too— unlike the West— is the rule rather than the exception in India, all my Indian friends, active in academic and in political life, meditate regularly and many are devotees of some Teacher, as Ramu Gandhi to Ramana Maharashi. Some of these masters have themselves been political activists, like Swami Hariharji Maharaj, who was a member of Gandhiji's first Congress, and who has since dedicated his life to the promotion of the *Bhagavad Gita* and founding schools based on its teaching. Sri Aurobindo, revered Teacher and author of many books of philosophy, was in his youth a political activist. Karan Singh recently became President of the Sri Aurobindo Ashram at Auroville. My old friend Arabinda Basu, a devotee of Sri Aurobindo, was for some years Reader in Philosophy at Durham. He it was who conferred on Karan Singh his Doctorate in philosophy, the title by which he chooses to be known.

With his own long experience of being a reigning Prince, he never fails to ask after, and send good wishes to, our patron, the Prince of Wales, himself a dedicated seeker for spiritual truth.

Another of Karan Singh's activities lies close to my heart, his work for the Indian Board of Wildlife, and above all his work for the preservation of the tiger. My friend, the artist Thetis Blacker, who accompanied me on my first visit to India, says she would not want to live in a world in which there were no tigers. And how can I, as a Blake scholar, fail to have reverence for that tiger 'burning bright', who is the glory of India?

□□□

Kanchi, Kashmeer and Sri Karan Singh

•

Jagatguru Sri Sankaracharya

Jagatguru Sri Sankaracharya Swamigal in a rare and benedictory felicitation sent from Kancheepuram, the exalted seat of His Holiest, has referred to a letter from H.H. Major General Sri Pratap Singh, Maharaja of Jammu and Kashmir, Dr. Karan Singh's grand father, to the Sankaracharya's Mutt on November 23, 1917, whose text is reproduced below:

"I have much pleasure in acknowledging receipt of your circular letter dated the 11th November 1917 forwarding therewith a printed copy of the Memorandum with its covering letter forwarded by the mutt to the Secretary of State for India & H.E. then Viceroy and Governor General of India regarding the Indian Postwar Reform Scheme which will receive my consideration."

"Sankaracharya Caritam" is a succinct biography of Sri Sankara Bhagavatpadacharya, written in Sanskit by Govindanatha a scholar of Kerala. Manuscript copies of this work exist in the Palace Library and in the Curator's at Trivandram (Kerala) and also in the India Office Library in London. This biography was at first printed in the Mangalodayam Press at Tiruchur (Kerala). In 1966, the work was again printed at the Geeta Press in Tiruchur and published by Divakaran Nambudri, a scholar of Tirupunitura (Kerala). This author of Sanka Caritam is ascribed to the latter half of the 17th Century, A.D. This work contains 561 verses, divided into nine chapters. The first two verses of Chapter IX are as follows:

सर्वज्ञशिष्यसंवुक्इझाकरो देशिकेश्वरः।
भूमिं प्रदक्षिणीकृत्य भूयः काच्चीपुरं गतः।।
जम्बूद्वीपस्य कुर्वाणे शोभां भारतमण्डले।
शास्तं काश्मीरनामानं देशं विद्योतभद्भृशम्।।

The first verse above states that Sankara after touring all over the country again reached Kañchipuram. The second verse speaks of Kañchi as a flourishing city and as having the name 'Kasmir also. Here a poet from the extreme south of India writes about Kásmir of the extreme North and indicates that Kañchi was also known as 'Kasmir'.

Kashmir is the Crest Jewel of our *Bharata Desa*. Kasmir, as a common noun means saffron. This strange variety of spice is produced mostly in Kashmir. Kanchi, when used as a common noun indicates a hook that joins the two ends of a metal-made ornament (belt-like) worn by women. Poet Govindanatha has perhaps hooked Kañchi with Kashmir.

Ujjvala Sánkara, the 16th Acharya of the Kañchi Sankaracharya Math, during his tour in Northern India visited and stayed in Kashmir for some time. He attained eternal bliss at Kalapuri on *Vaisakha-Sukla Ashtami* of the cycle year *Akshaya* (Kaliera-3468) *i.e.* 367 A.D. Since then Kalapuri has been known as 'Ujjvala Mahayati Pura'. This is confirmed by 2 verses found in 'Punya-Sloka-Manjari, compiled by Sarvajna Sadasiva Bodha—the fifty-sixth Acharya of Kanchi Sankara Math, (1524-1539 A.D.). The verses read as follows:

सूनुः शंकरकेशवस्य तपतीतीरो दभ्वों नैष्ठिकः।
श्रीमानच्युतकेशवः श्रितपदे वञ्चीश्वरे गीष्पतेः।
आदेशात् कृतसंयमश्च विमतानामूलमुन्मूलय-
त्राकाश्मीरमगान्महायतिरिति ख्यात्योज्ज्वलश्शंकरः।।32।।
अष्टत्रिंशदथातिवाह्य शरदः पीठे जगद्देशिक-
स्यासीद्दिग्रसवार्धिवहिनषु कलेर्यात्स्वक्षयेच्छे वृषे।

अष्टभ्यामपहषंशोकमजरं ब्रह्मैव यश्शाश्वतं
काशमीरेषु कलापुरे यदधुनाप्याख्यातेस्याख्ययां

About 1620 years ago, there lived an astronomer cum astrologer, by name Vidyavati, in Kancheepuram. He had a son who was a congenital deaf mute. In his late teens Vidyavati's son gained the power of speech and also the power to compose poetry because of the grace of Devi Kamakshi. When the boy was about nineteen years of age, Acharya Vidyaghana of the Sankaracharya Math in Kanchi got informed about the deaf-mute boy having turned into a budding poet by the grace of Devi. The Acharya sent word to the boy's parents to go over to the Math with their son. When they came the Acharya told the parents about his intention to initiate their son into the ascetic order and to nominate him as successor Acharya of the Math. The parents expressed their joy and accepted the guru's proposal. The initiation got completed in a few days. The youth was given the name '*Muka Sankara*' by the Acharya. After Vidyaghana's demise, *Muka Sankara* became Acharya in 398 A.D.

Muka Sankara made extensive tours through many parts of the country. He was greatly revered by Matrigupta, sometime ruler of Kashmir and his successor Pravarasena and by Vikramaditya (Sákari).

Abhinava Sankara, 38th Pontiff of the Sankara Math at Kañchi had been to Kashmir. He is said to have defeated in debate, Vakpati Bhatta, the greatest of the scholars in the court of the then ruler of Kashmir.

Coming to modern times, copy of a letter addressed to Sri Kañchi Sankaracharya Math from H.H. Major General Sri Pratap Singh ruler of Jammu & Kashmir, dated 23-11-1917 can be found on page 196:

The Kumbhabhishekam of the Kamakshi Temple at Kancheepuram was performed by His Holiness Sri Jayendra Saraswati Swamiji on 5th April, 1976. On this sacred occasion, His Holiness released an all comprehensive edition of Sankara Bhagavatpada's Saundaryalahari with text, nine Sanskrit commentaries, notes in English, prayoga of verses, Yantras and several illustrations. Dr. Karan Singh, has written foreword to this work. The following is an extract from that foreword:

THE PALACE.
JAMMU.

23. 11. 1917.

Dear Sir,

I have much pleasure in acknowledging receipt of your Circular letter dated the 11th November 1917 forwarding therewith a printed copy of the Memorandum with its covering letter forwarded by the Mutt to the Right Hble the Secretary of State for India & H. E. the Viceroy & Governor General of India regarding the Indian Postwar Reform scheme which will receive my consideration.

[illegible] His Holiness [illegible]

Yours faithfully,
[illegible]

Dr. Karan Singh

Manasarovar
Chanakyapuri,
New Delhi

The Maha Kumbhabhishekam of Sri Kanchi Kamakshi Ambal Temple is an event of great spiritual significance. Kancheepuram is one of the most holy cities in our great and ancient land and it has been blessed by a long line of sages coming down to the present Gurus, Sri Chandrasekharendra Swamiji and Sri Jayendra Saraswati Swamiji. It is a matter of satisfaction that on this great occasion, a new edition of Saundaryalahari, one of the masterpieces of Sri Adi Sankaracharya is being brought out . . . . I consider it a privilege to associate myself with this important publication."

"My homage on this occasion to Adi Sankaracharya. May the blessings of the Goddess Kamakshi continue to shower down on suffering humanity".

(sd.)
Dr. Karan Singh

New Delhi
March, 30, 1976

Dr. Karan Singh, is a well-read scholar, deeply mooted in our ancient heritage. His services to the country at large and to Kashmir in particular have been commendable. He stands as a distinguished entity amidst the statesmen who have strained their nerves for the betterment of the country.

May the grace of Devi Kamakshi and that of Sri Chandramouleeswara, the presiding deity of our *Peeth* grant long years of prosperous and healthy life to the former Maharaja of Kashmir.

□□□

Dr. Karan Singh's Contribution to Interfaith Dialogue

•

H.H. Sri Swami Satchidananda

His Holiness Sri Swami Satchidananda, founder of Sri Gurudev, Satchitananda Ashram and Integral Yoga Institutes in the United States, in his felicitation has talked about Dr. Karan Singh's work for the Temple of Understanding and the Interfaith movement.

"What I appreciate so much about Dr. Karan Singh, besides his great service to India, his statesmanship, his philanthropy, his extraordinary intellect and understanding of world philosophies, is his humility and his deep devotion and piety. His extraordinary character and great virtue enables him to understand that the essence of Hinduism is Sanatan Dharma, the Eternal Truth, and he sees this residing in the heart and center of all the great wisdom traditions."

I first met Dr. Karan Singh, over twenty years ago, in conjunction with the interfaith work we were engaged in. Both of us have been associated with the Temple of Understanding (of which Dr. Singh now serves as Chairman) for many years as well as other interfaith organizations. We have shared a common interest in promoting world peace through interfaith dialogue and have met regularly at these programmes as well as programmes sponsored by the Bharatiya Vidya Bhavan.

Thus, began a long and warm association that culminated in Dr. Singh's now yearly pilgrimages to Satchidananda Ashram, Yogaville since the past 10 years, where we share *bhajans*, *satsangs*, and worship at the Nataraja shrine that was established by Dr. Singh. The enchanting bronze Nataraja was shipped from Jammu and enshrined here in USA in a breathtaking setting amidst the Blue Ridge Mountains and overlooking the light of Truth Universal Shrine (LOTUS). Dr. Singh serves on our advisory committee for the LOTUS and our LOTUS Center for World Faiths. The LOTUS is unique in the world with altars for every major faith as well as altars for those less well-known and as yet unknown. The central symbol of the light or *jyothi* is a universal symbol, the one light that illumines all faith. the principle upon which the Shrine is based is: "Truth is One, Paths are Many."

What I appreciate so much about Dr. Singh, besides his great service to India, his statesmanship, his philanthropy, his extraordinary intellect and understanding of world philosophies, is his humility and his deep devotion and piety. His extraordinary character and great virtue enables him to understand that the essence of Hinduism is *Sanatana Dharma*, the *Eternal Truth*, and he sees this residing in the heart and center of all the great wisdom traditions. Dr. Singh's vision and commitment to promoting great understanding among people of all faiths has endeared him to the world's religious communities and all the major interfaith organizations.

Historically, there has been a confusion about the Interfaith movement—that its purpose is to form one universal religion. Interfaith organizations are not asking that you leave your religion to join another religion or become part of one universal religion. The Interfaith movement doesn't believe in that kind of conversion. Just because I love my mother, should I ask you to renounce your mother and only love my mother? I should know that just as I love my mother, you also love your mother. That is why in the name of Interfaith dialogue we are saying, "Let us love all our mothers." I believe Dr. Singh has helped to address this misunderstanding by his yeoman service in this field. He is able to communicate the very essence and purpose of religion and appreciation for all the diversities. This opens a very rich and inclusive dialogue and makes him a great diplomat and emissary. He engages in the work of the Temple of Understanding and in interfaith dialogue to bring people together so that they can remember the unity behind the diversity.

I particularly appreciate this aspect of Dr. Singh's life and service because I believe we are literally destroying ourselves in the name of religion. The purpose of any religion is to educate us about our spiritual unity. However, more people have been killed in the name of God and religion than in all of the natural calamities and world wars combined. That means that religion has gotten caught in the hands of egoistic groups who are fighting with each other, who are claiming that only their path is right.

We criticize each other's faiths proclaiming, "Mine is the best, yours is the worst," Even the same religious groups have splintered factions. Muslim factions in the Middle East are killing each other. It's happening everywhere. The Hindus and Buddhists are wreaking havoc in Sri Lanka. The Jews and Muslims are at each other's throats in the Middle East. Is that the purpose behind religion? Do you think our God will be happy? Because we are one in Spirit, it doesn't mean that you should renounce your own path or approach. That is not unity; that is conversion. Real unity means accepting all the various approaches, and that is what ecumenism or interfaith understanding is all about.

Dr. Singh has beautifully demonstrated in his own life how one can be loyal to one's religion, one's country, and at the same time love and respect another person's allegiances. As a great statesman and a great *bhakta*, he leads by example and demonstrates how we can love our own faith and respect another person's faith as well; there is nothing contradictory in that. You don't have to renounce one to love another. Ultimately, we all aim for the same truth while walking on different paths.

All the rivers, whatever direction they flow, with whatever speed they flow, are all running toward the ocean. They all have different names, different forms, and different colours, but originally they came from the ocean and they are going back to the ocean. Even our gutter water flows back to the ocean. The ocean doesn't say, don't come. It openly receives all the waters. Like that all the different paths are like different rivers flowing toward that one all-embracing Truth—the one Light, the one God.

There are many conferences now being organized world-wide to promote this kind of interfaith perspective and Dr. Singh has been at the forefront of many of these great gatherings. The time has come and the world has shrunk. We cannot separate ourselves and deny each other anymore because we are aware, more than ever, that we are a global village. It's time to understand each other better and to live as one global family.

When we fight in the name of religion, we divide ourselves in the name of God. This is terribly wrong. It is disconcerting enough that we separate ourselves by country, by region, by race, by language, by political beliefs, and so on. We have put labels that say, "This is my land, that's your land." We have even divided the sea, "My sea, your sea, you see?" Then we have even divided the sky, "this is our sky. Your flight should not go over our sky." How small our vision is, how little-minded we have become. We want to grab everything and label it as "ours."

When it comes to God, one will say, "Krishna is the best." Another will argue, "No, you are wrong; Jesus is the only way." Yet another will challenge, "Allah is the best." This kind of fighting is going on and on and has already killed enough people. It's not the religions or the founders of the religions—the sages and prophets who gave us these beautiful paths—that are dividing us. They want us to be together.

This is the very reason I admire Dr. Singh so much. He has been very active in politics and understands that arena completely, at the same time he has a greater vision. He realizes that we must do everything within our capacity to follow the principle that we should not and cannot divide ourselves in the name of God and religion. It is the people who make use of religion for their own benefit or political reasons, who are literally dividing humanity in the name of that which is supposed to unite us.

Truth is one. That is why my motto has always been, "Truth is One, Paths are Many." the great sages and saints have experienced the same truth but only expressed it in different ways. It does not matter, what name you give to the nameless Spirit. Because the Christians called the Spirit as Christ, they say Christ is the only way. Because Buddhists called the Spirit Buddha, they say the only way is through Buddha. The "only way" is to experience that Spirit—you are free to call it whatever you like. The only way to eternal peace and joy is to realize that Christhood or Buddhahood or Krishnahood. But when we miss that point, we fight in the name of Spirit.

God gave each of us a different costume, different makeup, a different role, in order to play our part in the world. But behind all these differences we are all one in Spirit. When we forget that and identify ourselves with the superficial differences, we lose sight of the spiritual oneness. So, religion asks us to get back to that original state. The very meaning of the word" religion" is to bind back; to get back to your original oneness.

When we argue about what is the right path and whose religion is best, there is something terribly wrong with our approach. We are looking at the superficial side of religion and forgetting to go deep into its foundation. If we did go deep, we would find that all the religions ultimately talk about the same God, the same Truth; but somehow we ignore that common base and continue to fight over the superficial aspects. It is time for us to recognize that there is one truth and many approaches.

The moment the understanding comes that essentially we are one appearing as many, all the other problems—physical and material—will be solved. Until then, they will never be solved, because the basic cause for all the world problems is the lack of understanding of this spiritual unity.

I can think of no greater tribute to this wonderful occasion of Dr. Karan Singh's 70th birthday, than to make a personal resolve to share the spirit of interfaith understanding and true sisterhood and brotherhood with one and all. In honour of Dr. Singh, let us join hands and wherever we go say, "We look different but we are all one in Spirit. Hello, brother, hello sister." We should embrace the entire universe with the understanding that God has a purpose for everybody. Nobody is superior and nobody is inferior. No religion is superior and no religion is inferior. We are all doing God's work. We should learn to live together and work toward one goal: to share and care, love and give. I cannot think of a better tribute to a great man who has nobly devoted his life to global humanitarian efforts. May God bless him, his wonderful wife, Princess Asha, and all the family with health and happiness, peace and prosperity.

❑❑❑

A Gentleman Scholar

•

K. Natwar Singh

An eminent Indian diplomat who has distinguished himself in the fields of scholarship and politics, having served once as Indian External Affairs Minister, has known Dr. Karan Singh not only as a poet-politician but also as a gentleman-scholar, the aspect he seeks to reveal quoting Machiavelli.

"I first set eyes on Karan Singh in July 1953 in Srinagar as an I.F.S. probationer. The 1953 I.F.S. batch was invited to tea by the Sadar-i-Riyasat. We spent a week in J &K. Even to our untrained minds, it appeared that all was not well in the state. Our patriotism was offended to see the Indian` flag being treated somewhat indifferently by the National Conference and Sheikh Abdullah's supporters."

To comprehend fully the nature of the people, one must be a prince, and to comprehend fully the nature of princes, one must be an ordinary citizen.

Niccola Machiavelli- 1469-1522

Few individuals have made so spectacular an entry into history as Dr. Karan Singh. At the tender age of 18 he became *Sadar-i-Riyasat* of Jammu and Kashmir. At 36 he became the youngest ever Cabinet Minister in Indira Gandhi's cabinet. To appoint him as Head of State, the Constitution had to be amended. A Governor had to be 35 years old.

His entry into the world also had a touch of class. He was born with a golden spoon in his mouth. And where was he born? In Cannes, the fashionable resort on the French Rivera, on the 9th of March 1931. The announcement of his birth was made in Srinagar by General Janak Singh, a minister in his father's government. The minister was a darbari with a sense of history. He recorded the arrival of the Heir-apparent in his diary thus:

> The 9th of March was the first bright day when the weather in Kashmir cleared after a long spell of bad winter. It was on this day that the newspapers containing the news of the Gandhi-Irwin agreement reached Srinagar. The people of Kashmir thought these happenings a good omen and believed that the future destiny of the Prince was bright.

The prince has lived to sustain the burdens of a 70th birthday, lightened by the refinements of an astonishing wide-range of interests-literary, musical, political and social. Karan Singhji carries lightly an air of cheery majesty. He is endowed with a benign nature. He gets a lot out of life and life has got a lot out of him.

As the tortuous history of Jammu and Kashmir unfolded after October 1947, Karan Singh became a participant in formidable and fateful events. In their midst he conducted himself with confidence and distinction. It really is amazing that he was not coarsened by the skilled and unceasing flattery of scores of courtiers. This odious tribe flourished and prospered in almost every Indian princely state. They were dedicated frauds and concentious intriguers.

I first set eyes on Karan Singh in July 1953 in Srinagar as an I.F.S. probationer. The 1953 I.F.S. batch was invited to tea by the *Sadar-i-Riyasat*. We spent a week in J &K. Even to our untrained minds, it appeared that all was not well in the state. Our patriotism was offended to see the Indian flag being treated somewhat indifferently by the National Conference and Sheikh Abdullah's supporters.

A few days later, on 9th August, Karan Singh took a very bold step. He dismissed the Sheikh and ordered his arrest. That act alone ensures him a place in modern Indian History.

Jawaharlal Nehru, was fond of the young *Sadar-i-Riyasat* and addressed him as Tiger or Yuvraj. On 10th August, 1953 he wrote to Karan Singh, following Abdullah's arrest:

I quite realize the great strain which you must have undergone during these few days. I think you have acted with wisdom and dignity.

In his book, "Heir Apparent", Karan Singh has this gem on these momentous events:

> I knew that what I had done was for the national good, and that all the danger and risks were worth taking if it served the country. Asha(his wife) had also sat up anxiously in her room all night. Slowly, I climbed up the steps and walked into her room. 'It is over' I said, and we both smiled. She sixteen going on seventeen, I twenty-two going on twenty-three. I was asleep almost before I hit the bed.

His book on Sri-Aurobindo was published in 1962. Nehru wrote the foreword. Karan Singh had established himself as an author at 31.

In 1967, he shifted to Delhi as a Cabinet Minister. He added colour to the Council of Ministers. I was then working in Indira Gandhi's Secretariat and saw him from time to time. After my marriage, a closer relationship developed. The houses of Kashmir and Patiala had been on friendly terms since the 1880s. My wife's grand father, Bhupinder Singhji got on well with Maharaja Hari Singh and made quite a splash when he went to Srinagar in 1926 for the investiture of Hari Singhji. He drove to Srinagar in a custom-built Rolls Royce. An English paper wrote:

> Nothing has been permitted to break the smooth flow of its graceful lines, every joint is welded, and to preserve the sweep of the body's bevelted top, the hood is completely concealed...

In 1970, the question of discontinuing the Privy Purses of the Princes acquired urgency, Dr. Karan Singh acted most honourably and kept away from the Quixotic outfit called the Concord of Princes, as did my father-in-law, Yadvendra Singhji of Patiala. Karan Singhji made a forceful statement in the Lok Sabha when the Privy Purse question was debated. He demolished the case that was made for the continuance of the Privy Purse by Dr. Karni Singh of Bikaner, himself no run of the mill parliamentarian.

Post-emergency there was a parting of ways with Indira Gandhi. About this time Karan Singhji took a wrong turning and the next 15 years saw him edged to the side lines. This did not bother him one bit. He, as usual behaved in a majestarial and stately manner, writing, lecturing, travelling and for a brief moment coming perilously close to the Sangh parivar. His inherent

Nehruism saved him and he returned to the fold. In the 1999 Lok Sabha election he gave A.B. Vajpayee a run for his money at Lucknow. His tenure as Ambassador to the USA was short but not insignificant. I had a small share in his being sent to Washington. The V.P.Singh government recalled him abruptly and unwisely. He had at one time set his heart on becoming Director General of UNESCO. He would have added lustre and brought learning to the job, but that was not to be.

Perhaps he peaked too early. I cannot but conclude that his full potential has yet to be realized. Perhaps, the wheel of fate will turn and we might still see him where he really belongs. I do not have to elaborate. For me, his friendship has meant a great deal, enriching and enlarging my life.

□□□

A Call For Dialogue: Among Civilizations and Faith Traditions

•

L.M. Singhvi

Dr. Singhvi is an eminent constitutional lawyer, Member of Parliament and is India's foremost intellectual statesman. A distinguished diplomat who served for seven years as India's High Commissioner in UK, he heads Indira Gandhi National Centre for the Arts and the High Level Committee on Persons of Indian Origin and Non-Resident Indians. He has the rank of a Central Cabinet Minister. Dr. Singhvi's article "A Call for diaologue" belongs to the area of inter-faith understanding and is based on his speech and the commitment pledge at the Plenary Session of the World Summit of Spiritual and Relgious Leaders at the U.N. in the year 2000.

"The First and final question which confronts our dialogue is: Do Religions and Spirituality have a real role to play in the prevention of conflicts and violence and in establishing durable peace. My answer is Yes and No."

The purpose of the recent Millenium Peace Summit at the United Nations was to create a world of amity and harmony so that we can fashion and construct a more inclusive world of goodwill, understanding, reciprocity, mutual respect and peace on Planet Earth. The Call to

Dialogue at the Summit was meant to look at the future of our faiths and the faith of the future in the light of the Past and the awareness of the Present.
A Call to Dialogue at the Summit was a call for building bridges between different faith traditions, to build defences of peace in the minds of men, women and children and to rediscover and reclaim our innate and intrinsic spirituality at a critical juncture in human history. That dialogue was in a sense, our moment of Truth, our Pledge of Peace, our Tryst with Destiny.

II

The tradition of dialogues itself is SACRED in India and is the foundation of human civilizations everywhere. In India at the dawn of human history, a perrenial *dialogue of the spirit* became a way of life. The Vedic and the Sramaṇa traditions of Dialogue go back to about seven to ten millenna. The *Upanishads*, the Jain Agamas and the Buddhist Jatakas are the finest and the most fragrant flowers of spiritual, philosophical, ethical and religious Dialogues. Equally so were the ancient traditions of dialogue in Socratic Greece and in Judaism, Zorastrianism and Christianity.

Many millenna ago, the Vedic, the Jain and the Buddhist worldview proclaimed that Truth was one, but it had many facets, many routes and many interpretations. The ancient Indian tradition celebrated the diversities of thought through a philosophy of pluralism and tolerance based on Non-Violence as the Supreme Religion. The composite creed and culture of Non-Violence, Compassion, Tolerance, Pluralism and Reverence for life arose in the quest of Peace and has become the living legacy of the best in the faith traditions in India.

III

In response to the Call to Dialogue at the UN Summit, we must recall the resonance of Swami Vivekananda's eloquent redefinition of Tolerance as Acceptance and as an affirmative and positive concept in 1893 in Chicago. I see before my mind's eye the inspiring example of Mahatma Gandhi whose life was his message. I remember Martin Luther King's unforgettable words that he spoke to me when we met in Geneva at the Peace on Earth *(Pacem in Terris)* Conference convented by His Holiness the Pope in the late 1960s. Martin Luther King told me of

Mahatma Gandhi, the great messiah of freedom and the apostle of Non-Violence, Tolerance, Justice and Peace: "*It was Mahatma Gandhi who brought the meaning of Jesus back into my life*". The ancient Vedic, Jain and Buddhist traditions as well as Zorastrianism, Judaism, Christianity, Islam and Sikkhism found their true apotheosis and renewal in the life and message of Mahatma Gandhi.

IV

If the Dialogue of Faith traditions and civilizations is not to be a dialogue of the deaf, if it is to be a fruitful and meaningful dialogue, if we as religious and spiritual leaders are to write a new chapter in the healing process in human history, our dialogue cannot be a dialogue of the clash of civilizations. We must sincerely reach out for each other and be infused and enriched by Love, Compassion, Sense of Duty. We must make our Dialogue constructive, effective and purposeful with an Agenda for Action for the future.

We cannot overlook the fact that the religions of the world have often been at loggerheads, they have often played a negative role, they have even allied themselves to colonialism, oppression, exploitation and apartheid. When there are religious riots, when terrorism claims its victims in the name of religion as in Kashmir, when religions altercate and attack each other, religions are diminished and brought into disrepute. We have, therefore to inculcate a new Culture of Peace, among religions. Religions must earn Reverence through Truth, Tolerance and Humility. First and foremost, Religions of the World must cease and desist from *treading on each other's toes*; they must make a treaty of permanent peace and avoid all mutual aggression.

V

We must celebrate the fact that the world is a rainbow of diversities. It is imperative that we must live and let live. If, I may put it bluntly, the first condition of a true dialogue in our common quest for peace is that all religious establishments and individuals must abjure and abandon the predatory concept of domination and conquest. If our shared sense of the sacred is to prevail, and if religions of the world are to serve the humanity and ameliorate the human condition, they must respect each other, they must reinforce each other, they must reciprocate and work together for a global ethic, for ecology, for eradication of poverty and for the reconstruction of human relations in a new international order, which must proclaim the primacy and the majesty of the Moral Law and the beauty and grace of the full range of human spirituality of which we find diverse manifestations in different faith traditions of the world.

VI

Let the Religions of the world "Unite for Peace" in common endeavour. They have nothing to lose but their prejudices. Humankind is born free but everywhere humanity is in chains. Let our solidarity in our common spirituality destroy the *Bastille of past prejudices.* Let us emancipate ourselves before we can establish Peace on Earth and make the world safe as a sanctuary for material progress and for the development of higher spiritual consciousness. Let us accept universal moral responsibility as the conscience-keepers of the world. Let us build a Forum of Conscience in the inner and outer space of the Cosmic order so that new priorities, a new Earth Charter, a Covenant against Ecocide and for Ecology, a new Constitution of Humanity may transform the Charter of the United Nations into a moral and spiritual charter of Togetherness, of Justice, Peace and Non-Violence for a sharing and caring world. Our Dialogue must be a *Dialogue of Togetherness*, which is the creed of our Times. As the ancient Indian seers put it:

संगच्छध्वम् संवदध्वम् संवोमनांसि जानताम्।

I would translate that invocation as follows:

> Let us walk together with a common goal. Let us converse with a common purpose. Let our minds meet together in the quest of true knowledge.
>
> and
>
> सह नावक्तु, सह नौ भुनक्तु, सह वीर्यं करवावहे।
> तेजस्विनाम् अधीतमस्तु मा विदिभावहे

I would translate that Vedic *matra* thus :

> Let us gather together and protect each other in a spirit of reciprocity and in our respective pursuits: Let us share and enjoy our togetherness. Let us strive and endeavour together. Let us together seek the luminous Truth in friendship and without jealousy and hostility.

VII

If violence, fanaticism, hatred and terrorism are allowed to be unleashed and perpetuated in the name of Religion, if our spirituality does not permeate our lives and is denied its due space in the world, if unbridled consumerism has the freedom to consume our civilization itself, if human lives are destroyed in the name of religions, if religions position themselves in the battle array of adversaries, if we end up by making the world a mere market and not one human family, religions will have no role to play in the New World, which is struggling to be born. But religions do have a role and are destined to play that role if they can work together in peace. Religions have a role to play in preventing conflicts and establishing peace if they can avoid their mutual recriminations and conflicts and observe the groundnorms of peace among themselves. Individuals must have the freedom of religion, but roselytising religions must ponder over the negative and counter-productive consequences of organized and overzealous evengelisation, which has a long history of creating tensions, violence and ill-will.

Let us speak not merely as men and women of this or that religion but as true representatives of Religion and Spirituality. Let us speak of a continuum of *Human Needs, Human Rights* and *Human Responsibilities.* Let us *proclaim our togetherness as the hyphen that joins us and the buckle that binds us.* Let our spirituality and shared human values be enthroned in our hearts and minds. Let us prepare a blue-print of Peace on Earth. Let us pledge ourselves to ensure that our Religions and our spirituality shall be a reservoir of human resources to enable us to work together to fulfill the sacred mission of Religions and Spirituality in the new Millennium and to contribute to the cause of the U.N. as an organisation consecrated for the purpose of building a new moral and spiritual edifice for our *Common Future.* The pledge and commitment which I have had the honour to assist in drafting must go beyond the spoken word; it must be inscribed on the canvas of our consciousness and etched in our hearts.

Dr. Karan Singh and Human Security

•

M.S. Swaminathan

Dr. M.S. Swaminathan, the agro-scientist Titan who led India's Green Revolution and many path breaking agricultural science projects in many other areas, is now the Chairman of the M.S. Swaminathan Research Foundation based at Chennai. He has taken up the vital issue of human security for his felicitation presentation.

"Dr. Karan Singh represents a rare combination of intellectual brilliance, spiritual depth and political acumen. His contributions to national development and human well being are many and varied. He is one of the few who view problems in their totality. Also, he is one of the few who integrate the spiritual dimension with ecology and economics. To Prof. Amartya Sen's "welfare economics", he has added the dimension of "welfare ecology".

Dr. Karan Singh represents a rare combination of intellectual brilliance, spiritual depth and political acumen. His contributions to national development and human well being are many and varied. He is one of the few who views problems in their totality. Also, he is one of the few who integrates the spiritual dimension with ecology and economics. To Prof. Amartya Sen's "Welfare economics", he has added the dimension of "welfare ecology".

He is an articulate exponent of the implications of the interactions between population and environment and of the need for human beings to live within the population supporting capacity of their ecosystems. In a volume designed as a tribute to his multifaceted contributions, I would like to deal with certain aspects of population, poverty and food security."

Planning From Below: Role of Village Level Socio-Demographic Charters

Thanks to rapid technological progress and the spread of democratic systems of governance, we have uncommon opportunities for overcoming poverty induced hunger. The goals of "food, literacy, water, health and work for all" can be achieved only if grassroot democratic institutions can be empowered to realise the vision that every new born child must have an opportunity for a productive and healthy life.

The goal of stabilising human numbers at a level not exceeding the population supporting capacity of an ecosystem can be achieved only by enabling local level democratic institutions to prepare socio-demographic charters for their respective villages. Also, greater attention is needed to human resource development. I will like to dwell at some length on these two issues.

The socio-demographic charters being planning tools at the grassroot level, should be prepared by the people themselves so as to better reflect their aspirations and priorities. A hierarchy of unmet needs can then be spelt out starting with the most pressing need. Plan implementation and funding mechanisms can concentrate on meeting the hierarchical needs in a phased manner. A sense of recognition and self-worth will promote community spirit in problem solving.

With such a broad aim of unity in goal and diversity in implementing strategies, the charters would tailor policies and programmes to suit the socio-cultural and economic needs of the area. The area specific issues shall be many and varied across situations. Yet, these issues can be grouped under broader issues that can form an integral component of the socio-demographic charter. These are:

Environment

Environment protection and the conservation and equitable use of common property resources are issues that are to a large extent amenable to local control. The degradation of environment in villages, towns and cities is now seriously threatening the sustainability of the eco-system. The local bodies need to incorporate in their plans, mechanisms to prevent loss of top soil, depletion of underground water, pollution of lakes and rivers, deforestation, loss of grazing lands, conversion of forests into agricultural land and air pollution. Waste management and sustainable life styles especially in the urban centres is needed because these have implications for the ecology of the rural areas. Both in urban and rural areas, houses should be designed in a manner that they harvest and conserve rain water. Incentives for promoting renewable energy sources should be introduced. Conservation of biological diversity and promotion of sustainable development should be the watchword. The steps necessary for managing the common property resources of the area in an equitable and sustainable manner will also have to be developed. The community should aim to live within the population supporting capacity of the ecosystem, Awareness should be spread that in the area of environment, short term solutions based on narrow sectoral considerations are counter productive and self defeating. The clear message should be that an attempt to raise the standard of living by depleting natural resources will invariably be accompanied by a progressive decline in the quality of life. Environmental issues by their very nature require long term perspectives, yet, if environment is taken for granted increasing devastation and havoc in the form of floods, drought, landslide famine, hunger, disease, and death cannot be prevented..

Hygiene and Housing

This would include, mechanisms for safe disposal and recycling of garbage, sewage and human wastes. Sewage treatment and waste disposal should form part of housing design. Water storage tanks and ponds should be disinfected to prevent breeding of mosquitoes and made mosquito-proof. In both rural and urban areas, water and electricity shortages are widespread. Housing designs should have inbuilt mechanisms for harvesting sun and rain. Methods of recharging ground water should also form part of the landscape.

Health Security

This would include reproductive health issues like maternal

and child health care services, gynaecological and sexual problems, safe abortion services, reproductive health education, AIDS and sexually transmitted diseases. It would also include provision of safe and affordable contraceptives with adequate emphasis on reproductive tract infection and follow up. Adequate emphasis would be given to the prevention of infant mortality and morbidity especially reduction of peri-natal mortality by ensuring deliveries at the hands of trained personnel. The quality aspects of contraceptive services will receive particular stress.

Education

This would ensure higher enrolment in primary schools, reduce dropouts with particular attention being paid to the girl child. Equal emphasis would be given to non-formal and technical education. Special attention would be paid to adult literacy, continuing education and skill upgradation. Awareness generation should be the long term aim of education so that effective attitudes and behaviour are fostered among the population.

Nutrition Security

This would aim at enabling access to balanced diets and safe drinking water. Special emphasis would be given to nutritional supplementation of pregnant mothers and under five children and to eliminating micro-nutrient deficiencies. The charters would focus on gender disparities with regard to nutritional intake. Since over 70 per cent of our population is dependant on agriculture, crop-livestock, integrated farming should be encouraged so that the crop diversity can provide for a balanced diet. Since forests provide many communities with dietary supplements and also food, the need to protect forests as a means of ensuring nutrition security should be emphasised. For ensuring economic access to food, greater attention is needed to both on-farm and non-farm livelihood opportunities. Priority attention should be paid to overcoming maternal and foetal under and mal-nutrition, so that children have adequate birth weight. Low birth weight children suffer from several handicaps, including retarded brain development.

Gender Code

Gender analysis focuses on understanding and documenting the differences in gender roles, activities, needs and opportunities in a given context. Gender analysis involves the disaggregation of quantitative data by gender. It highlights the different roles and behaviour of men and women based on gender attributes. These vary across cultures, class, ethnicity, income, education and time; gender analysis does not treat women as a homogenous group or gender attributes as immutable.

Women's needs are better understood when viewed in relation to men's needs and roles and to their social, cultural, political and economic context. In gender analysis women's roles in production, reproduction, and management of community assets and other activities are taken into account. Any change in one may produce beneficial or detrimental effects in others.

Gender analysis is important in the formulation of poverty assessments, environmental assessment and in sector specific project planning, monitoring and evaluation. Applied to development intervention, gender analysis helps to:

a. identify gender based differences in access to resources to predict how different members of households, groups, societies will participate in and be affected by planned development interventions,
b. permit planners to achieve the goal of effectiveness, efficiency, equity and empowerment through designing policy reform and supportive programme strategies, and,
c. develop training packages to sensitise development staff on gender issues particularly in designing training, knowledge and skill empowerment programmes.

The equal participation of men and women in policy making, project design and management may be impeded by cultural and legal constraints against women's participation and by women's relative lack of time and mobility caused by their workload and multiple roles. If participatory development is to benefit from women's contributions and meet the particular needs of women, a range of strategic and practical measures must be taken to overcome these barriers. Unless specific steps are taken to ensure the equal participation of men and women, women shall invariably get excluded. As a result, the projects would fail to benefit from women's contributions and also fail to meet the particular needs and interests of women.

The gender module would emphasise steps to end all forms of gender inequity and discrimination including adverse sex ratios, inequitable property rights, dowry, female foeticide and infanticide, higher female mortality and morbidity, higher female illiteracy, feminisation of poverty and food security for women. The village / town level socio-demographic charters can thus become powerful tools in bringing about the desired demographic transition speedily.

Imagining India of Tomorrow: Agenda 2007

Poverty persists under conditions where the human resource is undervalued, and land and other material resources are over-valued. The late Dr Mahbul Huq and the UNDP have rendered a valuable service by initiating the Human Development Reports. Focus on human development is the best way of getting national priorities right. In the year 2000 Human Development Report of UNDP, India ranked 128 among 174 nations in Human Development Index (HDI). Life expectancy at birth, adult literacy rate, school enrolment and per capita income are the criteria used for estimating HDI. In 1999, India occupied the 112th position in gender development index(GDI). GDI uses the same parameters as the HDI but adjusts for gender inequality. In the area of gender empowerment measure, which is based on seats in Parliament held by women, female administrators, managers, professionals and technical workers, and women's real GDP per capita, India's position is 95 among the nations included in the 1999 Report.

Without added and urgent attention to human development, it will be difficult to make progress during the coming *knowledge century* in improving food, livelihood and ecological security. In my view, we should aim to reach the 50th rank in HDI by the year 2007. Given the necessary political will and action, this is entirely feasible. I shall explain why.

During the last 50 years, the country has made considerable progress in areas relating to human well being. Life expectancy now is nearly 60 years, as compared to 44 years in 1960. Adult literacy is 50% compared to 34% in 1970. Infant mortality is 89 per 1000, down from 165 in 1960. The population of poor people fell from over 50% in 1950 to just over 30% now. However, the actual numbers of persons living in poverty virtually doubled, due to population increase. We have today as many illiterate and poor persons as the entire population of India in 1947.

Our record in the field of education is poor. Only two thirds of children aged 6-14 attended school in 1992-93 and only just over half the population completes more than 4 years of education. Our population is now one billion and the descried goal of TFR 2.1 is yet to be achieved in most States. The United Nations medium projection indicates that our population may reach 1.5 billion in 2050 and could reach 1.6 billion before it gets stabilised.

To quote Jawaharlal Nehru "We have to run twice as fast to stay where we are". Approximately 350 million adults in India cannot read or write. Infant mortality rates can and need to be reduced by another 80% or more. We will have another 500 million young people to educate and nurture by the middle of the 21st century. So while in percentage terms we may be better off, in absolute numbers the work left to be done is even greater than what we have accomplished till now.

I believe that looking back 100 years from now, India will have achieved rates of life expectancy, literacy and infant mortality comparable to that now prevalent in the most economically advanced countries of the world. But I am not heartened by this expectation. I find it totally unacceptable to say that our descendants a century from now will achieve that which we are perfectly capable of providing to our children and grandchildren today. I believe it is our solemn duty and obligation to make life better for all Indian citizens as fast and as much as possible.

This is why I propose that we set ourselves the inspiring goal of raising our position on the Human Development Index from 134th place to 50th place by 2007, the 60th year of our independence. This will require that we raise life expectancy by another 10 years, reduce infant mortality by two-thirds and raise adult literacy to 90%. We should also strive to reach the 40th position in GDI and 10th position in Gender Empowerment Measure.

Some of you may think that such goals are unrealistic and unachievable. But I beg to differ. India has already demonstrated in at least one field that our nation can accomplish what many people both inside and outside the country considered impossible. In 1965-66 we lived a "ship to mouth" existence. Two successive years of drought threatened the lives of up to 10 million people with famine. Few people believed that India was capable of feeding itself. Very few could conceive that millions of uneducated traditional Indian farmers could take to Modern agricultural methods speedily and enthusiastically.

These were the conditions under which India launched the Green Revolution. A fully committed government launched a massive programme to promote modern methods of cultivation. Hundreds of demonstrations were laid in small farmers fields. New organizations were established to produce hybrid seeds and fertilizers, build warehouses, purchase and distribute foodgrains. Agricultural education and research were revamped to focus them on meeting the nation's urgent needs. Above all, assured and remunerative prices were offered to farmers. Within five years foodgrain production increased by 50% and the country had achieved foodgrain self sufficiency at the prevailing level of purchasing power. Now the production of foodgrains has reached the level of 200 million tonnes.

This remarkable feat was accomplished at a time when the country was far less equipped in terms of power generation, roads, ports, science and technology, educational levels, industrial facilities, management capabilities and financial resources than it is today. If so much could be achieved by our people at that time, surely the nation is capable of far greater feats of accomplishment today, particularly since we can mobilise "people power" through *Gram Sabhas* and elected local bodies.

We see a glimpse of that untapped capability in the rise of India's software export industry, which grew 400-fold from a mere $10 million in 1983 to $ 4 billion this year and is projected to reach $ 12 billion by 2002. How do we extend such accomplishments to the basic area of human development?

First, it is important to recognize that the country already possesses the needed technological, organizational and financial resources to raise our position on the HDI to 50th place within seven years. We do not need to import technology. We do not need to borrow ideas or money from other countries. There is nothing wrong with borrowing strategies and techniques that have been successful elsewhere, but the idea that we should rely on foreign aid is totally counterproductive. If the Education Guarantee Scheme is implemented in such a way that it becomes community owned and managed, we can realise soon the goal of education for all.

Second, we need to redirect our national energies away from preoccupation with political competition to focus on national development. Today, the bulk of the country's energy is being sapped and wasted in political battles which enable parties and candidates to gain temporary victories, but which contribute nothing to the advancement of the poor people or the country. Let there be a common minimum political agenda agreed to by all political parties for raising literacy, employment, income, gender equity and life expectancy, for stabilising the population and for safeguarding the environment.

Third, we should recognize that we already have formulated and put in place many plans and programmes that are capable of achieving the goal I propose. We have excellent examples in education, as for example the schooling revolution in Himachal Pradesh and Mizoram and the Education Guarantee Programme in Madhya Pradesh (Public Report on Basic Education in India, The PROBE Team, Oxford University Press, 1999). Similarly the success of Kerala, Tamil Nadu, Andhra Pradesh, Goa and Mizoram in stabilising population has many lessons for the rest of the country. We however need more and better implementation and execution. The country should declare a national emergency for achieving a corruption free administration characterised by a high degree of accountability and efficiency.

Fourth, we should enable local bodies to:

- extend programmes to provide safe drinking water and vaccinations in every village and town and to develop a health security system based on the principle "prevention is better than cure"
- emphasise the need to restrict population size so as to live within the supporting capacity of the ecosystem.
- double the investment in education, especially pre-school, primary and adult educational programmes in rural areas,
- provide incentives to encourage the adoption of innovative teaching methods, including the establishment of Virtual Schools and Colleges involving the use of computers and active involvement of the private sector in rural pre-schools and primary schools.

The challenges facing India today are not for the weak or the timid. Nor is it a time to be discouraged or lose heart. This is the time for bold innovative action. Revolutionary efforts that destroy the status quo are necessary to remove barriers to progress, but they are not sufficient to realise our potential. Revolution needs to be supplemented by evolutionary efforts to consciously create the organizational foundations for a better common present and future. It is time to abandon half-hearted, half-way measures and show ourselves and the world what this nation can accomplish. In the emerging Knowledge and Innovations century, human development will hold the key to sustainable food and livelihood security as well as to national well being. It is time to inspire our youth, which represent the best part of the population, and fire them with enthusiasm to build a better India. The emergence of a caring, sharing and innovative India during this century is a prospect well within our reach. It is our duty and privilege to work for this inspiring cause. This is the most meaningful way of not only imagining but working for an India of Dr Karan Singh's vision. Dr Karan Singh's pathway of achieving human security integrates science, spirituality and society. This is the only sustainable pathway to enduring human well being.

□□□

A Tribute from Down Under

•

Sir Moti Tikaram

Sir Moti Tikaram K.B.E., C.F., former Ombudsman and retired President of the Fiji Court of Appeal and a former judge of the Fiji Supreme Court, is a thinker and scholar in his own right. In this tribute he highlights Dr. Karan Singh's keen interest and services to overseas Indians.

"I have the pleasure of being acquainted with Dr. Karan Singh for over Three decades. Notwithstanding his busy schedule of meetings, lectures and parliamentary activities it is amazing how he always finds time to meet friends and visitors from abroad. He is generous to a fault. His hospitality to and interest in overseas visitors is now a legend. Coming as he does from a princely family he nevertheless has the capacity to move with the kings and yet not lose the common touch."

To be invited to be amongst a galaxy of illustrious contributors to this volume to felicitate Dr. Karan Singh's attainment of the biblical three scores and ten is a great honour indeed. More so when the galaxy includes people of stature, standing and eminence in their own right straddling as do the sub-continent and beyond.

They are better equipped to make an in-depth analysis of Dr. Singh's multifaceted personality and his long and varied contributions in a multitude of fields in India and aboard.

This humble contribution comes from a relatively minor player so to speak from the far flung islands of Fiji in the South Pacific. But such is the strength of Dr. Singh's personality that he leaves a deep and abiding impression in every country that he has visited and this includes Fiji which he visited in1969 in his capacity as Minister of Health and Civil Aviation. It speaks volumes for his foresight and commitment that he saw to it that Air India continued its service to Fiji notwithstanding many odds against it continuing to do so. Unfortunately, the service stopped soon after Dr. Singh's tenure ended. Such was Dr. Singh's interest in overseas Indians and their problems and their evolving culture that he regarded the service as a two-way link in maintaining cultural contact whilst promoting understanding. This small article is therefore a simple but sincere tribute to Dr. Singh for making Indians proud wherever they lived of his many and varied contributions in the international field.

Interest in Overseas Indians

I have had the pleasure of being acquainted with Dr. Singh for over 3 decades. Notwithstanding his busy schedule of meetings, lectures and parliamentary activities it is amazing how he always finds time to meet friends and visitors from abroad. He is generous to a fault. His hospitality to and interest in overseas visitors is now a legend. He is ever willing to share his thoughts with them. Coming as he does from a princely family, he nevertheless has the capacity to move with the Kings and yet not lose the common touch.

Sense of Humour

His sense of humour adds sparkle to his pleasant but dynamic personality. On one occasion I remarked to him that I noticed that he was back in Parliament (Rajya Sabha). He responded smilingly—"*You know politics is like diabetes - once it catches you it never leaves you*".

On another occasion I observed that an idea mooted by a certain public figure was patently absurd. He agreed but added "*You'd be surprised how many fools would nevertheless subscribe to such ideas*".

Geeta's Wiseman

Another endearing trait that I have admired in him is his capacity to take success and defeat in its stride. When he lost an election I wrote to him commiserating because I felt Parliament would miss his valuable contribution to debate. Unperturbed he replied "but I still have many other creative avenues to pursue". He truly conforms to Geeta's description of a wise man *i.e.* one who is not overwhelmed by pleasures of success nor dejected by the sorrows of defeat.

Humility

When I received the 2nd volume of this autobiography titled "*Sadar-e-Riyast*" he asked me for my comments. I replied that his autobiography deserved better and wider readership abroad because he had set the record straight on a number of issues involving his leadership in Kashmiri affairs, and that this is not likely to be achieved because the obscure title would be meaningless to Westerners leave alone many Indians. Instead of taking umbrage he wrote back and thanked me saying that the publishers had agreed to take out a combined volume entitled "Heir Apparent".

Mastery of English

Dr. Singh is recognised in India and aboard as a scholar, writer, statesman and also an authority on Hinduism. Besides his fluency in Hindi (though his mother's tongue is Dogri) I dare say that it is through his mastery of the English language that he has been able to portray Hinduism and Indian philosophy abroad in good light.

It was through a little book containing a collection of Dr Singh's "*Contemporary Essays*" published by Bhavans in 1971 that I first got a glimpse of a unique personality with vibrant views expressed through chaste English. Dr. Singh's autobiography and his subsequent publications and in particular his "*Essays on Hinduism*" all testify not only to his creative thoughts but also to his command of English. No matter how complex the subject, clarity is a sovereign virtue with Dr. Singh.

Love of Nature

One has to read only parts of his writings to appreciate his discerning eye and his immense powers of observation translated through his facile expressions and fine turn of phrases. His love of nature and its beauty is symbolised by his fascination with mountains. No one can be left unmoved as by the following observations of his:

> "Their poise, unhurried and imperturbable, provides a welcome contrast to the rush and bustle, the envy and intrigue, of daily life. I have had occasion to travel to the ends of the earth, and have found that all great mountain ranges—the Himalaya, the Alps, the Andes—share this very special quality of expanding human consciousness. It was the stunning natural beauty of Kashmir that first taught me to ask deeper questions leading into the heart of the mystery that is life. In my early years my religious feelings were largely confined to the traditional devotionalism of my mother—genuine but somewhat limited. Looking back, though, it is clear that the sheer physical beauty of Kashmir—its mountains and valleys, rivers and forests, paddy fields and winding mountain tracks—helped to sharpen my awareness of beauty, to make me more responsive to the softer and finer aspects of the human spirit that are so often steam-rollered into the dust by hammering insistence of the life of the moment".
>
> (See pages 17 & 18 of Dr. Singh's "Autobiography" published by Oxford University Press in 1994)

On Hinduism

Dr. Singh is keenly aware that religion has the potential to both divide as well as to unite. He has always emphasized Hinduism's role to unite by distilling its true essence from the Vedic scriptures. He has done much to dispel the notion that Hinduism is a sectarian, parochial and dogmatic faith. In his book on "Hinduism" he argues that it is a religion of an immanent ad transcendal god. He focuses on Hinduism's ideal of universalism and love for humanity in an age of armed conflict and mutual annihilation. Dr Singh has distilled 5 basic concepts from the Vedic scriptures and after discussing them at length he summarises them beautifully in a paragraph of his book. This paragraph is worth quoting. It reads—

> "*These five concepts from the Vedanta—the all-pervasive Brahman; the Atman which resides in all beings; the concept of the human race as members of a family; the idea that all religions are essentially different*

paths to the same goal; and the concept that we must work for the welfare of society as a whole and not only for ourselves, when taken together provide us with a comprehensive world-view which will greatly help in the process of globalisation upon which we have embarked".

Cultural Ambassador

Dr. Singh is not only an illustrious son of India but is also an eminent international figure. His contributions have enriched the lives of many, including myself, both inside India and outside it. To me and numerous others he has been a guide, philosopher and friend. He continues to be, par excellence, India's unofficial cultural ambassador at large.

□□□

Experimental Studies of the Psychological Effects of Medicine

•

Roger Walsh

Professor Roger Walsh of the Department of Psychiatry and Human Behaviour, University of California, along with Dr. Frances Vaugham, presents results of some significant studies of psychological effects of meditation as his felicitation to Dr. Karan Singh.

"While there is much to admire about this man, we have particularly appreciated his interest in integrating the best of East and West, the spiritual and scientific. In particular, Dr. Singh has supported transpersonal psychology, a field dedicated to bring contemporary scientific studies to bear on perennial wisdom and practices such as meditation. With this contribution of his in mind we would like to contribute a review of contemporary meditation."

Meditation research surged in the latter part of the twentieth century as East and West met in a new way. Over 1800 publications, including several hundred research studies, have appeared and have documented a wide array of effects on personality, performance, perception and physical and psychological health, as well as on physiology and biochemistry.

Psychological Effects

The range of experiences that can emerge during meditation is enormous. Experiences may be pleasant or painful, and intense emotions such as love or anger can alternate with periods of calm and equanimity. Although the idea of meditation as simply a relaxation response is a vast oversimplification, the general trend as meditation practice continues is toward greater calm, positive emotions, and perceptual and introspective sensitivity. Advanced experiences include profound peace, concentration and joy, intense positive emotions of love and compassion, penetrating insights into the nature of mind, and a variety of transcendent states that can run the gamut of classical mystical experiences.[1,2]

Enhanced perceptual ability allows insight into psychological processes and habits. One of the first insights is how extraordinarily out of control, unaware, fantasy-filled, and dreamlike our usual state of mind is. Classical claims that the untrained mind is like a "Wild drunken monkey" and that taming it is "the art of arts and science of sciences" soon make sense to the beginning meditator. To date most knowledge of meditative experiences has come from personal accounts, and there has been little systematic phenomenological research.

However, there have been a large number of experimental studies of meditation's effects on personality, performance, and perception. Intriguing findings include evidence for enhanced creativity, perceptual sensitivity, empathy, lucid dreaming, self actualization, a positive sense of self control, and marital satisfaction. Studies of TM (Transcendental Meditation) suggest that it may foster maturation as measured by scales of ego, moral and cognitive development, intelligence, academic achievement, self-actualization and states of consciousness.

A fascinating study of perception examined the Rorschach test responses of Buddhist meditators ranging from beginners to enlightened masters.[2,6] Beginners showed normal response patterns, whereas subjects with greater concentration saw not the usual images, such as animals and people, but simply the patterns of light and dark on the Rorschach cards. That is, their minds showed little tendency to elaborate these patterns into organized images, a finding consistent with the claim that concentration focuses the mind and reduces the number of associations.

Further striking findings characterized subjects who had had an initial experience of *nirvana* and thereby reached the first of the four classic stages of Buddhist enlightenment. At first glance their Rorschach tests were not obviously different from those of non-meditators. There was, however, a difference in their accounts of the test: These subjects viewed the images they saw as creations of their own minds and were aware of the moment-by-moment process by which their stream of consciousness became organized into images.

Interestingly, the initially enlightened subjects displayed evidence of normal conflicts around issues such as dependency, sexuality, and aggression. However, they showed remarkably little defensiveness and reactivity to these conflicts. In other words, they accepted and were unperturbed by their neuroses.

A meditator at the third stage of enlightenment gave reports that were unique in four ways. First, this meditation master saw not only the images but the ink blot itself as projection of mind. Second, she showed no evidence of drive conflicts and appeared free of psychological conflicts usually considered an inescapable part of human existence. This finding is consistent with classic claims that psychological suffering can be dramatically reduced in advanced stages of meditation.

The third and fourth unique features were that this master systematically linked her responses to all ten cards into an integrated response on a single theme. The result was a systematic teaching about the nature of human suffering and its alleviation. In other words, the meditation master transformed the Rorschach testing into a teaching for the testers.

Physiological Variables

Physiological research began with sporadic investigations of spectacular yogic feats such as altering body temperature and heart rate. When some of these claims proved valid, more systematic investigation was begun. The introduction of better controls led to the recognition that many physiological effects initially assumed to be unique to meditation could actually be induced by other self-control strategies such as relaxation, biofeedback, or self-hypnosis.[7] This led some researchers to assume prematurely that there is little that is unique to meditation or its effects.

For example, initial studies of metabolic effects reported marked reductions in metabolic rate—as shown by reduced oxygen consumption, carbon dioxide production, and blood lactate levels—and suggested that transcendental meditation led to a unique hypometabolic state. Subsequent studies confirmed a reduced metabolic rate, but better controls suggested that the effects were not unique to meditation.[2]

The cardiovascular system is clearly affected.[2,4] During meditation the heart rate drops, and with regular practice blood pressure also falls. Meditation can therefore be a useful treatment for mild high blood pressure, but the benefits dissipate if practice is discontinued. Certain practitioners can increase blood flow to the body periphery, thereby raising the temperature of fingers and toes.

Tibetan Tumo masters who specialize in this are reported to demonstrate their mastery by meditating semi-naked in the snows of the Tibetan winter.

Blood chemistry may also shift.[2,4] Hormone levels may be modified, lactate levels—sometimes regarded as a measure of relaxation—may fall, and cholesterol may be reduced.

In summary, it is clear that meditation elicits significant physiological effects. While a few studies of TM have reported distinct patterns of blood flows and hormone levels, overall it is not yet clear to what extent the physiological effects are unique to meditation.

Electroencephalograph (EEG)

The most common measure of brain activity during meditation has been the EEG. This provides a measure of cerebral electrical activity that is valuable but gross, comparable to measuring activity in a city by placing a dozen microphones around it. While it remains unclear whether there are patterns unique to meditation, intriguing findings have emerged.

With most meditative practices the EEG slows, and alpha waves (eight to thirteen cycles per second) increase in amount and amplitude. In more advanced practitioners even greater slowing may occur, and theta (four to seven cycles) patterns may appear. These findings are consistent with deep relaxation.

Not only do the brain waves slow but they may also show increasing synchronization or coherence between different cortical areas. Some TM researchers suggest that this provides a basis for enhanced creativity and psychological growth.[1]

However, it is always difficult in EEG research to extrapolate from brain waves to specific states of mind, and it is usefully humbling to realize that increased coherence can also occur in epilepsy and schizophrenia.

Some skeptics have attempted to explain (away) meditation as merely the effect of drowsiness or even sleep, but this explanation fails for several reasons. While meditators, especially novices, may become drowsy, this is recognized by contemplative traditions as a specific trap: the "defilement of sloth and torpor," as Buddhists picturesquely describe it. Second, the experience of non drowsy meditation is very different from sleep. Finally, the EEG pattern of meditation is quite distinct from that of sleep.[4,8]

It is increasingly recognized that the left and right cerebral hemispheres have distinct, though overlapping, functions. Because meditation may reduce left-hemisphere functions such as verbal analysis, meditation might involve either a reduction of left-hemisphere activity and/or an activation of the right hemisphere. There is preliminary evidence of some enhanced right-hemisphere skills in meditators such as the ability to remember and discriminate musical tones. However, EEG studies suggest that while there may be relative left-hemisphere deactivation during the initial few minutes of a sitting, thereafter both hemispheres seem to be affected equally.[8,9]

Yogis and *Zen* practitioners may respond differently to sensory stimulation, in ways consistent with their respective methods and goals of practice. *Yogis*, whose practice involves internal focus and withdrawal of attention from the senses, showed little EEG response to repeated noises. Zen monks, however, whose practice involves open receptivity to all stimuli, showed continued EEG responsiveness to a repeated sound, rather than habituating to it as non–meditators would.[4] Although other studies have found less clear cut differences,[8] these findings remain intriguing because the electrophysiological data are consistent with both the different goals and experiences of *Yogis* and *Zen* practitioners.

Moreover, the lack of EEG habituation in the Zen monks is consistent with other reports. Continuous freshness of perception is characteristic of both Maslow's self-actualizers and contemplatives who practice, for example, the Buddhist's "mindfulness" or the Christian's 'sacrament of the present moment.

Therapeutic Effects

Many effects of meditation seem beneficial and research suggests that it can be therapeutic for various psychological and psychosomatic disorders. Responsive psychological disorders include anxiety, phobias, post-traumatic stress, muscle tension, insomnia, and mild depression. Studies suggest that mindfulness meditation can both reduce the symptoms of depression and reduce the relapse rate.[16,17,18] Regular long-term meditation seems to reduce both legal and illegal drug use and to help prisoners by reducing anxiety, aggression, and recidivism,

Psychosomatic benefits may include reduction of blood pressure, cholesterol, and the severity of asthma, migraine and chronic pain.[2,3,10]

These therapeutic effects may reflect enhanced general psychological and physical health. In fact, TM meditators use less than normal amounts of psychiatric and medical care, and meditators in their mid-fifties measured twelve years younger on scales of physical ageing than members of control groups.[11] Of course how much of this superior general health is actually due to meditation and how much to associated factors such as prior good health and a healthy life-style is unclear.

One well-controlled study clearly demonstrated dramatic effects on the aged. A group of nursing-home residents whose average age was eighty-one and who learned TM performed better on multiple measures of learning and mental health than did residents who were taught relaxation, given other mental training, or left untreated. Most striking, however was that after three years all the meditators were alive, whereas only 65 per cent of the untreated residents were still alive.[1] For thousands of years yogis have claimed that contemplative practices increase longevity, a claim that can no longer be ignored.

The most startling research claim is that meditators can exert "action-at-a-distance." TM researchers see fundamental reality as a field of consciousness. They therefore argue that minds are interconnected and that meditation groups of sufficient size can influence non–meditating individuals and society at large. Several studies report that TM groups have beneficially influenced social problems. These benefits include reduced rates of crime, violent death, traffic accidents, terrorism, and when a group meditated in the Middle East, the intensity of conflict in Lebanon.[12]

These findings are certainly dramatic. However, most of this and other research on TM has been conducted by members of the TM organization.

Unconscious biases can easily affect research findings, so studies by researchers independent of the TM organization are essential. If the findings of "action-at-a-distance" are independently and reliably confirmed, then the implications—for everything from philosophy and physics to peace and politics—will be remarkable.

In summary, meditation may produce a large number of effects and therapeutic benefits. However, some experimental designs and control groups have been less than ideal, most meditation subjects have been mere beginners by traditional standards, and it is often unclear whether meditation is necessarily more effective for clinical disorders than other self-regulation strategies such as relaxation, training, biofeedback, and self-hypnosis. On the other hand, meditators often report that the practice is more meaningful, enjoyable, and easier to continue than other approaches and fosters an interest in self-exploration.[2,10]

Complications

A general principle in psychiatry states that any therapy powerful enough to be helpful is also powerful enough to be harmful. This seems to hold true for meditation, though serious casualties are rare. While meditators may experience psychological difficulties at any stage, problems are more frequent in beginners, those doing intense practice without adequate supervision, and in people with pre-existing psychopathology. Some difficult experiences may ultimately prove to be cathartic and beneficial, a process TM calls "unstressing."

The range of difficulties is wide. It may include emotional liability with episodes of anxiety, agitation, depression, and euphoria. Psychological conflicts may surface and somatic symptoms such as muscle or gastrointestinal spasms may appear. Meditators may ruminate obsessively or be confronted by painful existential questions. On rare occasions defenses may be overwhelmed, resulting in a psychotic break, especially in those with a history of previous psychosis.[13] Advanced practitioners may also experience difficulties, although they are more likely to be subtler and to involve existential or spiritual concerns.[14]

Development at any level involves challenges.

Given that meditation can produce both benefits and difficulties, can we predict which people will be affected? Studies of TM suggest that those who persist successfully share certain traits. They are more interested in internal experiences, more open to unusual ones, and feel high self-control. They may be less emotionally labile and possess high concentration and alpha-wave activity. They seem less psychologically disturbed and more open to recognizing and acknowledging unfavourable personal characteristics. Future research may identify those people who will respond optimally and those at risk for negative effects, as well as means of enhancing favourable responses.

Exactly how meditation produces its many effects remains unclear. Many mechanisms have been suggested. Possible physiological processes include lowered arousal and increased hemispheric synchronization. Possible psychological mechanisms include relaxation, desensitization, dehypnosis and development of self-control skills, insight and self-understanding.[2] Perhaps the most encompassing explanation is the classic one: namely that meditation fosters psychological development.

Conclusion

While much has been learned experimentally about meditation, research is still in its early stages. As yet relatively little can be said about the relationships between the traditional goals of meditation and experimental measures. More attention has been given to heart rate than heart opening. Future research will need to pay more attention to advanced practitioners and their transpersonal goals such as enhanced concentration, ethics, love, compassion, generosity, wisdom and service.[15] The vision of a mutually enriching bridge between meditation and science remains only partly realized, but it also remains worth seeking.

REFERENCES

1. Alexander, C. et al. (1991). *Growth of Higher Stages of Consciousness*. In C. Alexander et al. (eds.). *Higher Stages of Human Development*. New York: Oxford University Press.

2. Shapiro D., & Walsh, R. (eds.). (1984). *Meditation: Classic and Contemporary Perspectives*. New York: Aldine.
3. Kwee, M., (ed.). (1990). *Psychotherapy, Meditation and Health*. London: East-West.
4. Murphy, M. & Donovan, S. (1997). *The Physical and Psychological Effects of Meditation*, 2nd ed. Sausalito, CA: Institute of Noetic Sciences.
5. Alexander, C. Rainforth, M., and Gelderloos, P. (1992) *Transcendental Meditation, Self-actualization and Psychological health: A Conceptual Overview and Statistical Meta-analysis. Journal of Social Behavior and Personality* 6:189-247.
6. Wilber K. Engler J. & Brown, D. (eds.). (1986). *Transformations of Consciousness: Conventional and Contemplative Perspectives on Development*. Boston: New Science Library/Shambhala.
7. Shapiro, D. (1982). *Comparison of Meditation With Other Self-control Strategies: Biofeedback, Hypnosis, Progressive Relaxation. American Journal of Psychiatry* 139: 267-74.
8. West, M., (ed.). (1978). *The psychology of Meditation*. Oxford: Clarenden press.
9. Earle, J. (1981) *Cerebral Laterality and Meditation. Journal of Transpersonal Psychology* 13:155-73.
10. Kabat-Zinn, J. (1990). *Full Catastrophe Living*. New York: Delcorte.
11. Orme-Johnson, D., & Alexander, C. (1988). *Critique of the National Research Council's Report on Meditation*. Fairfield, Iowa: Maharishi International University.
12. Orme-Johnson, D., et al. (1988). *International Peace Project in the Middle East: The effect of the Maharishi Technology of the Unified Field. Journal of Conflict Resolution* 32:776-812.
13. Epstein, M., and Lieff, J. (1981). *Psychiatric Complications of Meditation Practice. Journal of Transpersonal Psychology* 13:57.
14. Wilber, K. The spectrum of pathologies. (1993). In R. Walsh & F. Vaughan (eds.) *Paths Beyond Ego: The transpersonal vision*. New York: Tarcher/ Putnam.
15. Shapiro, D. (1990). *Meditation, Self-control, and Control by a Benevolent Other.* In M. Kwee (ed.) *Psychotherapy, Meditation and Health*. London: East-West, pp. 65-123.
16. Walsh, R. (2000). *Asian Therapies*. In R. Corsini & D. Wedding (eds.) *Current Psychotherapies*. 6th ed. Itasca, IL: F.E. Peacock, pp. 407-444.
17. Smith, W., Compton, W., West, W. (1995). *Meditation As An Adjunct to a Happiness Enhancement Program. Journal of Clinical Psychology* 51 (2):269-273.
18. Teasdale, J., Segal, Z, & Wiliams, J. (1995), *How Does Cognitive Therapy Prevent Depressive Relapse and Why Should Attentional Control (mindfulness) Training Help? Behavioral Research Therapy* 33 (1):25-39.

Culture, Development and Democracy: Towards Coherence in South Asia

Ponna Wignaraja

Dr. Ponna Wignaraja, Chairman, South Asian Perspectives Network Association and Vice Chairman, Independent South Asian Commission on Poverty Alleviation takes a close look at culture, development and democracy in South Asia, major concerns of Dr. Karan Singh.

"The complex concept of social justice and its links to self-reliance and dignity is deeply ingrained in our culture. As growth is generated we share. Sharing and caring are deeply ingrained values. The practice was that a just ruler would always ensure that available food was adequately distributed. At all levels of society food was shared. This was our food security system."

Dr. Karan Singh and I were part of the pre-Independence generation in South Asia. As the Independence process unfolded we, along with many other intellectuals and practitioners, helped re-inforce what can be termed "dissent" in the best sense of the word, from conventional received wisdom on development and democracy, in our respective geographical and intellectual "spaces" As early as the 1950's, we had begun to realise that there was a deeper challenge to nation building in South Asia than in merely continuing values, processes and institutions from the colonial period. Despite our formal elitist educational backgrounds, we instinctively realised that in the reign of dogmatism at that time, such undogmatic and innovative dissenting voices such as ours had to find expression, if South Asian countries were to move forward and avert the kind of multifaceted crisis that is upon us now.

Unfortunately, Dr. Karan Singh and I did not meet till many decades later. It was only in the 1990's that we entered into a mutually re-inforcing dialogue on our dissenting ideas. With other colleagues we tried to give coherence to our respective dissenting voices and go beyond dissent into formulating holistic transitional strategies and practical actions, to respond to the deepening multifaceted crisis that was facing all South Asian societies."

Dr. Karan Singh had been saying:

> "It has been my view for a long time that, South Asian relations have not really received the in-depth attention that they deserve. Obviously, because, all of us have been under Western domination, the relations between our countries and the Western countries tend to be academically and intellectually closer than between South Asian countries themselves. This is a historical phenomenon and I think the time has now come when we must start getting over this and begin a process of rediscovering the cultural and civilisational roots of the South Asian identity. For the first time every square mile of South Asia is governed by South Asians. This is an opportunity to develop our own perceptions. I think the time has now come when we have to understand the essence of the great religious philosophies and how they have influenced South Asian history and civilisation. The challenge is to see if we can develop composite cultures in South Asian countries. What we need to embark on is a dialogue with people from around South Asia to achieve some consensus. Is it possible for us to make a creative contribution in which we can perhaps structure a new kind of consciousness involving a harmonious symbiosis between science and spirituality, between material progress and the enrichment of the mind, between the outer life of action and the inner life of consciousness?"

As early as 1953, I myself had stated in an article on "The conflict between economic rationality and cultural values" (Civilizations, Vol. 3, No. 1).

"While considerable thought has been expended in recent years in attempting solutions to the numerous immediate problems confronting developing countries, very little attention has been placed on the reality that development takes place within an established cultural pattern. The process of cultural change that is set in motion during economic development tends for most part to be ignored. When it is recognised, it is merely hoped that time will bring about the necessary adjustments."

In 1975, I joined with four other South Asian colleagues in another study entitled "Towards a theory of rural development" (G.V.S. De Silva, Wahid-ul-Haque, Niranjan Mehta, Anisur-Rahman, Ponna Wignaraja). We collectively stated:

> The concept of development is presented in this study in terms of fundamental humanistic values rather than narrower techno-economic notions of development. The core of this concept is the de-alienation of man vis-a-vis the material forces of production and society, and a purposeful growth of human personality. Such humanistic philosophy has often been considered at the subjective level, but its historical validity is becoming increasingly apparent. For one thing, disillusionment with the quality of life in today's economically advanced societies is growing among their own people, and this growing alienation can be traced to the specific nature of their accumulation process and the social relations on which, it has rested. For another thing, the developing nations of today are confronted by a world historical framework, in which the ideological driving force for accumulation, pertaining to the economically advanced societies, no longer offers a viable road to accumulation itself for the former. The compulsion for seeking alternative-driving forces for accumulation, even in its narrower conception, is therefore, mounting.

In the same study, in advocating participatory democracy as the other side of the nation building coin, we also stated, that this is not formal voting of representatives into power évery few years and passive obedience, thereafter, by the people. It is not government for the people, but more fundamentally by the people, with devolution of power. We were also of the view that common South Asian spiritual values should inform our perspectives of development and democracy.

Instead of these issues providing a point of departure for a new vision and actions, many false debates were entered into. Critical issues which needed to be analysed in depth and reconciled were presented as dichotomies.

Demystifying false debates and the current multifaceted crisis

The realisation that South Asians should have an opportunity to think on South Asian problems uncluttered by ideologies and processes from far distant places, no matter, how rational they may appear to be, had dawned on some of us nearly a quarter century ago. That is how SAPNA come into being. From small beginnings, there are now a critical mass of a 100 individuals and institutions in South Asia who are probing the South reality and setting a perspective through our Network. After the establishment of the India International Centre South Asia Project in 1997, a sub-project of their larger Asia Project, we began a systematic effort along-with members of our respective networks to find the common ground in our thinking,.

The President of India on the eve of 50 years of Independence reinforced with a strong statement, the need for coherent thinking and action to respond to the crisis in India (for that matter in all South Asia). He stated it would appear that the lack of a vision has led to a sharpening of the contradictions in society. Extreme poverty was leading to violence and an unmanageable polity, despite technological progress. We South Asians should have articulated a culturally relevant vision much earlier. Groups of South Asians should have got together and systematically looked at our reality, looked at our civilisational rhythm and collectively, tried to see what should we do, not only in the long run, in terms of social transformation, but what could we be telling those currently in power, on a shorter time bound transition. This is something that cannot be done by individual "experts". We must collectively, even at this late date, probe the richness of South Asian culture, with its values, knowledge systems, the relationship between people, people and nature and institutions and find relevant answers. At Independence we did not probe in sufficient depth what kind of democracy, what kind of development, we need to have or how to initiate and manage a complex process of social transformation.

Whatever dissent to simplistic imitative mainstream thinking and action came from the margin not from the system. Unfortunately, this peripheral dissent itself had no real coherence. Even at this late date, we have to realise our collective creativity and get a collective consensus on a coherent alternate modernity. There seems to be many visions. Some visions appear to be progressive on the surface, but are really only marginally reformist. Some visions are fragmented and the actions are more so.

We are in practice still tinkering with conventional thinking and action and afraid to let go. We were promised One World, but it never really emerged. Then there are sharp contradictions that have resulted from our uncritically accepting either the neo-classical framework of thinking in relation to development or elements in the Marxist framework or the Westminster style democracy. Both of these were somewhat alien to us and South Asian cultures. These were narrow, even in their own terms, and many categories were missing in their frameworks. We ended up with a mish mash of the theory and practice. There are much more fundamental common values and processes in South Asia, which could have guided our nation building exercises and social transitions. Instead of imitating other cultures, we should be informing the world with our fundamental values and lessons from success cases and best practices on the ground.

At independence we also got caught up in another false debate that had no relevance to our reality. Let me try to put these issues in simple though not simplistic terms. Historically, there was this tremendous cultural resurgence that brought independence to most South Asian countries. It took the form of a political movement, which also had a holistic approach to life of the people. It was to lead not just to political independence, but to a good life for all. Mahatma Gandhi was the inspiration and catalyst. But the debate at that time, put again simply, revolved around capitalism vs. socialism or modernism vs. tradition. The result was an eclectic mix of strategies and policies.

The focus was not on how to take Gandhianism, as a point of departure, and go on to our own brand of South Asian modernity. Gandhi never said, "do not go to modernity" He did not say — go back to a romanticised tradition. He Provided a very forward-looking kind of alternative modernity — starting at the base of our societies and in terms of fundamental cultural values. He said "the world has enough for everyone's need, but not for everyone's greed" and "break the barriers between mental and manual labour". These were based on culturally rooted values and perspectives. He died before the initial holistic vision matured in practice.

The way the debate proceeded was polarisation between

Nehru's "Bhakra Nangals are the new temples of India" to Gandhianism being a kind of a romantic going back to the *charkha* and staying at the village and so on. There was no analysis. Within Gandhianism itself there were many sub-strands of thinking and action. There was the *Sarvodaya* or harmony model, as well, as *Antyodaya*, which accepted contradictions and conflict, which had to be mediated. The *Antyodaya* strand was the one that reflected the class, caste contradictions in our society and where we had to start with the poor. The poor, of necessity, held on to traditional values and knowledge and kept alive a kind of a momentum of struggle. They now inform the new social movements in South Asia. The new social movements are a form of positive dissent to mainstream ideologies of "top down" democracy, development and liberalisation. In another sense these social movements are also a very positive factor in the way civil society in our countries, are now responding, to globalisation, to the further polarisation of society by the rich getting richer and poor poorer and to the inability of our States to manage these contradictions. They are raising mass consciousness.

Looking back, another phase of the old debate, went on between neo-classicism and Marxism, as if these were the only two options that were available to us in our development strategy and polity. We vacillated between a kind of "top down" bureaucratic planning or leave everything to the market. We did not question the underlying ideological orientations in terms of our cultural values and institutions. We imitated the centralised decision making processes in both systems — the centralised state or the boardrooms. We went in for globalisation and thought we could tranquilise the poor with safety nets, welfare and charity. The poor are not asking for welfare and charity. They are asserting the right to work, the right to food, right to information and access to resources.

Even today, the fundamental issue of culture is blurred in the discourse on development, by adding "social" to narrow economics and a kind of humanism to economistic and technocratic approaches to development. To take a holistic view of development processes, one had to unlearn and re-learn from the ground. One had to challenge the system. The system can be ruthless in dealing with dissent. Dr. Karan Singh has gone through his own struggle. Unfolding events in South Asia and elsewhere however has proved how right he and others like him were to highlight the interrelationship between culture, development and democracy in South Asia.

Confronting Academic Imperialism

We are pitted against an equally ruthless system of academic imperialism. We have to confront the challenges in South Asia at the beginning of the millennium not only in our actions, but also on how to re-vision our thinking. We need new methodologies of inquiry and a paradigm shift.

The alternative pathway to a kind of culturally relevant development and democracy in our own context, has to be accompanied by a new pattern of development with growth. "No growth" and these words like "Hindu rate of growth" are derogatory. We should not even repeat this, just because somebody from outside had used these words. At a low level of growth we could have dignity, in our culture. From the new social movements in South Asia, the poor are showing every day even at low rates of growth, they can save and they can invest. They can initiate even in narrow economic terms an accumulation process, where growth, human development and equity are part of the same process. You do not have to grow through only public sector or private sector activities and then redistribute. The poor can also contribute directly to growth. In all our cultural efforts and I say cultural in the broader sense, it is not a matter of growing first and then redistributing after. Redistributive justice is simply not the issue. The real choice is not between growth and welfare. We need to see who is capable of generating growth and how?

The complex concept of social justice and its links to self-reliance and dignity is deeply ingrained, in our culture. As growth is generated we share. Sharing and caring are deeply ingrained values. The practice was that a just ruler would always ensure that available food was adequately distributed. At all levels of society food was shared. This was our food security system. And I am putting this into very simple words so that there is no misunderstanding on the kind of message that one has to deliver, when talking of the cultural dimension. At the most basic level South Asian societies were not "greedy", "dog eat dog", "competitive", 'survival of the fittest" societies. The fact that they are becoming this way as a result of the pressure of globalisation and consumerism should not make us lose sight of the fundamentals.

Taking another illustration — the gender dimension in development and democracy — I think there has been historically, Manu notwithstanding, always a sense of complementarity between men and women in South Asian cultures. Women struggled for equality and gender equity. Without formal literacy poor women are demonstrating that they can keep their saving books. They know exactly how to calculate leakages from the family earnings. They can save even at low levels of income.

They know how to use the savings wisely. If there is food in the house, the child eats first, because the mother makes sure of that. She even feeds the drunken husband before she will eat. These are very strong and powerful cultural values. They know they must not take credit from money lenders or other external sources, before saving and learning to use savings wisely. They learn to repay, as a matter of self-respect, if they borrow.

In South Asian cultures, the fundamentals include this more holistic approach. Instead of taking such an approach intellectually and in practice in all spheres, we merely took a cartesian and additive approach. What did we mean by "Economic" and "Social" development? Now some say "Human Development". When you identify with the base of our economies and polities, what you see is that, if people, particularly the poor do not work, they do not have an income, they do not eat, their family does not eat, and if their family does not eat, they fall sick, and if they fall sick, this is not a matter of just improving a little bit of health here and giving a little bit of charity there, through fragmented "human development projects". It becomes a vicious cycle. It is being recognised increasingly, as we learn from the ground that, we have no choice but to take this more holistic approach. This was deeply ingrained in the culture, but got diffused, with colonial penetration, academic imperialism, cartesian approaches to knowledge and the narrow economistic view of development. To get out of this vicious cycle, we need rigorous social mobilisation and real participation and not "tool kit" approaches.

The reason for being more assertive now is that the new social movements in South Asia, which, as mentioned, are a form of dissent from mainstream thinking and action, are reflecting some of the coherence of our common South Asian values and civilisational rhythm and providing the lessons from the ground. They are for instance reviving and giving scientific validation to the traditional knowledge system. The scientific validation to the knowledge that we had is increasingly available. This scientifically validated knowledge has to be widely disseminated. In this knowledge system there are, for instance positive cost effective strategies of nutrition and biotechnology. In terms of many other elements, not only related to health and so on, but also wisdom, governance and literacy, the knowledge and choice of technology is there.

Towards Coherence in Meeting the Intellectual Challenge and that of Practice

In 1998, collaboration with Dr. Karan Singh and his colleagues in the India International Center, South Asia Project and SAPNA attempted to identify and sharpen, as a step in the search for further coherence, the real intellectual issues that pose the challenges to South Asians today. We need to identify the real challenges in relation to how we understand our South Asian reality. Challenges in relation to how we set the vision, both for the long term as well as, the shorter term. The time horizon becomes very important, otherwise we are confusing the short and the long term solutions and the marginal reformist with the more fundamental transformative changes that are required. This could not be done without new analytical tools. What is the methodology we use for probing the reality? Is it the same cartesian single discipline analysis, couched in new semantics or do we take a holistic interdisciplinary approach to social change, using the methodology of social praxis.

The point of departure was to go back to our experiential learning and drawing the hard lessons from macro micro best practices and success cases on the ground, in South Asia. A group of twenty-five South Asians met, in Colombo under the auspices of SAPNA and IIC in a brainstorming session lasting several days. It was clear we needed a new Social Contract to manage the transition, from the reality to the vision. The old Social Contract between labour and management, and the Welfare State was now outdated. It is now unsustainable, even in the Western industrial societies, where it originated and which we imitated. It started with a Social Contract between the management and the workers in the organised sectors. It was broadened through Keynesian thinking in capitalist societies. Socialist Countries also had adopted a similar welfarism delivered from the top by the State. We adopted that old social contract based on redistributive justice and welfare and now we cannot afford it. It is not necessary for us, particularly when we have the possibility of a superior culturally rooted social contract, for development and eradicating poverty.

In South Asia, we do not need to take surpluses generated by the poor from the base of the economy, send it upwards through state taxation or private profit and then re-distribute it. And that is what was called redistribution with growth, "trickle down", etc. We know "trickle down" has not worked and that our bureaucratic systems were incapable, of sustaining redistributive processes to reach the poor. Our systems and our institutions, which we borrowed from the West in the name of representative democracy and economic development and centralised planning and so on, were incapable even of establishing that old social contract on a sustainable basis. That social contract, was a soft process because it was dependent on an aid relationship based on expectations of massive transfer of resources from industrialised countries. This dependence led to the neglect of our own resources—the people's creativity, their knowledge system, their values and also South Asia's natural resource base. In the case of the poor, additionally we wasted their efficiency, their capacity to save at low levels of income and generate a different pattern of pro-poor growth at the base of our economies. The massive transfer of resources from industrial countries did not take place effectively.

We discussed the concept of "pro-poor growth" at this first SAPNA/IIC meeting. It was a culturally relevant pattern of growth. It started with simplicity and austerity, gave savings priority over credit and consumerism. It is not the growth that takes place through decisions in the boardrooms of the private sector or the public sector and is then redistributed. It is a growth that mainly comes from below. It is based on efficiency of the poor, their creativity and knowledge. They keep their surplus in their own hands. It is part of a three-sector model, rather than a two sector model. That is where the Western economists and even the Western social scientists and their counterparts in our countries went wrong. They advocated a two-sector growth model for us. The poor were to be tranquilised with safety nets, welfare and charity. Safety, welfare and charity can only be a residual or supplementary strategy. There has to be a three-sector model, particularly when 40-50 per cent of our people are in the informal sector and poor. The old compulsions for public and private accumulation alone are not adequate for us. The poor have shown they can also contribute to growth. They are not the problem and can be part of the solution. At this meeting the role of civil society came into the discussions on decentralisation and governance. It was found even in civil society there are many contradictions. There is a great deal of confusion. They are coming up with single solutions, single "entry point" solutions to this multiplicity of problems and multifaceted crisis. Civil Society organisations also need to get their act together. The discussions re-inforced the need for new kind of coherence and partnership, even within civil society organisations. We decided at least on a few limited issues let us discuss in-depth and be agreed. Civil Society cannot work alone. The state is also needed, but a re- structured state. Our culture gave guidelines for this too, on how to build new partnerships and coalitions. How to share power.

As South Asian problems mounted, the two networks met to plan a second brainstorming session in New Delhi, in 1999. Dr. Karan Singh chaired the session. As poverty increased and our polities became unmanageable we felt, it is necessary now to call a spade a spade. We were now fifty years into Independence and needed to learn the harder lessons from history. There were no soft options. We discussed South Asian civilisation and 50 years of making mistakes and limited successes in evolving participatory development and democracy. But the real question was what have we learned from the ground, the commonalties with which, we can begin a re-visioning process. We are good at repeating ourselves on all the things that are wrong with our society but the challenge is to agree on what to do at 9 o'clock on Monday morning, where do we begin to transform our societies in a more orderly way.

A Concluding Message

Apart from these collective efforts, in our reflective personal dialogues, Dr. Karan Singh and I have spent many hours asking ourselves when are we going to articulate a coherent set of values that can then inform those who have power at the top, as well as, other actors, in development and in the management of our polities, in the transition, There is no choice if the contradictions in our societies are not sharpened further. Can we convey these ideas to the younger generation and how? Youth alienation leading to violence is a new threat to the very fabric of our societies. Let me conclude this Felicitation Message by saying that, there has to be a transition from our almost unmanageable reality towards a culturally rooted vision. Visions abound in our South Asian Culture. Social changes also do not occur any more by violent revolutions. When they do, we have seen that they may not be sustainable and may lead to societal collapse. We cannot continue with ad– hoc marginal tinkering in the name of reforms. For us there has to be a transition in the course of the "long revolution" to social transformation.. It could be a more orderly transition but for this the approach has to be culturally relevant. We are now in a position to articulate in a rudimentary fashion the framework of a coherent concept of alternative modernity.

The Heads of State of all SAARC countries in 1991 began to feel the same sense of unease that has been expressed here. That was when they set up the Independent South Asian Commission on Poverty Alleviation. It is called an Independent South Asian Commission on Poverty, but in reality it was a Commission on Development, taking into consideration political realities and need for cultural relevance. It should have been named that way, but that would have been too threatening for the system. So it was titled in terms of poverty. The contents of the Report specify how to evolve a coherent transitional strategy to an alternative modernity and manage it. It was a unanimous Report by fifteen South Asians. By accepting the Report's recommendations, the SAARC Heads of State took over ownership of this culturally relevant and practical strategic thrust.

This showed it was possible to get coherence and political acceptance. This was a silver lining in the "long revolution"

I hope, Dr. Karan Singh, with his links within India and elsewhere will devote the rest of his active life in pursuing the messages and recommendations in the Report of the South Asian Commission and help reinforcing the emerging coherence, which has gone well beyond dissent from received wisdom, towards a practical alternative modernity.

❑❑❑

. . . And Thus Speaks Dr. Karan Singh

The Global Society

"It is my firm conviction that mankind today is transiting into an entirely new phase of civilization, which may be called the global society, a transition as important, if not more so, as the earlier ones from nomadic to agricultural, from agricultural to industrial and from industrial to post-industrial society. Besides, with the rate of change having immensely accelerated due to the technological explosion, major transformations, which in an earlier age would have taken several centuries, are now compressed into a few decades. This gives human consciousness insufficient time to adjust to the new situation; hence the dangerous lag we witness today between the emergence of a global society and its acceptance by the vast mass of humanity."

The Concept Of Time

"The Hindu concept of time is cyclical, not linear. The universe is *anadi-ananta*, without beginning and without end, going through recurrent phases of manifestation and dissolution. It is quite extraordinary how the Hindu concept of time is becoming more comprehensible with recent developments in extra-galactic cosmology. Each day of Brahma, the creator principle in the Hindu trinity, consists of four billion, three hundred and twenty million years, and the night of Brahma is of a similar duration. Thus, the entire universe is a process of the outbreathing and inbreathing of Brahma, corresponding to alternating periods of manifestation and dissolution."

Hinduism And Its Challenges

"The entire history of Hinduism, looked at from a certain angle, can be seen as a constant process of challenge and response. to each major crisis, Hinduism reacted, first by briefly withdrawing into a shell and then, with its unparalleled capacity for assimilation and regeneration, by a new resurgence. This happened with the Jain and Buddhist movements, with the early Christian missionaries and, to a lesser extent, with the Muslim advent. But with the arrival of the British, first as traders and finally as imperial rulers, Hinduism was confronted with the most critical of all the challenges it had faced in its long and eventful history."

Swami Vivekananda

"The other feature of Swami Vivekananda's life was the contribution he made to the spread of Hindu thought abroad, specially in America. Prior to his advent, it was only a handful of Western Indologists and scholars who had any real insight into the Hindu ethos, while among the general public, there flourished all sorts of grotesque impressions regarding this great religion. Vivekananda pioneered a new awareness of Hinduism in the West. His eloquent and able presentations of the essential truths that underlie Hinduism, and his broad approach of the essential unity of religions, combined to make him a unique spokesman of the eternal East to the bustling technological culture of Western society."

Shri Ramana

"Unlike Vivekananda, Sri Ramana never concerned himself with social service or reform movements. He seldom ventured outside his abode at Arunachalam, and yet such was his spiritual presence that he commanded veneration from all sides. The thousands who trekked to see him were often content to do just that, because in the Hindu tradition even the sight of a holy person—*darsana*—has its own spiritual merit."

Sri Aurobindo

"According to Sri Aurobindo, man is the result of aeons of evolution from unicellular organisms up through mineral, vegetable and animal forms. However, he is by no means the end-product of evolution. Sri Aurobindo postulates a further evolutionary thrust from man with his mental faculties to superman with suparmental faculties. Indeed, he holds that it is only with the next quantum leap in the evolutionary adventure that mankind will break out of its present impasse and fulfill its spiritual destiny."

Science And Technology

"Mankind faces a complex dilemma at this stage of its evolution. Science and technology, if wisely used, have given him for the first time the capacity to abolish deprivation and poverty, illiteracy and disease, unemployment and inequality from the face of the earth. On the other hand, the same science has also given him the power to destroy not only the human race but perhaps all life. There is a great churning of the collective consciousness of humanity, and a tremendous urge for new certitudes to take the place of the old bulwarks that are collapsing. In such a situation, all religions face a fundamental challenge. Hinduism, with its tremendous capacity for regeneration and reinterpretation, should not have anything to fear. Indeed, India, with its rich and varied religious heritage as well as the most distinguished pool of scientific talent in the developing world, should be able to give the right lead to humanity at this crucial juncture."

The Unity Of The Race

"Science and technology have now converted what was once only a vision in the minds of seers into a concrete reality. Time and space are shrinking before our eyes, and the extraordinary photograph of Earth taken from the moon shows our planet, as it really is, a tiny spaceship hurtling through the endless vastnesses of space, so beautiful and yet so fragile. The essential unity of the race that inhabits this planet, based upon the fact of 'humanness' itself, is thus a concept that is growing increasingly relevant as this century draws to its close and mankind struggles desperately to survive its own technological ingenuity."

Spiritual Realisation

"Howsoever diverse the circumstances, howsoever hostile the environment, Hinduism believes that there is within the human psyche the unquenchable spark of divinity that can, sooner or later, be fanned into the blazing fire of spiritual realization. This concept endows every individual with a dignity that immediately places him, in essence, above and beyond social customs and traditions."

Among Billions of Galaxies

"Among billions of galaxies in the universe, one is ours; among billions of stars in this galaxy one is ours; among billions of human beings in this solar system one of them is ourselves, but such is the grandeur and mystery of the Atman that it can move towards a comprehension of the unutterable mystery of existence. We, who are children of the past and the future, of Earth and heaven, of light and darkness, of the human and the divine, at once evanescent and eternal, of the world and beyond it, within time and in eternity, yet have the capacity to comprehend our condition, to rise above our terrestrial limitations, and, finally, to transcend the throbbing abyss of space and time itself."

Vasudhaiva Kutumbakam

"The *Upanisads* have a beautiful word for the human race, *amrtasya putrah* (children of immortality), because we carry within our consciousness the light and the power of the Brahman, regardless of our race or colour, our creed or sex, or any other differentiation. That is the basis of the concept of human beings as an extended family: *vasudhaiva kutumbakam*,"

Five Concepts of Vedanta

"Five concepts from the *Vedanta*—the all-pervasive Brahman; the *Atman* which resides in all beings; the concept of the human race as members of a family; the idea that all religions are essentially different paths to the same goal; and the concept that we must work for the welfare of society as a whole and not only for ourselves—

when taken together provide us with a comprehensive world-view which will greatly help in the process of globalization upon which we have embarked."

Poverty vs Armaments

"Science and technology have given us tremendous power, but that power can be used for benign or malignant purpose. We can abolish poverty and hunger, malnutrition and misery, illiteracy and unemployment from the face of this earth by the end of this century. It can be done quite easily—seven days' expenditure on world armaments can abolish hunger in Africa, ten day's expenditure on world armament can abolish the debt of Latin America. But, instead, thousands of billions of dollars and roubles and pounds and rupees and other currencies are going into the manufacture of weapons of mass destruction every year."

The Worship of Power is not Enough

"The worship of power, of science, is not enough. Hitler's gas chambers were an example of science and technology; the Hiroshima and Nagasaki atom bombs were an example of science and technology. We now have a single nuclear warhead packing the power of 1,000 Hiroshima bombs, and there are 50,000 such nuclear warheads on Earth today. Are we not standing on the threshold of a major disaster? Are we not on the verge of the *mahapralaya*, great deluge, or *mahagni* great fire or whatever mode of destruction will finally develop? At such a time we can survive only if we have an alternative ideology to the present one which has led mankind to this position. I claim that the *Vedanta* in fact provides such an alternative ideology. Even at this stage, even at this late hour, if we can imbibe some of the universal truths of the *Vedanta* we can perhaps reverse the processes of destruction."

Reversing the Mad Rush to Destroy

"We must never forget that power by itself is neither good nor evil; there is the *daivi sakti* and there is the *asuri sakti*, thc benign power and the malign power. The worship of power, of science, is not enough, we also need to recapture wisdom, compassion and understanding. We can now survive only if we have an alternative ideology to the one which has led mankind to this position, and if we boldly act in harmony with that ideology. The *Vedanta* provides such an alternative world-view,; and if even at this late hour we can imbibe some of its universal truths, we can perhaps reverse the mad rush towards destruction and begin the long, slow climb back to sanity."

A Caterpillar and A Butterfly

"Can you imagine what it is like when a caterpillar, an ugly, land-bound worm, goes into a chrysalis and a miraculous metamorphosis takes place so that it emerges as a beautiful, radiantly coloured butterfly? That is the sort of metamorphosis that the *Upanisads* envisage for human consciousness. We change from our earth-bound consciousness into this bright, multi-coloured consciousness, which can still alight upon the ground like a caterpillar but can also fly into the air which the caterpillar could not."

Capacity for Renewal

"The reason our Indian cultural tradition has come down unbroken for thousands of years is that it has the capacity for spiritual renewal from age to age. No philosophy or religion that does not have the capacity for renewal and renaissance can really meet the requirements of a changing society. It has to have the inner elasticity and breadth to cover the new developments, and there also have to be men and women who, in their own lives, live and illuminate these great truths."

Kuruksetra Within

"Let us remember that Kuruksetra is not only a plain in Haryana. The outer Kuruksetra is still there, of course, but the inner Kuruksetra is within each one of us. It is within our psyche that the *asuri* and *daivi* powers are drawn up in array against each other, and it is within the heart of our consciousness that this battle has constantly to be fought."

The Conflicts Are There

The conflicts are there. There is no easy path to greatness or to spiritual realization, either individual or collective. We must always remember the Vedic exhortation: *Caraiveti, Caraiveti* (Move on, Move on). Imagine human consciousness as a great current that is flowing down through the dark channels of time. If we do not swim upwards against the stream, we will be carried down to the rapids and the waterfalls below. There can be no standing still for man. Man is a transitional being, half way between the animal and the divine. Man's destiny is to move onwards to the next stage of evolution, for then only can our divine nature be fully developed. But, in order to move upwards, we have to struggle. If we have faith and reverence, then, with the sound of the divine flute echoing in our ears and the voice of the divine charioteer resounding in our hearts, we can move resolutely onwards towards the divine destiny that awaits us."

The Final Collapse

"The outstanding feature of the last quarter of the twentieth century is the final collapse of the materialistic paradigm that had dominated the world for many centuries. The Cartesian-Newtonian-Marxist paradigm has finally collapsed, and in the post-Einsteinian period, with quantum mechanics and Heisenberg's Uncertainty Principle, with Stan Grof's Extended Cartography of the Psyche, and so many other exciting and interesting developments, we find that the ancient vision of the mystics is again being recaptured. This too solid matter dissolves into waves of probability, and all materialistic philosophies, whether Marxist or capitalistic or of any other brand, have failed. Humanity gropes for a new model, a new philosophy and a new paradigm to replace the old: in fact, for a new consciousness"

And A Miscalculation

"No bomb has so far been invented that would destroy only the Russians and the Americans. All of us, whether we live in Asia or Africa, in the Arctic areas or at the ends of the Earth, will be effectively eliminated, In fact, those people on whom the bombs fall may be luckier because they would go instantaneously, whereas millions of others would die lingering deaths longing to be released from their torture. And this can happen not necessarily through a political decision. A miscalculation, an accident, a flock of geese, an earthquake, a malfunctioning computer—anything can now do it."

No One Knows the Answer

"Many thinkers have pointed out that, whenever there is a major transition, there is a period of reaction and crystallization. Can we afford that type of crystallization in a world bristling with nuclear weapons? Will there be a substantial enough transformation of consciousness on Planet Earth in time to prevent its destruction? Or is this particular adventure in consciousness, as Arthur Koestler has pointed out, doomed to failure? Is man a creature programmed for self-destruction, and not even a graceful exit like the dinosaurs but a malignant one, taking all life with it, not only collective suicide but terricide? No one knows the answers"

For A Coherent Philosophy

"We have got to understand that all these great religious traditions draw their sustenance from the same centre. We have got to move towards the concept of the unity of all religions, Finally, there is the concept of the welfare of all mankind, regardless of whether they live in the East or the West, the North or the South. These were some of the insights which we find in the Hindu tradition. We can go to other religious traditions and also non-religious traditions in order to develop a coherent philosophy."

The Parallel Movements of Peace

"It is not enough to be involved in a movement for outer peace: there has to be a parallel movement of inner peace within each one of us. In our own lives, we must move towards a realization of the truth at the core of our being, the higher consciousness that is the birthright of each individual born on this planet, 'the light that lighteth every man that cometh into this world'. In the crucible of our individual consciousness alone can the poison be contained, transformed into nectar and released into society and the world.'

Lord Siva to appear again. In this age, it is not realistic to expect the great Lord Siva to appear once again and drink the poison for us. We have now passed that stage in evolution. Now that we have reached the state of self-individuation, we have got to drink the poison ourselves. Each one of us has to integrate the poison within our psyche, and convert it by the power of our spiritual striving into nectar."

Religion to be Valid

"Let us not forget that for any religion to be valid in the nuclear age it must have both these aspects: it must have the eternal truths and it must also have the capacity for creative reinterpretation and regeneration."

Between Collapsing Past and Unborn Future

"Remember that the demoniac forces are there deeply embedded in the human psyche, and today, with the possibility of nuclear destruction staring us all in the face, we find ourselves precariously poised between a past that is collapsing and a future that refuses to be born. We find ourselves in a position of extreme danger."

Endangered Earth

"Planet Earth, embattled, endangered, polluted, is yet the mother that has nurtured and nourished our race for millions of years from the slime of the primeval ocean up to the rsis and the saints. The most remarkable photograph ever taken is the photograph of earth taken from the moon. It shows us as we really are, a tiny speck of life and light against the unending vastnesses of outer space. Will we convert this beautiful jewel into a burnt-out cinder, or will we cherish it as the cradle of the higher consciousness?"

Harmonious Human Beings

"We need the mind to be illuminated by *jnana* (wisdom); the heart to be flooded by *bhakti* (devotion); the will to be disciplined by *karma* (action); and the psyche to be spiritualized by *raja* (practice). It is only if we are able to develop all these four elements of our personality that we will achieve that capacity to function as integrated and harmonious human beings, capable of building a new, global civilization on planet Earth."

We Need Fear No Evil

"The path ahead is difficult and dangerous, but that is inevitable in any great undertaking; and, as long as we have courage and faith, we need fear no evil. The goal of individual salvation and collective transformation may be far away, and may need many generations to achieve. But we must press on undeterred, summoning all our material, moral, intellectual and spiritual resources to this most important of all undertakings. Let us recall that immortal verse from the *Katha Upanisad* which exhorts us to arise, awake and move onwards across the sharp and difficult razor-edged path laid out by the great spiritual beings of past ages:"

The Erosion of Values

"The erosion of values in our country now is something that has been virtually accepted, and I say this with a sense of sorrow: because wherever one goes, not only is corruption virtually accepted as a way of life, it has virtually become a philosophy of life. It is rampant in all spheres of activity, not just in politics. May be in politics it is a little worse than most, for obvious reasons. But in all spheres of activity there has been this widespread erosion of moral and spiritual values. To some extent this is true the world over, but is specially tragic for a country like India, which has from the beginning of its civilization sought to base itself upon certain spiritual moral values."

Educational System and Multi-religious Traditions

"The multireligious situation in India is a reality which

will not go away. Instead of approaching the whole problem from a negative viewpoint, it would be far better to take the bull by the horns, and convert what is sometimes looked upon as a major 'problem' into a positive asset for the new Indian that is struggling to be born. This can only be done, if our educational system gladly accepts the multiplicity of our religious tradition."

Creative Co-existence

No nation can continue to grow if its central concepts become fossilized and it loses the capacity for creative reinterpretation of its philosophical roots. The great secret of Indian civilization, which has survived so long lies precisely in its capacity for such periodic reformulations. It is no longer good enough for us to try and hide behind an outmoded concept of secularism. What is needed is a deeper understanding of the importance of religion in the life of our people, and the formulation of a new and dynamic interpretation of secularism which would ensure the creative co-existence of our many religions, all making a positive contribution to the rich and varied mosaic that is India."

Shedding The Shackles

"In a world rushing headlong into the twenty-first century we are now called upon to make a major effort to shed the shackles of corruption, superstition and obscurantism that have bound us for long, and to mobilize our inner and outer resources for a decisive leap into the future. The main instrument for this process will inevitably be the educational system."

The War in Human Affairs

The history of all races and nations is full of battles and wars, whether these are internal conflicts or external invasions. It would require the latest generation of computers to work out the amount of bloodshed and deaths inflicted by human beings upon each other through all ages. The causes of these conflicts have been many and varied. Some wars have resulted from the ambition of individuals or groups to dominate society; others from an attempt to fight against injustice and tyranny. There have been wars flowing from the megalomania of tyrants, and also wars of national liberation and freedom. Sometimes it is possible to demarcate those guilty of starting conflicts; often the issues are so complex that a clear-cut verdict is virtually impossible. But the fact remains that war has always been a major factor in human affairs."

The Dilemma of Mankind in Nuclear Age

"It should now be clear that a major war can no longer be looked upon as an acceptable way of settling international disputes. Peace and international understanding are now not merely a moral necessity but a categorical imperative for the sheer survival of the human race. The ancient vision of the seers regarding the establishment of peace on Earth must now be converted into reality, if mankind is to survive into the next millennium and benefit from the benign application of the amazing advances in science and technology that have taken place over the last few decades. Any philosophy which evades this central question of possible nuclear annihilation cannot claim to cope with the dilemma of mankind in the nuclear age."

Human Welfare

"The goal of human life is a dual one: the spiritual release of our individual souls from bondage, and also the welfare of society and the world. This welfare is not interpreted in any narrow racial or religious terms; it is defined as the welfare of the many, the happiness of the many. Thus, our spiritual quest must manifest not only in our internal spiritual practice but also in our external activity devoted to peace and human welfare."

The Golden Bridge

"We stand today at a crucial crossroad of destiny. The old is dying, and the new is struggling to be born, and it falls to our generation to seek the golden bridge whereby humanity can cross the dark and perilous waters that surround us."

Globalization and Global Consciousness

"While the movement towards globalization is gathering momentum, the global consciousness that is required to sustain the new civilization has still not emerged adequately. Thus, a most dangerous situation has arisen, caused by the lag between the growth of globalization and its acceptance by the vast masses of humanity, particularly political leaders. It is here that the great religious traditions of the world have a crucial and urgent role to play. While religion has been a fountain-head of great inspiration in many creative spheres of life—music and dance, philosophy and the fine arts, literature and architecture—it has also been a source of tremendous internecine strife. But despite this history of conflict the great world religions do provide invaluable insights into a higher form of human consciousness, which need to be creatively re-articulated in the light of present requirements."

Spiritual Realization

"Spiritual realization cannot take place simply on the intellectual or theoretical plane. It is only when one dives into the depths of the heart — the *hridaya-guhayam*, as the *Upanisads* have it — that one can hope to transcend verbalization and enter the actual experience.

Let us always remember that the spiritual transmutation is an eternal and on-going process. As Maulana Jalaluddin Rumi says in his great *Masnavi*:

"Wherever I look there are torches and candles,/ Wherever I turn there is tumult and shouting,/ For the world today is heavy and in travail/ Seeking to give birth to the eternal world."

Multi-dimensional Dialogue

"It is incontrovertible that much that is great in human civilisation—art and architecture. law and literature, dance and music, moral codes and religious texts—can be traced back to one or other of the great religions, without which human civilisation would have been greatly impoverished. On the other hand we are forced to admit that, tragically enough, more people have been killed and tortured, persecuted and ill treated in the name of religion than in any other name. This is a negative legacy which we must now decisively shed if humanity is to move onwards towards a sane and harmonious global society into the future. In its place what we need is an on-going multi-dimensional dialogue between the great religions of the world."

Sharing The Gifts

"If all the great religious organisations of the world were to divert a substantial portion of their funds towards poverty alleviation, it would go a long way towards removing the grave disparities that we find today which will increasingly become a source of conflict and tension in the years and decades ahead. We must share the gifts that the divine has showered upon us with our less fortunate fellow humans, particularly women and children who represent the more vulnerable section of our societies."

Degradation Of Natural Environs

"We must reiterate our commitment to safeguarding the natural environment, which is a divine gift to the human race. Indeed it is a resource which belongs to entire humanity and must be preserved and protected for generations yet unborn. The degradation and depredation of our natural environment has been one of the most tragic features of the 20th century. The havoc caused by deforestation, desertification and intolerable pressure of population growth is causing widespread distress. Global warming is proceeding rapidly, the glaciers are melting, and within the next two decades several island countries are in serious danger of disappearing from the map of the world. In this background, it is essential that religious and spiritual leaders should commit themselves to the preservation and enhancement of the natural environment, and spread the environmental message among their followers."

To Access the Divine Within

"Religious and spiritual leaders must surely draw the attention of humanity to the inner core of light and luminosity that lies at the heart of all human beings.

Regardless of their race or religion, sex or nationality, the human psyche today is fractured and fragmented, and can be healed only by the inner processes of meditation, prayer and introspection which are to be found in all the great religious traditions of the world. Let us never lose sight of this fundamental truth enshrined deep within the recesses of our consciousness, for it is only to the degree that through a profound inner dialogue we can access the divine within ourselves."

Shackles of Poverty And Hunger

"Humanity today stands at a crucial crossroad in its long and tortuous destiny on Planet Earth. It now has the resources and technology to abolish hunger and illiteracy, want and unemployment from the face of the earth within the next two decades. But what it lacks is the wisdom and compassion to achieve this goal. We have broken the space barrier, explored the planets and are reaching out for the stars themselves, but we have not been able to break the shackles of poverty and hunger, despotism and malnutrition that still hold over half the human race in servitude."

The Positive And Negative Aspects

"We cannot deny the fact that there are also some very negative aspects. Drugs and drug trafficking, terrorism and arms trafficking, sexually transmitted diseases, and a steady diet of horror and violence, ultra-consumerism and hyper-promiscuity, a curious obsession with death, disaster and dinosaurs on film and television, all represent dangerous and negative trends. Whether we like it or not, the processes of globalization have become virtually irreversible, and as we enter the third millennium A.D., we must seriously consider how the positive aspects can be highlighted and the negative ones counteracted."

Creative Restructuring of UN

"At present the five permanent members of the Security Council represent just about 1/3 of the human population, while 2/3 are placed in a secondary position. This situation emerged at the end of the war when the victors understandably arrogated to themselves a special status. However, the world has changed dramatically since then. It is clearly anomalous that countries like Germany and Japan with their amazing post-war resurgence, huge nations like India and Brazil, and the whole African continent should remain outside the place of permanent membership of the Security Council. A creative restructuring of the United Nations is long overdue."

Transcending Traditional Animosities

"It is truly amazing that countries of Europe which were literally at each other's throats for a thousand years have, as a result of economic compulsions and enlightened political leadership, transcended their traditional animosities and forged an economic, monetary and quasi political union. It is my sincere hope that this will be the path adopted in South Asia, the region to which I belong, so that the recently acquired nuclear capabilities are put to creative rather than destructive purposes."

"The European Union is an astounding example of the manner in which centuries old animosities—for example between Germany, France and Britain—have been overcome thus heralding a new era of peace and rapid economic development in Europe. That is the path that we need to follow if we are really to expect a global power shift to Asia in the 21st century."

Repaying Debt to Nature

"We have to repay our debt to nature by reversing our narrowly anthropocentric policies of exploitation and dominance, and begin the long process of nurturing the Earth and healing her wounds. If this is not done, actors and subjects alike will be overwhelmed by the processes of environmental destruction. The population bomb is also ticking away, specially in those countries that can least afford these exponential rates of growth, and if this trend continues, the world will face a major food and water crisis in the course of the next century which can cause domestic and international havoc and chaos. Already starvation has become endemic in many parts of Sub-Saharan Africa."

Peace, Weapons And Warheads

"Peace and harmony have been sought by humanity ever since the dawn of civilization. And yet the whole of human history, from the very earliest times, is replete with wars and violent conflicts from the tribal right up to the international level. All religions preach peace, but in fact religion has been one of the major sources of violent conflicts down through the centuries, and remains so even today. Science was supposed to help establish peace, but it has created increasingly deadly weapons of mass destruction, to the extent that a single nuclear warhead now packs explosive power equal to one thousand of the bombs that obliterated Hiroshima and Nagasaki half a century ago."

Despite the Great Peacemakers

"Despite the great peace-makers like Lord Buddha, Emperor Ashoka, Jesus Christ, Lord Mahavira, and, in our own day, Mahatma Gandhi, there seems to be no appreciable decline in the human propensity towards violence. Indeed, this twentieth century has surpassed all records of violence, killing and maiming more human beings than in the last ten centuries put together. Arthur Koestler suggests that as a result of an engineering defect in the human cortex, man is a creature programmed for self-destruction, while the poet A.E. Housman ends a memorable poem with the following lines:

"The troubles of our proud and angry dust
Are from eternity and shall not fail
Bear them we can, and if we can, we must,
Shoulder the sky my lad, and drink your ale."

Creative Power

"All the great traditions of the world tell us that there is, deep within our consciousness, a creative power that if invoked and honoured can bring about a transformation which may appear to be miraculous. The lives of saints and seers drawn from all the great religious traditions of the world bear this out, and though it may be unrealistic to expect such capacities in ordinary people, it does impel us to look deeper into this whole problem of peace in its varied dimensions."

Divine Spark and Modern Psychology

"With the development of depth psychology in the West, particularly with C.G. Jung who must be ranked as one of the most creative thinkers of this century, modern psychology has also at last realized that our conscious minds are simply like the surface of an ocean, constantly buffeted by waves and typhoons, harbouring in its depths numerous creatures, friendly as well as deadly. Deep within, we are told by the spiritual and mystic traditions of humanity, there resides the divine spark which, under certain circumstances, can be fanned into the blazing fire of spiritual realization."

Family Relationship

"If our family relationships are full of conflict and struggle, we are unlikely to be able to find inner peace or make any contribution towards establishing it in society. Family relationships have two basic dimensions, the husband-wife relationship and the parent-children relationship, in both of which tension and strife seem to be becoming increasingly widespread."

Status of Women

"An important point here revolves around the status of women. Particularly in developing societies, this status is still far from satisfactory, and women tend to be relegated to an inferior position. In the West, I sometimes get the impression that the pendulum has swung in opposite direction, perhaps to compensate for past injustices. What is needed is a harmonious balance between the two. In the Hindu tradition,we have the remarkable concept of *Ardhanarishwara*, Lord Shiva as half man and half woman.

This, creative fusion is ideally reflected on the social plane in the concept of the wife as *ardhangini*, equal sharer and partner in the adventure of life. Thus neither the traditional Eastern custom of the woman walking three paces behind her husband, nor the curious Western practice of their walking three paces ahead, is satisfactory. Walking side by side is symbolically the ideal arrangement."

Peace Mechanism And Nation States

"The quest for world peace is now no longer merely a mystical vision or an idealist utopia. It has become a sheer necessity for the very survival of the human race. The growth of weapons technology has been so awesome that with nuclear weapons we can destroy not only the human race but all life on this planet. Even a non-nuclear conflict like the Gulf War caused massive casualties and appalling damage to the biosphere and environment of our planet. Therefore, it is imperative for us to find mechanisms for a peaceful resolution of disputes between nation states."

Ageing As An Asset

"Ageing is sometimes termed a `problem': but the way I look at it is that older people represent a national asset. With their experience and their maturity, if that could be used for creative purposes, they can do a great deal for the development of society and of the nation."

Youth is A Wonderful Thing, but

"Bernard Shaw said that "youth is a wonderful thing, what a pity it is wasted on the young", because they do not really appreciate or understand its importance. If, when people are young ,they adopt good food habits, proper exercising, refrain from poisoning themselves either through tobacco or alcohol or drugs, if they live a physiologically fitter life, it would help them in their old age. As you grow older what you have done, your *karma* in this very life catches up with you. Ultimately the body responds to the sort of treatment you have given your body when you were young."

Family Values in the West

"In the West you have social security, but family values do not seem to be there. My American friends on being asked `Where are your parents?', might say "Well, the last we heard, they were out in Arizona, maybe we will catch up with them during Thanksgiving". It is unbelievable that there should be such a lack of rapport, of interest, of concern, of feeling between parents and children as is often found in the West. The emotional sustenance that can be achieved through inter-personal family relationships is entirely missing."

Possessiveness

"Ideally, older people should be friends, philosophers, and guides to younger people. This point is seldom stressed, particularly while addressing older people. It needs to be made, because nothing is more corrosive in life than possessive, dominating behaviour. It can lead to nothing but disaster and pain for everybody concerned: the sooner everyone realises this, the better."

Growing And Keep Growing

"As your experience grows, and if your mind is open and you are able to absorb the many subtle variations encountered in daily life, then you continue to keep growing. As the poet Browning says "grow old along with me, the best is yet to be".

The Journey from Womb to Tomb

"We are living at an exciting time in human destiny. It is a privilege to be alive at this time when human beings have reached the moon, and the planets, and are reaching out towards the stars. Science and technology is changing the texture of life in front of our very eyes, and people say, "we are bored" because their minds are moving in unidimensional grooves. They have not learnt that life is not a meaningless journey from the womb to the tomb, but an extraordinary adventure of consciousness."

In The Islands of Luxury

"We live in islands of luxury in a huge ocean of suffering and deprivation. The *Vedas* tell us there ate two elements of our lifework, *Atmano mokshartham, Jagat hitaya cha*. We work for the liberation of our own souls, but also for the welfare of the world. The two things are linked: if you are involved in socially useful work, that itself can become a powerful means of spiritual development."

Approaching Death With Dignity

"We must look upon death itself as the ultimate learning experience. To approach death with courage and dignity is very important. Unfortunately there is no education for death, the one inevitability that faces each one of us at the end of the road. Nobody talks about it, nobody teaches you about it. It is not supposed to be mentioned, it is unplanned, unpredictable. We have to face death as Nachiketas faces Yama, the Lord of Death in the *Kathopanishad*. We have got to face death with dignity, with courage, We must look upon death as a great learning experience."

Negative And Positive in Globalization

"Globalization, with both its positive and negative implications, is now an irreversible process. With accelerating globalization, not only have the barriers between nations and peoples been overcome, which is a positive development, there has also been a massive collapse of any kind of coherent value system, so that generations are growing up without any clear guidelines for thought and action. As a result, despite the glittering and unprecedented achievements of science and technology during the 20th century, it has been the most lethal and destructive in all of human history."

Fanaticism And Fundamentalism

"Whole populations are being indoctrinated into the necessity to kill and die for their religions, so that thousands of young people are growing up convinced that their highest destiny is to destroy other young people belonging to different religions. Surely this situation is no longer acceptable to any sane and humane society. It is up to religious leaders to respond creatively to this challenge, to transcend the barriers of hatred and exclusivism, fanaticism and fundamentalism, and move towards a new era based on respect for all the great religious traditions of humanity."

The Plurality of Paths of The Divine

"There are multiple paths to the divine. From the dawn of recorded history the quest for the divine has been a major dimension in all the world's great civilizations. The divine has been accessed in different ways, described in different words and portrayed in different forms. This plurality of paths to the divine is one of the most striking features of human history."

Planet Earth In The Classrooms

"The stunning photographs of Planet Earth taken from outer space should hang in every classroom, board room and parliament around the world. That shows our world as it really is, a tiny speck of pulsating life amidst the infinity of outer space, and is par excellence the symbol of the emerging global society. It does not reveal geographical, racial or religious differences; it shows our planet as a spaceship hurtling through time-space with all of humanity on board."

Inner Core Of Effulgence

"We must rejoice that though we are all transitory residents of a small planet hurtling through the cosmos, we each encapsulate a spark of consciousness which can be fanned into the blazing fire of spiritual realization transcending the throbbing abyss of Space and Time itself. To achieve this we need to address a dimension that is often overshadowed by the glitter and glamour, the speed and stress of our modern society. We must rediscover the inner core of effulgence that sparkles within the heart of all human beings, regardless of their race or religions, sex or nationality, and to which saints and seers from every religion have left ample testament."

Stepping Into The Same River Twice

"Over the last century, science and technology have so accelerated the speed of time that the future is upon us even before we realize that the past has disappeared. Indeed the old saying "that you cannot step into the same river twice" has now to be changed. In the new millennium we cannot even step into the same river once, because in the very act of stepping in, the river has already changed. The speed with which the information technology revolution is transforming our lives is quite astounding."

Asia's Gift To The World

"Historically Asia, stretching from the Mediterranean to the Pacific, has been the birthplace of most of the world's great cultures and, without exception, of all the world's great religions. The four Indic religions — Hinduism, Jainism, Buddhism and Sikhism, the four West Asian religions — Zoroastrianism, Judaism, Christianity and Islam, and the three East Asian religions — Confucianism, Taoism and Shintoism — were all born in Asia, although subsequently some of them travelled to the West. Not only has Asia been the birthplace of the most sublime philosophies in human civilisation, it has also produced some of the greatest architectural marvels in the world — the Great Wall of China and the Angkor Vat Temples in Cambodia, the Borobudur in Indonesia and the Taj Mahal in India; the great Hindu temples of South Asia and the rock cut caves of Ajanta and Ellora, these and numerous other architectural wonders are part of Asia's gift to the world."

Asian Contribution in The History Of The Human Race

"We should not fall into the common error of thinking that Asia has produced only philosophies and temples. Many of the great inventions of science also came from Asia— paper, ceramics and calligraphy from China, and the zero from India, to give only some examples—without which all the marvels of modern science and technology would not have been possible. While discussing copyright and intellectual property rights with my Western friends, I point out that if they were to give India one cent for every time they use the zero, we would need neither Western trade nor Western aid, and the same is true for China with every sheet of writing paper! Centuries ago Asia achieved high levels of expertise in medicine, astronomy, phonetics, linguistics, metallurgy, architecture and other fields too numerous to catalogue, and though many of these achievements may have been attenuated in the long and tortuous corridors of time, they must be given their due place in the history of the human race."

"Third World" As An Obnoxious Terms

"I consider it to be an obnoxious expression, describing us as the "Third World". The Western powers arrogate to themselves the first category, the Communist, countries of the now defunct Soviet Union were placed in the second, and the rest are lumped into a sort of third class category. If we talk of a power shift to Asia in the 21st century, the first thing that will need to be done is to overcome this mindset and to realize that in the modern world, although countries may be on different levels of development, there is no scope for condescension. Also, Eurocentric terminology such as "Middle East" and "Far East" need to be replaced by the more appropriate terms of West Asia and East Asia. This is not merely semantics, but part of a deeper shift in consciousness, the necessity for which Asians themselves often fail to recognise."

Global Society: Do we need to . . . . ?

"In the emerging global society, while economic growth is certainly a necessity, do we really have to accept the hyper-consumerism and ultra-promiscuity with which our electronic media is constantly bombarding us, along with lethal doses of horror and violence on cinema and television which surely are wrecking havoc with our collective consciousness, specially of younger, more impressionable generations? Do we not need to temper technology with wisdom, corporate profits with compassion and military might with humanistic values?"

The Moments Of Transition In History

"Moments come, which come but rarely in history, when quite perceptibly one age draws to an end and another dawns, when we stand precariously poised between a collapsing past and an indeterminate future, when established landmarks disappear and we often seem to be adrift on a limitless ocean, when waves of change crash constantly against our mental beaches, when, to survive, human civilization needs not merely a linear progression in its thinking but a paradigm shift in its consciousness. We have, in fact, reached just such a crucial crossroad."

Globalisation: The Negative Face

"In this vast drama of human evolution that is now being played out on the global stage, there are, as in most dramatic situations, both positive and negative forces at work. The negative ones are too obvious to need reiteration. The recrudescence of ethnic and religious animosities, the globalization of the malign underworld of drugs and international terrorism, the exponential spread of the AIDS pandemic, the multi-billion dollar arms trade, are all indications that unless illuminated by wisdom and compassion, this latest transition could well end in disaster, particularly as we have succeeded in gravely damaging the thin envelope of life-sustaining biosphere that surrounds our globe."

The Plus And Minus Of Tourism

"Tourism is thus a positive force for economic growth and development, for cementing ties of friendship between the people of the world, and for furthering the emergence of a harmonious global society. In all fairness, however, I must also point out that there *are* some negative factors involved. Many areas and destinations are very vulnerable to ecological pollution, and tourists often leave behind them a horrible trail of debris which ruins beaches and threatens forests. Equally important are the cultural factors involved, in which sheltered societies are exposed to attitudes and lifestyles which play havoc with their traditional cultural patterns. Imaginative planning and adequate care are needed to offset these negative factors."

Two Roads Of Human History

"We stand poised at a crucial moment in human history. The two roads so eloquently described in the *Katha Upanishad* open up before us. One seeks through peace and understanding, compassion and friendship, the possibility of a new and harmonious global society. The other leads through fanaticism and terrorism, bigotry and conflict, to disaster and destruction. Which road humanity will take will depend ultimately upon what you and the millions of people with whom you come into contact in your daily lives, decide."

Global Society And The Goddess Mahalaxmi

"I would like you to imagine Goddess Mahalaxmi's figure superimposed upon that photograph of Planet Earth. The Goddess is seated upon a great white lotus, which is born in the muck and darkness of the underworld but comes out clean and glittering, rather like human consciousness has emerged in the course of evolution from primeval matter. She is dressed in spotless white, the colour of the higher consciousness. She is full-breas ted and deepnavelled, because she is the World Mother. Her eyes are like lotus petals, the most beautiful shape for a woman's eyes in Indian iconography, and in her hands she holds a pair of lotus flowers, symbols of the human psyche that sleeps in the darkness of ignorance but awakens when the sun of knowledge rises. She is being bathed from both sides by divine, six tusked elephants that are pouring ambrosia over her from golden jars.

For the emerging global society we need holistic, healing images to offset all the violence and horror that we are bombarded with day and night"

Towards Realisation And Liberalization

"Howsoever glorious the outer iconography, real spiritual growth has to take place within the inner recesses of our consciousness. As the Upanishads say, 'Within the furthest golden sheath resides the immutable Brahman, the resplendent light of lights. It is this that the knowers of the Atman know'. I look upon spiritual life as the essential foundation for our outer activities, as the centre from which they should all be constantly referred. It is by thus centering our lives and consciousness that we can hope to move towards realization and liberation in this very lifetime."

To Lord Siva

I am your plaything.
You can breathe into me
the fire of eternal life,
and make me immortal;
or You can scatter my atoms
to the far corners of the universe
so that I disappear for ever.

You can fill me with light and power
so that I shine like a meteor
against the darkness of the midnight sky;
or You can extinguish my spirit
so that I sink for ever
into the deep and fathomless ocean of time.
You can set me among the eternal stars
resplendent with your divine fire;
or You can hurl me
into the abyss of darkness,
so that I can never again be visible
to mortal eyes.
You can come to me
with the glory of a thousand cupids;
or You can turn from me
and leave me stranded
in a grey and ghastly desert of despair.
You can smile at me
with the radiance that kindles the universe;
or You can open your eye of fury
and reduce me to a heap of ashes.
I am your plaything;
the choice is yours.

(Karan Singh)

❐❐❐